BUSINESS DOCUMENTS

Their origins, sources and uses in historical research

BUSINESS DOCUMENTS

Their origins, sources and uses in historical research

John Armstrong and Stephanie Jones

MANSELL PUBLISHING LIMITED
London and New York

First published 1987 by Mansell Publishing Limited
(A subsidiary of The H.W. Wilson Company)
6 All Saints Street, London N1 9RL, England
950 University Avenue, Bronx, New York 10452, U.S.A.

British Library Cataloguing in Publication Data

Armstrong, John
  Business documents : their origins,
  sources and uses in historical research.
  1. Business records
  I. Title   II. Jones, Stephanie
  651.5   HF5736

  ISBN 0–7201–1846–8

Library of Congress Cataloging-in-Publication Data

Armstrong, John, 1944–
  Business documents.

  Bibliography: p.
  Includes index.
  1. Business records—Great Britain—Handbooks,
manuals, etc.   2. Business enterprises—Great Britain—
Archival resources—Handbooks, manuals, etc.   3. Business
records—Handbooks, manuals, etc.   4. Business enterprises
—Archival resources—Handbooks, manuals, etc.   I. Jones,
Stephanie (Stephanie Karen)   II. Title.
HF5349.G7A76   1987   651.5   86–28451
ISBN 0–7201–1846–8

Printed in Great Britain by
Whitstable Litho Ltd., Whitstable, Kent

Contents

Illustrations

The original size of most of these illustrations was foolscap, 16¼ x 13½ in approx. (413 x 343 cm).

Preface

This book arose from the honorary activities of the authors on behalf of the Business Archives Council. The Council is dedicated to preserving historical business records, disseminating information about them and encouraging their use to study the development of business. It had frequently been noted that among many professional archivists 'business records' were a Cinderella class: neglected, misunderstood and little-loved. One of the reasons for this is that there is no general guide to the location or interpretation of this class of records readily available to the archivist, whereas there are many sumptuous volumes relating to manorial records, the records of central or local government, church and school records. In a very small way the present volume is intended to start to rectify the omission by providing an introduction to some types of business document.

The book makes no claim to be a comprehensive guide to all types of business document. Rather, we have used three criteria for the selection of types of document. First, only those which were created internally within a business organization either for its own use or to satisfy an external requirement have been included. This has meant that we have not dealt with some sources which are invaluable to the study of business, such as the trade press or the financial journals. Although of undoubted utility they were created by bodies external to the firm and for this volume we have ignored them. The second criterion is that the documents are not specific to only one trade, industry or service; rather they are documents which most firms were likely to create at some time in their history and which were general to a whole range of industries. Thus we have not discussed industry-specific documents such as bills of lading, insurance proposals or weavers' tickets. Thirdly we have chosen the most informative documents which have survived most frequently.

The basis on which we chose the specific examples of each business document was fourfold: the documents should be readily available to researchers; they should be drawn from a range of companies and industries; the specific document should be fairly typical of the type; and that the document had not previously been drawn upon in writing a published business history. Thus the examples are typical, novel, readily available and give an idea of the range of business documents.

Perhaps it should be stressed that although we have covered fifteen different types of documents, this in no way exhausts the range that is generally available — even setting aside the mass of industry specific documents — and that there are many more which could be illustrated and discussed. We have chosen only the most important. On the other hand, it is rare for all types of document to have survived for any particular firm. The norm is for piecemeal survival for any company. In general, the earlier the date the less likely the particular document is to survive. Even where the particularly favoured company can boast specimens of all the types covered in the book, it is unlikely to have a complete run of those records which were periodically created, such as diaries or balance sheets. This is borne out too well by the number of business histories which stop or start at apparently odd dates — in fact, dictated by document availability — or simply ignore completely some key aspect of running a business because documents no longer exist relating to that functional area for the particular firm. This patchiness of document survival is not always an insuperable problem. In some cases different documents will contain the same sorts of information. Where more than one document has survived, this allows corroboration; where there are gaps in one set of records, other documents may fill them. For example, if chairman's reports have not survived, they may well have been embodied in the board minute books; if balance sheets no longer exist, it may be possible to reconstruct them using the financial records such as journals or ledgers.

Throughout the book we have tried to keep in mind the needs of both the archivist or record keeper and the researcher. The order of the documents was a subject of some discussion. We considered arranging them in the order that they would have been created, which would have meant prospectuses first, followed by articles of association, then registers of directors and shareholders' lists. However, we decided that the most appropriate order was that which would be of most value to the researcher investigating a company's history. Thus we have arranged the entries from the general to the particular. Those in the early part of the book, such as the prospectus, the articles of association and the board minute book, give an overview of the firm at the level of general strategy and the broad areas of product or service, capital structure and business policy. Those towards the end of the volume usually only give insights into particular functional areas, such as staffing, premises or technology. Thus the researcher who knew almost nothing about a particular business should tackle the documents in approximately the order in which they appear in the book.

There is one piece of advice we wish to pass on to the novitiate researcher. In general, before approaching a specific company for advice or permission to consult its archives, it is best to have already consulted those documents which are available in public repositories such as the PRO, Companies House and the Patent Office. In this way the researcher can show commitment to, and knowledge of, the company's history and is more likely to gain entry if demonstrating previous investigation of some sources. The researcher may be in a position to add to the company archivist's knowledge, information which the in-company people do not know and thus can add to their understanding of their own past. The other advantages to the researcher of tackling the external sources first is that they will give some indication of the functional areas which are of most significance to the particular firm, the key dates, and the issues and controversies which need following up. Time spent in the in-company archive will thus be used more efficiently and profitably. A word on what may seem trivialities. Business firms remain fairly conservative, those in the City of London particularly so, and it behoves the researcher to approach cautiously and thoughtfully. The best initial approach is by letter giving as precise details as possible of what is required and establishing the enquirer's bona fides. Any visit should reflect the need to appear more like a businessman than an academic; politeness and respect will achieve much more than a brash, aggressive stance. The records belong to the company so the researcher will have to respect its policy on closure periods and allow the company to read the work prior to publication. An offprint should be sent to the company with thanks after publication.

In general, archivists are keen to see their archives used, though it should be stressed that they have also to fulfil numerous duties internal to the firm, and on occasions complain of the low usage rate of business archives.[1] This volume is intended to promote such serious usage by explaining the documents and suggesting ways in which they could be used. Provided the researcher approaches a company archivist with consideration and forethought, the archivist will be only too keen to find sources and help the research along.

This book primarily discusses British business documentation. However, many of the points made on the original purpose, contents and uses of these records apply equally to foreign business documents. Any firm, no matter in which country it was based, kept letters or files of correspondence. Whether the businessman was English, American or Japanese, the reasons for doing so were similar. This is equally true of business diaries or agency agreements: individual directors and entrepreneurs kept their own personal records and recollections for the same reasons and in similar manner as we have explained irrespective of their nationality. Agency agreements are similarly international. As explained in Chapter 15, many firms found the agency system of particular value in overseas trade. Just as UK firms used agents abroad to sell their exports, find cargoes for their ships, or drum up business for their financial services, so foreign firms reciprocated in the UK: Singer, the pioneering American sewing machine company, set up numerous agencies throughout Europe in the nineteenth century.

Patents are another area where a remarkable degree of international conformity exists. Apart from socialist/communist regimes where private property in products or processes is politically unacceptable, most countries have broadly similar patent legislation serving the same purposes as in the UK and providing similar privileges. The remarks made in Chapter 12 on the purposes of a patent, the information specified, and its value to the historian apply equally to German, French or American patents as to British. Since licences largely derive from patents and much of the legislation about them is in patent law, they are similarly international. A prime use of a licence by the inventor is to permit a firm in another country to use the process or manufacture a product under controlled conditions. Indeed, the example quoted in Chapter 13 is truly international: German and British companies allowing an Austrian to use their patents under licence.

Staff and premises records are such broad categories that any business, whatever its nationality, created and maintained some examples of these. Insurance is world-wide with London as the centre, and therefore proposals, policies and plans for insurance occur for companies in all countries. Similarly, architects' drawings and diagrams, records of wage rates and conditions of employment are documents common to companies in all countries, although described in Chapters 11 and 14 essentially from a British viewpoint. Even the apparently peculiarly British system of company registration with its terminology of 'directors', 'articles of association' and 'shareholders' is not restricted to the UK. Britain took to its imperial possessions much of the basic paraphernalia of company law. Because the UK was the first nation to industrialize and pioneered modern business practices, many nations based their company laws, consciously with modifications, on the British model, just as British committees in the late nineteenth century or early twentieth centuries took cognizance of developments in practice in other industrial countries. Thus there is much convergence on company law. The language will differ, but a *compagnie* in France, an *aktiengesellschaft* in Germany, or a corporation in the USA are broadly similar institutions, with share registers and boards of directors under a chairman, *président, Vorsitzender*, or president respectively, which created broadly similar classes of documents to those described in Chapters 1 to 3, 6, 7, 9 and 10. Companies all over the world kept minutes of the proceedings of their directors as British companies did. They had chairmen who made speeches or issued statements, ensured registers were kept of shareholders, and that books of accounts were maintained. Some foreign examples have been used, for instance the French engineering company in Chapter 5 whose chairman's statements were utilized to show the causes of their decline and rebirth, and Australian examples in both Chapters 3 and 5. There are important differences in the timing of the introduction of specific pieces of company law from country to country, the detailed requirements on creation and retention of particular documents, the specific titles assigned to particular roles, type of capital or accounting entry, but broadly most companies in most countries created documents similar to those in this book, for similar purposes and containing similar information which have been, and could be, used in similar ways by historians of many nationalities.

Now is a particularly apposite time for this book. There has been an upsurge of interest in the UK in business history in recent years. On the academic front, a Business History Unit was established at the London School of Economics in the late 1970s with the aim of promoting the systematic study of business history, and in the last couple of years regional centres for the study of business history have been established by Coventry Polytechnic for the Midlands and by Bristol Polytechnic for the west country. The journal *Business History* received such a wealth of articles and books for review that in 1986 it expanded from three to four issues per annum. This increased activity on the research side has been complemented by a growth in the number of business history courses available both at undergraduate and post graduate level in British universities and polytechnics

This renaissance in academic interest has been mirrored by increased awareness of the value of business records and the necessity of preserving them for future generations. Ironically, a period of rationalization and reconstruction with high levels of unemployment and large numbers of firms ceasing operations leads to a growth in the volume of business records at risk and those becoming available for study. There has been, therefore, even more call on the services of bodies such as the Business Archives Council (BAC) to preserve and publicize such collections. It has responded by bringing out books on banking records and the archives of 1000 of the oldest registered companies, and by enhancing its output of pamphlet and periodical literature. The increased interest in business history has also been spurred by historical accident. The 1880s and 1890s saw booms in the conversion of partnerships into joint stock companies and of companies going public. Thus the 1980s and 1990s saw and will see household names celebrating the centenary of either their incorporation or flotation. This promoted an interest in their history and in some cases the publication of a centenary volume or a focus for their advertising in their longevity and tradition, and the durability of the appeal of their product. Thus businesses themselves have become more concerned with their own history and keen to preserve and publicize their records, appreciating the practical value of old advertising material and a long tradition.

The UK is not alone in this upsurge of interest in business and company history and the sources from which it is written. Although many of the European countries were very early in establishing economic archives — for instance, the Netherlands in 1914 – it was not generally until after the Second World War that societies of business historians or associations of business archivists were started.

Among the earliest were those in Germany, the Netherlands and the Scandinavian countries — Sweden had a Business Archives Association in 1955, Finland in 1960 and by the 1960s a whole host of other countries were forming such bodies — in 1968 alone a Business Archives Council of Canada and a Business History Society of ·Japan were founded. This led eventually to the formation of a committee on business archives as a sub-group of the International Council on Archives in 1978. Many of these bodies issue newsletters, bulletins or journals and, even where there is no society of *business* archivists, the archives association of the country often contains such individuals and there is an active interest in such documents. For example, a recent volume of *American Archivist* was devoted almost entirely to corporate records and archives. Despite this growth in awareness of historic business documents and their uses, very little has been written on their origins and nature and no guide to a wide range of such records exists. Hopefully, this volume will blow away some of the mist around such material, make it easier to understand how and why the documents came into existence, and give some ideas to researchers on how to use them.

We wish to acknowledge our indebtedness to many people. For the idea, to the BAC and particularly our colleagues on the Publications Working Party; for the initial impetus to translate the idea on to paper and for reading many of the sections in draft and improving them enormously both in expression and content, John Orbell, chairman of the Publications Working Party, whose good sense is much appreciated; to all the many archivists whom we harried and haunted, for allowing us to consult their collections, especially the staff of the Guildhall Library; to the companies who granted us permission to reproduce their documents; for rapid and accurate word processing to the ladies at Ealing College, especially Giuliana Taborelli and Sylvia Crowther; and finally but not least to Veronica Higgs at Mansell for tact and forbearance. We hope this book at least partly reimburses the vast overdraft of help we have run up. For all omissions and opinions, the authors are solely responsible; for all errors, each blames the other.

Notes

1. See Edwin Green's plea for historians to make more use of the Midland Bank archive: E. Green, 'Bank Archives for Historians: The Case of Midland Bank's Archives', *Business Archives*, No. 49 (1983) pp. 1–9.

Layout of material

Each of the fifteen documents described are laid out in a standard format in order to facilitate using the book as a reference aid. The facsimile example of the particular business document comes last, and we have tried to present it in a form as close as possible to the original document. We have retained the original language and spelling, even where this is now archaic, and tried to keep the pristine layout and typeface or writing. Thus, we hope to give the reader as authentic an example as a reproduction will allow. The reader should be able to get the flavour and feel of the original document.

The first section of each chapter discusses the original reason for the creation of that type of document. As explained in the Introduction, the general factors causing business documents to be created can be classified under a few main headings but it is also important to know the precise purpose for which each was created, in order to show whether it has a particular bias which the researcher needs to take into account. It is similarly crucial to be aware of whether the purpose of the document changed over time and thus if the original bias was exaggerated or ameliorated. The second section in each chapter gives the most easily accessed sources of that particular type of document. Where a company is still trading and maintains its own archive, many of the documents included in this volume should be found there. Wherever possible we have tried to give also a number of archives or libraries external to the company which contain the documents in order to facilitate finding examples. A list of names, addresses and telephone numbers of public repositories will be found towards the rear of the book under 'Useful addresses'. We have also indicated where collections are partial, incomplete or may have been weeded. This section does not pretend to be a comprehensive finding aid, but rather a guide to those archives which contain the largest collection of a particular class of document which are readily visited. It has to be said that the London-based researcher starts at a distinct advantage since most of the best collections are to be found in the national repositories and libraries based in and around the capital.

The next two sections are linked in that they show the sort of information which documents of that type usually contain and the uses to which the material therein can be put. Here again we have tried to show the sort of information that a typical document of this class would normally contain, and must be excused for the rogue example which falls at the outer ends of the normal distribution. We have also shown when and how the amount of information disclosed has changed over time and why these changes have come about. Equally importantly, we have indicated where particular types of information are not included and why this was so. When discussing possible uses for the information contained in each type of document, we have given not only those uses which existing scholarship exemplifies, but also ideas both for different topics of research and particular problems which are of current interest that would be illuminated by a study of the specific type of document.

Penultimately we have tried to show how the various documents interrelate to each other. Although we have treated each type of document separately for reasons of exigency, it is important to appreciate that originally they made up an interrelated set which complemented and elucidated each other. We have attempted to explain how these documents were interrelated and how the weaknesses, omissions or biases of one document may be countered by using other business documents. Finally, we have given examples of the type of historical works that have been written making use of the document being discussed. Again we make no claim for comprehensiveness and acknowledge our own biases. We have used examples which are readily available and which the reader can easily use to discover the type of research which has drawn heavily on the particular type of document. We apologize in advance to any authors who feel slighted because their work was not cited: we intend no disrespect.

We have assumed, hoping to be proved wrong, that some readers will not avidly devour the book from cover to cover but, rather, dip into it to elucidate one particular document. We have, therefore, tried to make each chapter stand on its own. This has resulted in some iteration, for example under the subheading 'Sources', but we preferred this to frequently referring the reader backwards or forwards to some other section which we find intensely irritating.

Introduction: document creation

The number of business documents surviving from before 1800 is very small indeed. The trickle of business documents increases in the early nineteenth century, becomes a wide stream in the late nineteenth century and threatens to become an unmanageable torrent in the twentieth century. The paucity of the early period is not simply a function of time, salvage drives and Hitler's Luftwaffe. It reflects the development cycle of business in Britain. The 'industrial revolution' is the historian's shorthand for a complex of interrelated developments which caused industry to become a dominant source of employment and income and which pushed agriculture into a secondary role as wealth creator.[1] It was this period which saw the number of businesses grow and, as the Victorian period progressed, so did the number of firms.

In the early phases of industrialization, scared by the speculative fever which reached a peak in the South Sea Bubble, the government took drastic action which effectively restricted businesses to the partnership form,[2] unless the individuals involved were rich or politically influential. The corollary of this strict government control on the formation of joint stock companies was that it largely abdicated responsibility for monitoring or guiding the running of business affairs and left it to the law courts to sort out contracts and torts. Toward the middle of the nineteenth century the government eased the rules on the formation of joint stock companies but insisted on unlimited liability. It was in the third quarter of the nineteenth century that the government abandoned its previous caution and introduced easy formation of limited liability joint stock companies. Many commentators have remarked how liberal the rules were, the most unrestrictive in the world at the time, so that within a quarter century the government removed virtually all checks on company formation.[3]

Surprisingly no great rush of industrial corporations followed, and it was not until the 1880s and 1890s that significant numbers of British manufacturing businesses began to adopt joint stock form and limited liability.[4] Prior to this, many trading or manufacturing firms required relatively small sums of fixed capital which they easily raised from informal sources such as family or friends. Circulating or working capital was available from banks, trade credit or merchant banks.[5] Thus they did not need to go outside their immediate circle for capital and did not need to attract the 'blind' investor who required the safety of limited liability because he did not necessarily know the entrepreneur. This had the attraction to the family firm of ensuring its control and was reinforced by the prevailing business morality which believed that creditors should have the guarantee of a businessman's fortune to back up his judgement and so minimize the creditors' risk. Transport required large sums of fixed capital, for example railways, shipping and canals, and it was among these that limited liability was first generally used to raise finance from a wider and less involved public.[6] By the 1880s and 1890s, firms required greater amounts of fixed capital as more capital-intensive methods of production were being adopted. This provided an impetus to seek capital outside the normal informal sources, from the formal capital market, preferably via debentures or preference shares which did not carry the same voting rights as equity. To take advantage of this source of rentier capital, the firm normally needed to have limited liability. This was brought home to the investing public by a number of notable crashes of firms with unlimited liability such as the City of Glasgow Bank 1878 when shareholders had to find over £27 for each £1 they had invested in the firm.[7] Additionally, by the 1890s some individuals had become aware of the profits that could be made by company promotion, aided by the low yield on government stock, a temporary distrust of foreign investment, and the poor returns on land which drove investors to seek new receptacles for their surplus capital.[8] During the twentieth century, government policy has proceeded in the opposite direction to the Victoria era, progressively tightening up the regulations on company formation, requiring a greater level of disclosure and restricting companies from certain activities. From the document creation point of view, therefore, the government's role has shifted from virtually a total lack of interest to being the most significant external influence on businesses in determining what records should be kept and thus what documents are originated which may survive to be of historical interest.

There have been three main influences on businesses which have caused them to keep records and create documents. Each of these overlap and in some cases reinforce each other and thus in practice are not separate. However, for ease of analysis they will be dealt with individually in turn. The three factors are: the role of law in requiring the creation and retention of certain documents; the rules of the stock exchange which required minimum levels of disclosure for publicly quoted companies; and the creation of records for the internal control of the firm, what might now be called management information, to provide data on which to base policy, guide day-to-day operations and record decisions made.

Legal requirements

Until the passing of the Joint Stock Companies (Registration) Act of 1844[9] there were only three ways of forming a legally acceptable joint stock company in England for most industries: private act of Parliament, crown charter, or letters patent administered after 1825 by the Board of Trade (BOT).[10] All were expensive and time-consuming and required the businessmen to have, or be willing to buy, parliamentary influence. In an unreformed Parliament before 1832 this did not come cheaply. Although shipowners were able to take advantage of the sixty-fourths provision, this was obviously a very restricted privilege peculiar to this industry.[11] Thus until the middle of the nineteenth century the vast majority of English businesses remained partnerships. Statute law laid down no requirements for such partnerships, assuming that civil law could take care of any breaches of contract, disagreements between the partners and disputes between partnership and customers. Since partnerships had unlimited liability and so were unlikely to raise capital other than from the partners themselves or their immediate family and friends, governments felt there was no need for legislation and laid down no rules requiring any general classes of documents to be created. Although firms in some industries were required to make returns, mostly of output for calculation of excise duty, these were very industry-specific and in no way constituted a general requirement to create or keep records.[12]

For those companies brought into being by one of the political devices, the requirement to keep particular records was laid down either in the enabling act or in their charter. However, there was no standard practice. The individual acts and charters varied enormously depending on the balance of interests in the House at the time, or the individuals who were instrumental in steering the venture through the political process. Some parliamentary companies, such as the Stockton and Darlington Railway of 1821, were required to keep 'proper Books of Account'[13] and others, like the Forth and Clyde Navigation, by virtue of receiving government loans were required to keep accounts and submit extracts of assets, debtors, revenues and costs annually to the Exchequer.[14] Others had no such stipulation to keep any particular set of books. Thus there was no general requirement to keep any class of documents placed on the early parliamentary or chartered companies, though Pollins has argued for the railway companies that by the mid-1840s there were a standard set of clauses inserted in most bills requiring books of account to be kept, balance sheets to be prepared and some other records began to be required.[15] A significant change in policy occurred in 1845 when the Companies Clauses Consolidation Act[16] required all parliamentary companies which were created thenceforth to keep 'full and true accounts', balance them regularly, present a balance sheet to the shareholders' meeting half yearly, and maintain a number of other books, for example a register of directors.[17] Although by modern standards these are minimal requirements and indeed they were less rigorous than current best practice, the principle is important in marking uniformity of treatment and recognizing that record keeping was an important aspect of company behaviour to provide shareholders with adequate information.

A key date in the process of record creation is 1844 for it marks the first occasion on which government required standard documentation from firms in a wide range of industries. The Joint Stock Companies Registration and Regulation Act[18] passed in that year made the formation of unlimited liability joint stock companies legal, cheap and easy (only banks and insurance companies were excluded: the former were granted the right to incorporation in a separate Act of the same year,[19] which required somewhat stricter reporting requirements than the general Act). To obtain joint stock form the business was required to file with the Registrar of Joint Stock Companies basic information about the firm. This brought into being the first across-the-board requirement for standard information from all firms wishing to avail themselves of this opportunity. This in turn meant the creation for every company of a standard set of documents. Registration was a two stage process. Provisional registration was obtained by a number of subscribers applying but full registration was only granted when the deed of settlement had been signed by at least 25 per cent of subscribers, by number and capital. The information required included the name and purposes of the company, its registered address, its proposed capital and how it was to be made up, names, addresses and occupations of directors and the deed of settlement, effectively the company's constitution.[20] Once registered, the company was required to submit a list of shareholders with their names, addresses, occupations and number of shares. When the company was fully operational it was required to keep books of account, maintain a register of shareholders and list of directors, all of which were to be open for shareholders' inspection.[21] The company's deed of settlement was required to make provision for the keeping of board minute books recording the attendance of directors, their proceedings and the minutes of such proceedings, and general provisions on the keeping of company records and papers.[22] The 1844 Act also required the directors to make up a 'full and fair' balance sheet at least once a year which was to be presented to the shareholders in general meeting as well as a copy being sent out to the registered address of each shareholder at least ten days before the meeting.[23] Finally, the Act required certain returns to be made to the Registrar of Joint Stock Companies, namely the lists of shareholders half yearly and the annual balance sheet. These returns, together with the documents lodged at the initial registration stage, were available for inspection by the general public on payment of the appropriate fee to the Registrar.[24]

This Act is, therefore, a turning point in the history of business document creation for it brought into being a mass of material on every joint stock company which was registered. Since some of it was submitted to a government agency, there was a high probability of it surviving as government departments have a greater continuity than private firms. Many of the documents submitted to the Registrar survive today; for companies still trading in Companies House in the City, or at least its Welsh outstation; for companies which have ceased business in the BT 31 and 41 papers at the PRO.

The 1844 Act remained in force until the late 1850s when the government changed its tack drastically. Within half a dozen years from being cautious and conservative over company formation, it threw away nearly all restraints and created one of the most liberal regimes in Europe. Between 1856 and 1862 a series of Acts were passed which allowed joint stock companies in all industries to take limited liability cheaply, simply and with a minimum of disclosure. Registration became a one-stage process, by filing a memorandum of association signed by seven shareholders stating only the company's name and objects.[25] In record-keeping terms, these Acts might be seen as an advance on the 1844 Act, for they laid down 'model' regulations which included much fuller provisions for creating and keeping financial records and the presentation of reports and accounts at the general meetings.

> The Directors shall cause true Accounts to be kept:
> Of the Stock in Trade of the Company
> Of the Sums of Money received and expended by the Company
> Of the Credits and Liabilities of the Company.
> Such Account shall be kept, upon the Principle of Double Entry, in a Cash Book, Journal and Ledger . . . The Directors shall lay before the Company in General Meeting a Statement of the Income and Expenditure for the past year. . . Statements so made shall show arranged under the most convenient Heads, the Amount of gross Income, distinguishing the several sources from which it has been derived, and the amount of gross Expenditure distinguishing the Expense of the Establishment, Salaries, and other like Matters. . . A Balance Sheet shall be made out in every year.[26]

This Act also required that the minutes, resolutions and proceedings of general meetings of the company be entered in appropriate books, thus ensuring the creation of another class of business record.[27] However, there were a number of omissions compared to the 1844 Act and some clauses in the earlier Acts were omitted from the 1862 Consolidating Act. This reduced the range of books required to be kept and returns which had to be made. For example, although the 1856 Act required, on similar lines to the 1844 Act, that board minute books be kept,[28] this provision was dropped entirely from the 1862 Act. Similarly, the stipulation in the 1856 Act that accounting records should be kept on the double-entry principle[29] was absent from the 1862 Act, as was the requirement of the 1856 Act for minute books recording the proceedings of general meetings.[30] There was no requirement in the Acts of 1856–62 that the balance sheet be sent to the Registrar of Joint Stock Companies, a departure from the practice established in 1844, although it continued to be recommended in the model regulations that it be presented at the general meeting and a copy pre-circulated to all shareholders.[31] Finally, the model regulations, including the extract quoted above, were not compulsory on all companies. Although they were recommended, and indeed were deemed to apply by default if a company did not indicate to the contrary in its articles of association, a company could alter or omit any of the clauses as it chose providing this was clearly spelt out in its articles and a copy duly submitted to the Registrar.[32] Thus in a number of ways the 1862 Act gave companies greater discretion in the business documents they chose to keep and reduced the returns they had to make. Only banks and insurance companies were subject to stricter disclosure, being required to publish half-yearly statements of assets and liabilities, authorized, issued and called-up capital.[33] The Acts of 1856–62 were of more significance for record survival than record creation. The vast majority of companies continued to keep full sets of accounts, drew up balance sheets, kept minute books and the full range of company records, but since they were compelled to send in fewer returns to the Registrar their survival depends not upon the cautious policy of a long-lived government department but entirely on the firm which created them which was much more exposed to short-term commercial exigency.

This state of affairs continued effectively unchanged until the turn of the century for the majority of companies, although in 1870 life assurance companies were required to prepare, file with the BoT, and make available to shareholders annual revenue accounts and balance sheets and quinquennial actuarial valuations.[34] Public utilities, such as railways, gas works and electric companies, in a series of Acts between 1868 and 1882 were also required to publish and file balance sheets and revenue accounts.[35] The Companies Act of 1900[36] tightened up the process of company formation in a number of ways. It insisted that all prospectuses be submitted to the Registrar before issue and laid down strict guidelines on what was to be disclosed in them.[37] As a result of this stipulation, prospectuses became uniformly informative documents containing a mass of detail about directors, their remuneration and shareholdings, contracts entered into, vendors, underwriting commissions and promotor's fees. In addition, the Act re-introduced two-stage registration. Stage one required that before a company was legally created it had to send to the Registrar not merely the normal documents such as company name, purposes and the memorandum of association but also whether it intended that a specified minimum amount of shares had to be applied for before the company would be formed. If no minimum was specified by the company, the Registrar assumed 100 per cent. Stage two was when the company had achieved the requisite level of applications; the Registrar was so informed and the company came into legal existence.[38] This significantly increased both the amount of documentation being created at the genesis of a company and the amount of information disclosed. The only exemption to this was the 'private' company. Although such an entity did not strictly come into being until the 1907 Companies Act, companies which did not issue a prospectus because they were not seeking capital from the public were exempt from the disclosure provisions, so implicitly there were two types of limited companies. The 1900 Act laid down other record-creating requirements to gladden the heart of latter-day researchers, namely that within one month of formation all companies had to file with the Registrar details of all share allotments, including those not issued for cash but in payment for some consideration, such as a patent or contract; the Registrar had to be informed for precisely what the shares had been payment. The Registrar also required information on all mortgages and charges against the company's assets within twenty-one days of their creation. Additionally, all directors had to record with the Registrar their consent to act as such and, where the articles required a minimum share qualification, had to put in writing a binding undertaking to take up the requisite number.[39]

However, there was still no provision for the filing of annual returns of balance sheets or other financial documents once the company was established. This was not rectified until 1907 when the Companies Act of that year re-introduced the requirement that all companies file with the Registrar an annual audited balance sheet,[40] so bringing the state of disclosure nearly back to where it had been between 1844 and 1856. There was one important exception to this rule and that was the 'private company' which was given formal recognition for the first time.[41] Providing a company was able to fit itself into the criteria which defined a private company, it was exempted from the necessity of filing most of these returns, such as balance sheets. The Consolidating Act of 1908, which drew together in one Act all the extant clauses from the company legislation of the past forty-five years, re-established the necessity of the company keeping a board minute book to record the proceedings and resolutions of its directors and managers.[42] Further document creation was insisted upon in 1928 when the Companies Act of that year required, in addition to the other returns, that a profit and loss account be laid before the shareholders in general meeting[43] to accompany the balance sheet, and all shareholders and debenture owners were entitled to receive copies of both free on demand[44] so increasing the number created and the likelihood of some surviving. In 1929 it was stipulated that the auditors' report and the balance sheet be sent to the shareholders a week previous to the meeting.[45] Although the balance sheet was to continue to be filed with the Registrar, there was no similar provision for the profit and loss account, so its survival rate is lower. This Act also re-imposed on the directors that they ensure the company kept proper books of account, and insisted on more detail being given on the breakdown of assets in the balance sheet, such as a distinction between fixed and circulating assets, a separate figure for goodwill and investments in subsidiary companies.[46] As a result, balance sheets from 1930 are more informative but, because no rules were introduced for a similar level of disaggregation for the profit and loss account, that document remained very uninformative with often one figure for all categories. A point well made by Sir William McLintock, an eminent chartered accountant, in evidence before the Greene Committee in 1925: 'it is not the practice with, I suppose, one company in a thousand ever to disclose their profit and loss account except by totals'.[47]

Despite a number of committees and some pressure for reform in the 1930s, little was done which affected the document creation activities of firms before the Second World War put such matters on ice for the duration. It was not until 1948 that a new Companies Act reached the statute book.[48] It had some significance for record keeping in that all companies had to send copies of their profit and loss account to the Registrar and more detailed guidelines were laid down as to how the balance sheet and profit and loss account were to be set out.[49] This Act is usually more remembered for its insistence that auditors belong to one of the professional bodies recognized by the BoT[50] but it also played a part in increasing disclosure although maintaining the private company's exemption from the need to file accounts with the Registrar.[51] This was not repealed until the 1967 Companies Act[52] when *all* registered companies were required to file annual accounts.

In general, then, company law has had a great impact on the preservation of business documents for the stipulation that companies file certain documents with the Registrar has resulted in a rich deposit of information about business that might otherwise not have survived. It is a great pity that company law was not more consistent in its requirements and that such a large lacuna exists in the middle to late nineteenth century. In terms of document creation, company law was less important for, as Hadden says, 'the standards set by the best firms have usually been far in advance of the strict legal requirements in the companies acts.'[53] Company law attempted to round up the stragglers, companies which avoided disclosure through inefficiency or for dubious reasons.

The Stock Exchange

The second influence on the type of business documents created was the requirements of the London Stock Exchange. In the early nineteenth century the informal association of dealers in a narrow range of government stock and the shares of a few chartered trading companies became more formalized with new premises in 1802 and a committee of trustees as well as a general purposes committee. The Exchange was increasingly dealing and issuing shares of financial and industrial companies, especially during the bursts of railway activity in the 1830s and 1840s; later, insurance companies, iron, cotton and coal firms were quoted.[54] In recognition of this widening in the range of industrial securities the Railway Department, under its secretary, Mr Slaughter, was renamed in 1864 the Share and Loan Department.[55] However, the real growth in the promotion of the shares of domestic industrial firms did not come until the last quarter of the nineteenth century when family firms and partnerships began looking to the Stock Exchange to raise more capital or put a value on their business.[56]

Since the long-term functioning of the London Stock Exchange depended upon the continuing confidence of a large number of investors, it was in the Exchange's interest to set rules to try and ensure that the companies which were traded on its floor did not bring it into disrepute. Therefore, by the 1880s the Committee of the Stock Exchange included in its rules clauses specifying the requirements for companies wishing to have their shares traded on the Exchange. Among these was the prerequisite that certain documents had to be lodged with the secretary of the Share and Loan Department before the Stock Exchange Committee would appoint a 'special settlement day' (the date when the shares were first traded on the floor of the Exchange.[57] Since if a company failed to provide these documents its shares would not be traded, this provided sufficient incentive for most firms to make the effort.[58] In the 1880s the documents that had to be lodged included the company's prospectus and articles of association; statements from the company giving details of allotment and deposits received; certificates from the company's bankers verifying these details; and copies of the share certificates and letters of allotment.[59]

If a company also wanted its share price included in the Stock Exchange list, that is given an 'official quotation', the Committee laid down additional requirements. However, these did not insist on the creation or lodging of additional documentation but rather specified that certain information had to be included in the documents such as the prospectus and articles of association.[60] Thus in the late nineteenth century the Stock Exchange did not bring about the creation of any significant new types of records. Those documents it required to be lodged — the prospectus, the articles of association — would have been created by the company in any case to comply with the Companies Acts. Also, the Exchange was only interested in receiving documents at one point in time, when the company sought the right to have its shares dealt in. The Exchange did not concern itself with dynamic record creation — the creation and maintenance of records within the firm on a regular basis. The beneficial side of the Stock Exchange requirements is that it affected document preservation by providing another repository for a range of business records, and one which survived largely intact to provide a vast source for latter-day users now available in the Guildhall Library, London.

The position of the Stock Exchange in influencing document creation did not fundamentally alter in the twentieth century. The Exchange continued to be mainly concerned to receive certain papers when a company raised more capital from the public or sought the privilege of having its shares traded there. Over time, the Stock Exchange increased drastically the amount of information it required and thus the amount of paper that had to be lodged before a special settlement day was appointed or an official quotation granted. For instance, in the early twentieth century it included the requirement that a company's articles of association contain a clause agreeing to circulate to all members at least seven days before a general meeting the balance sheet and report of the directors.[61] In this the Stock Exchange marginally anticipated the similar stipulation of the 1907 Companies Act. Similarly in 1929, the Stock Exchange added the requirement that the articles of association of all companies include provision to send out a profit and loss account to all members;[62] again this is merely a reflection of the same injunction in the Companies Act of that year. Thus the Stock Exchange did not pioneer any new forms of document creation but rather followed the movement of actual or anticipated company law. Similarly, apart from the creation of balance sheets, profit and loss accounts and directors' reports, with by implication the necessity of maintaining records from which these could be compiled and constructed, the Stock Exchange never took an active role in suggesting or stipulating any guidelines on internal record creation on a day-to-day basis which would improve the making of decisions or financial control. It perceived itself only as the guardian of the investor in a narrowly defined way.

The main benefit of the Stock Exchange's role in retrospect was in building up a vast archive of those documents which it required to be lodged with the secretary of the Share and Loan Department — the prospectuses, directors' reports, balance sheets and, later, profit and loss accounts. In addition to these regular remittances, companies were required to send copies of all letters or notices about scrip issues, rights issues, intentions to convert or redeem stock, reports of annual meetings in the financial or trade press, court rulings affecting the company's financial standing or voting procedures, or any other document which might materially alter an investor's view of the company's share price. In this way the Exchange endeavoured to build up a complete picture of the financial activities of its companies. In 1882 the secretary of the Share and Loan Department, Sir Henry Burdett, began issuing *Burdett's Official Intelligence* which was an annual abstract of the financial information submitted to his department during the year.[63] This was the forerunner of the *Stock Exchange Year Book*. Although there had been previous *Stock Exchange Year Books*, such as that published by Thomas Skinner from 1875, they had not been compiled from inside information and had not had the Exchange's blessing.[64]

These requirements, of course, only applied to companies who were seeking, or had acquired, a quotation on the Stock Exchange, that is 'public' companies in modern parlance. The Exchange also tried to influence document creation in the wider world of non-quoted joint stock companies. On a number of occasions its members gave evidence to parliamentary enquiries on the changes it considered necessary in company law. It put forward a most thorough set of proposals to the Register of Joint Stock Companies in early 1866, when it suggested ten points that needed consideration.[65] They were all intended to increase public confidence in joint stock companies by requiring the Registrar to vet more positively a proposed company's articles and directors, by outlawing some of the worst current practices, such as manipulation of the market in its own shares by a company, and by setting minimum requirements for subscriptions and deposits before a company could be considered fully registered. In addition, the Stock Exchange recommended fuller public disclosure of changes in the structure of companies, for example their boards or capital, and suggested publication of such alterations in the *London Gazette*.[66] It may seem strange that the London Stock Exchange should be in favour of government intervention in company formation and operation, given the popular view of businessmen as fervent advocates of *laissez-faire* in the nineteenth century. However, as in other examples, businessmen did not talk with one voice and when they found their particular interests in jeopardy they were not reluctant to come forward to request governmental action. In this case the Stock Exchange had to maintain the confidence of its existing investors to have a long-term future; more than this, the more far-sighted members were trying to extend the range of investors in its shares. Joint stock form and limited liability were two devices which aided this, but with an ever greater separation of ownership and management the Committee of the Stock Exchange appreciated the value of a favourable public image for the joint stock company and a higher level of disclosure, if not to inform the non-active shareholder, at least to counter the claim that information was not made available.

Thus both directly and indirectly the Stock Exchange influenced document creation and retention; directly, by insisting on receiving copies of certain papers it compelled all public companies to create those specific records and effectively required them to keep books containing the data from which to draw up the requisite documents, so creating a back-up level of internal documentation. Indirectly, the Stock Exchange influenced public opinion by contributing to the debate on the requirements for forming joint stock companies and advocating much fuller disclosure and thus record creation and circulation. The better-managed companies adopted such recommendations even when they were not backed by the force of law.

Of course the London Stock Exchange was not the only formal market for raising capital in the UK in the nineteenth century. A number of provincial stock exchanges developed during the boom in railway promotion in the 1830s and 1840s, as in Liverpool and Manchester in 1836, Leeds and Sheffield in 1844.[67] They had no formal connection with the London Stock Exchange and were free to draw up their own regulations about the requirements for granting a company a special settlement or a quotation, and for the period up to 1900 these varied significantly from those of London. Until the 1860s it 'involved little more than exhibiting the scrip to the committee for an exchange'.[68] There was a tightening of the requirements by some provincial stock exchanges following the legislation of the late 1850s which made limited liability easily available. Liverpool and Manchester laid down similar conditions to the London Stock Exchange for a special settlement, that is they were mainly concerned that companies should disclose to the exchange various details of the capital issued and the exchange stipulated that minimum proportions of the capital should be issued. The requirements were stricter for firms requiring quotations as well as special settlements, and were more valuable to the historian in causing documentation to be produced and lodged. For example, prospectuses, memorandum and articles of association, shareholders' and directors' lists and latest reports all had to be submitted. However, many of the smaller exchanges had virtually no requirements, and even on the larger provincial ones if a company already had a quotation in London or one of the other large provincial markets its shares would be readily accepted without the need to submit the usual paperwork.[69]

Towards the end of the century some of the provincial exchanges became aware of the need to tighten requirements and tended to follow most of the new practices established in London. There remained considerable diversity between the various provincial exchanges. The formation of the Council of the Associated Stock Exchanges in 1890, which included the eight largest provincial stock exchanges, endeavoured to implement uniformity in the requirements for quotations.[70] For example, in 1895 the Council recommended, *inter alia*, that certain clauses should be included in the articles of association of all quoted companies, including the necessity of printing and circulating balance sheets and directors' reports to all shareholders prior to the annual general meeting.[71] Again in 1910 the Council was urging its members to adopt the same rules as London on disclosure and thus the creation and lodging of documentation. This proved unacceptable to a number of provincial exchanges and the best the Council could do was to recommend London rules and accept that individual committees might waive some of them.[72] By the 1920s the larger provincial exchanges such as Liverpool and Manchester had adopted the same rules as London and thus required the filing of the same documents.[73] Although many of the smaller provincial markets continued to vary both in their apparent requirements and in practice from London, this was less true of the disclosure rules, the main sticking point being over the proportion of an issue allotted to the public. Thus by the 1920s the provincial stock exchanges were requiring roughly the same documents to be sent in as London. They therefore had a similar effect on document creation as the London Stock Exchange, that is to say they did not pioneer the creation of any classes of documents or introduce the necessity of maintaining any classes of books internally in the firm. Rather, their main importance to the present-day historian is that they built up a set of documentation on the smaller, less national companies which were traded on the provincial markets, some of which still exists today, mainly in local authority record offices.

Internal record creation

There were a number of factors influencing a business when it came to creating and maintaining internal documentation systems. External to the firm was the requirement of company law to keep and/or file specific documents, if the business was a registered company. The rules of the Stock Exchange about disclosure of mainly financial information applied to those companies whose share prices were quoted and imposed a need to prepare and circulate some data. The articles of association of a company, although self-imposed, had the force of law. Most contained clauses requiring the directors to keep specific books and records (see page 45 for an example from the Oakerthorpe Iron and Coal Company) placing a further onus on the company.

However, external factors were only the most obvious pressures on firms to create records. Any partnership or company with commercial acumen appreciated the value of a comprehensive set of books as an aid to good management. A permanent record of decisions made, especially those with long-term consequences, was required to ensure continuity of direction. Data on which to base management decisions was needed, such as the effect on sales of changes in prices, or on costs of investment in new machinery. The firm found it valuable to maintain records of previous experience in certain countries or regions, or of dealings with particular firms or types of activity when contemplating any new course of action. This required the preservation of historical data in order to calculate trends and perceive significant shifts. Control of employees or subordinate business units necessitated the creation of methods of transmitting instructions, receiving regular reports and ensuring careful recording of incomes and expenditures. Although of little significance until quite recently, record creation also came about in order to communicate to the workforce and keep it informed, via the house magazine. Thus there are many internal reasons for creating and preserving documentation, over and above external requirements.

Some features of a business are likely to determine the quantity and quality of documents created internally. One of the most important was the pattern of ownership. A firm run by its founder, perhaps employing only skilled labour and no other white-collar workers or managers, was likely to be able to operate on a very low level of documentation. Since the owner was in regular daily touch with all aspects of the business, and indeed carrying out himself most of the managerial roles — marketing, sales, personnel and financial — he knew experientially most of the important information and did not need to commit it to paper. This was reinforced by the lack of necessity to report to any other partner on his activities, or to ensure continuity of action by any parallel decision maker. Once a firm moved from a sole proprietor to a partnership, the need for documentation leapt dramatically. Each partner had to ensure the other was kept informed, or preferably consulted beforehand, on policy decisions.[74] The profits of the business were no longer the income of one man, and so records had to be kept to ensure only genuine business expenses were paid from the partnership funds. It mattered little if a sole proprietor paid his wine merchant from ousiness funds or if he paid for a piano with a bill of exchange drawn upon the business,[75] but it would have caused significant problems in a partnership if such transactions were not carefully recorded and the relevant sum deducted from the appropriate partner's profits. When one partner was absent from the business, perhaps on the road drumming up sales, collecting payment or seeking out new sources of raw materials, this was likely to generate correspondence as the partners reported on their respective activities. The assumption of company form, apart from bringing the pressure of company law to bear, also necessitated another quantum leap in document creation. For now there might exist a separation between ownership and management. Admittedly this was not usually the case in nineteenth-century English industrial companies. Leaving aside those formed to provide transport or public utilities, most industrial companies before 1914 were conversions of existing family or partnership-run firms, in which the partners became directors *and* shareholders.[76] In these cases the managers continued to be the owners. However, when there was a separation of ownership and control, it increased dramatically the onus on the directors to keep records of their decisions and actions, and their impact on the business, as in theory they could be held accountable by the shareholders for their stewardship. In practice, of course, the majority of shareholders played no positive role in the affairs of the company and, providing it announced steady or slightly increasing profits and a similar dividend, it was unlikely to suffer any complaints from the owners. A similarly high level of document creation was likely to occur when one firm acted for another as an agent or intermediary. This was particularly true for shipping agents who found cargoes for shipping firms, and merchant partnerships which sold or bought on their principal's behalf.[77] The agents needed to keep the principals informed of what was being done in their name and at their expense and so there was likely to have been a large amount of correspondence and financial reports generated between the two firms.

Size was another characteristic of a business which had a direct effect on the amount of documentation created. When the firm was small, the amount of information generated was so little as to need minimal recording: it was the common consciousness of the group of people working in it. As the firm grew in size, so did the amount of information created. There were more employees, more customers and more suppliers, necessitating the creation of separate books for all three. This was emphasized when the firm branched out on to more than one site. Documents were required from head office to control, inform or motivate the other plants. In like vein the outposts were required to report back to the main factory. There was too much work for a single proprietor or even a couple of partners. The simplest solution was to resort to a functional division of labour among management based on separate departments each concerned with only one functional area.[78] The board, in order to take an overview, needed to be kept informed and this required vertical reporting systems. When managerial specialization had developed further, the decision takers found themselves so compartmentalized that horizontal communication systems were also needed. Informal means of communication were insufficient to ensure that decisions were known and acted upon throughout the firm, so more formal methods of documentation had to be created and implemented. The problem of extended lines of communication became even greater when a firm became a multinational owning plants in a number of countries. If it did not implement strict, formal control systems it was likely to find itself with ailing subsidiaries which drained capital from the parent company. Similarly, a policy of diversification was likely to put a strain upon existing communications and require a re-think of documentation.

For an individual firm, another factor in its record creation and preservation policy was the influence upon it of the practice of other firms. Since the law made no attempt to lead but rather lagged behind best practice, being concerned only to outlaw the very worst practices, it provided little guide to firms. Instead they learnt from each other partially through the transfer of employees who took with them knowledge of their employer's current practice, and more importantly through the informal managerial networks. It was not uncommon to have interlocking partnerships in which an individual was a partner in a number of different businesses, therefore spreading his risks and widening his interests. This was continued and enlarged in the joint stock company where the non-executive director was common and individuals were normally on the board of a number of companies, perhaps because of familial links or friendships, perhaps because the firms had some working relationships. Through these informal connections, partners and later directors could and did bring ideas on documentation from one firm to another and thus encourage the average practice closer to current best practice.

Professional bodies began to make their influence felt in the last quarter of the nineteenth century when existing bodies began introducing tighter rules about membership, insisting applicants pass a qualifying exam and adhere to ethical codes, and many new ones were formed, for example the Institute of Chartered Accountants in 1880 and the Chartered Institute of Secretaries in 1891.[79] Their members were gradually accepted into industrial employment because they were recognized as having technical white-collar skills and were bound not to reveal trade secrets to competitors. These bodies attempted to codify their disciplines and press forward with research into new techniques and practices. They also disseminated current techniques and proposals for improvements through learned journals and newsletters.[80] In this way they kept their members abreast of current developments and thinking and they in turn suggested new methods of book-keeping or record creation. This process is most clear in the accounting field where professional accountants moved into industrial jobs and reformed book-keeping practices, introduced new costing systems and made changes to financial reporting procedures.[81] A similar impact was made in the twentieth century by the emergence of a professional personnel function culminating in the formation of the Institute of Personnel Management in 1946 but having pre-First World War roots in the Association of Industrial Welfare Workers.[82] Part of the professionalization process introduced by the members of this body was to introduce personnel records — cards and files on each employee — codify and systematize rates of pay, improve communications between the workforce and management, and introduce various methods of work or performance measurement as the basis of piece rates or bonuses. All of these activities involved the creation and retention of new forms of documentation.

In more recent times, another body of individuals which had dramatic impact on the firm's record creation and preservation policy has been the consultant. Their effect has not always been beneficial to the researcher. Although in some cases they have recommended the introduction of new types of documentation, in their search for cost savings they have also not infrequently recommended the discontinuation of some systems and worse still the clearance and disposal of old records having no current usage.

In the last few years technology has had a contradictory effect on the creation of business documents. On the one hand, the photocopier has meant a proliferation of copies of documents, which should increase the likelihood of their survival, and various new forms of record preservation such as microfilm and microfiche should make the storage and updating of documents easier and cheaper. On the other hand, the single most important innovation in business since the Second World War, the computer, is having a quite opposite effect in that it is reducing the amount of business documentation that is created and preserved in paper form.[83] This is reinforced by innovations such as microfiche where there is a great temptation to dispose of the 'hard copy' once it has been committed to microfilm and retain only the plastic copy. In the early days of the electronic information-processing age, the clumsy modes of input to the computer required the creation of additional paperwork in the form of coding sheets, punching instructions or somesuch. The data to be processed needed to be put on punched card or magnetic tape for feeding into the processor unit. However, there has been a minor revolution within electronic data processing in the last few years. Now data does not need to be separately encoded but can be typed directly in from a modified typewriter keyboard; this eliminates the necessity for the intermediate stage and the creation of the punching sheet. This, however, is no real loss since these documents were seen as essentially ephemeral and were not likely to be preserved once the data on them had been input. Of more significance is the advent of the VDU screen used in conjunction with the keyboard, for this allows material to be created which may never appear in paper form, but only exists as rearrangements of the magnetic field on a 'floppy disc' or within the computer's main memory. This trend is compounded by the advent of networking and the electronic office. For in such a set-up, the businessman will not need to write letters on paper or keep a physical diary; he will keep his appointments in the appropriate file on his desk-top work station and communicate with his colleagues directly from his keyboard to their electronic mail box. No paper will be involved. The sender will use his keyboard or 'mouse', the recipient will read it on his screen and reply in the same way. Although it is much too premature to talk of the paperless office as anything more than a dream for the future, there is no doubt that some classes of business records, such as ledgers, journals, letter books, diaries and staff records, are threatened with extinction in paper form. Others are likely to be with us for some decades if for no other reason than the legal requirements of company law and the Stock Exchange. Those records which are now fast disappearing as physical artefacts stand less chance of long-term preservation in electronic form. The cost of computer memory is still expensive and there is a ruthless drive to erase unneeded files to make room for fresh requirements, and although the computer spawns vast quantities of computer print-out that too is often perceived as ephemeral — to be used and recycled. The last few years of the twentieth century may well see not merely a revolution in office practice but also a drastic reduction in the amount of business records preserved for the use of later scholars and historians.

Notes

1. There are many general works on the process of industrialization. Among the best is P. Mathias, *The First Industrial Nation* (Methuen, 2nd edn, 1983) which contains excellent bibliographies at the end of each chapter.
2. E.V. Morgan & W.A. Thomas, *The Stock Exchange: Its History and Functions* (Elek, 1962) pp. 37–8.
3. P.L. Cottrell, *Industrial Finance 1830–1914: The Finance and Organization of English Manufacturing Industry* (Methuen, 1980) pp. 45 & 54.
4. L. Hannah, *The Rise of the Corporate Economy* (Methuen, 2nd edn, 1983) pp. 19–23.
5. Cottrell, op. cit., pp. 13–16.
6. M.C. Reed, 'Railways and the Growth of the Capital Market' in M.C. Reed (ed.), *Railways in the Victorian Economy: Studies in Finance and Economic Growth* (David & Charles, 1969); J.R. Ward, *The Finance of Canal Building in Eighteenth-Century England* (Oxford UP, 1974).
7. R.N. Forbes, 'Some Contemporary Reactions to a Banking Failure', *Three Banks Review*, No. 121 (1979) p. 46.
8. J. Armstrong, 'Hooley and the Bovril Company', *Business History*, Vol. 28, No. 1 (1986) p. 19.
9. 7 & 8 Vict. c. 110.
10. Cottrell, op. cit., p. 40.
11. Ibid., p. 9.
12. For example, soap and candle makers, see A.E. Musson, *Enterprise in Soap and Chemicals: Joseph Crosfield and Sons Ltd 1815–1965* (Manchester UP, 1965) pp. 26–7.
13. H. Pollins, 'Aspects of Railway Accounting before 1868' in A.C. Littleton & B.S. Yamey (eds), *Studies in the History of Accounting* (Sweet & Maxwell, 1956).
14. D.A.R. Forrester, 'Early Canal Company Accounts: Financial and Accounting Aspects of the Forth and Clyde Navigation 1768–1818', *Accounting and Business Research*, Vol. 10 (1980) supplement, p. 116.
15. Pollins, op. cit.
16. 8 & 9 Vict. c. 16.
17. Ibid., clauses 115 to 118.
18. 7 & 8 Vict. c. 110.
19. 7 & 8 Vict. c. 113.
20. 7 & 8 Vict. c. 110, clauses 4 & 7; Morgan & Thomas, op. cit., p. 127.
21. Ibid., clauses 33, 34, 37, 49 & 50.
22. Ibid., schedule A, clauses 16, 21, 22 & 28.
23. Ibid., clauses 35, 36 & 42.
24. Ibid., clauses 11, 18 & 43.
25. Morgan & Thomas, op. cit., p. 130; Cottrell, op. cit., p. 54.
26. 19 & 20 Vict. c. 47, table B, clauses 69 to 72.
27. Ibid., clause 40.
28. Ibid., table B, clause 61.
29. Ibid., table B, clause 69.
30. Ibid., clause 40.
31. Ibid., table B, clauses 72 & 73; 25 & 26 Vict. c. 89, clauses 81 & 82.
32. 25 & 26 Vict. c. 89, clauses 14 & 15.

33. 21 & 22 Vict. c. 91, clause 4.
34. 33 & 34 Vict. c. 61.
35. For example, 34 & 35 Vict. c. 41; 45 & 46 Vict. c. 56.
36. 63 & 64 Vict. c. 48.
37. Ibid., clauses 9 & 10; Cottrell, op. cit., p. 73.
38. Cottrell, op. cit., pp. 72–3.
39. 63 & 64 Vict. c. 48, clauses 10 & 14.
40. 7 Edw. VII c. 50, clause 21.
41. Ibid., clause 37(1).
42. 8 Edw. VII c. 69, clause 71.
43. 18 & 19 Geo. V c. 45, clause 39(3).
44. Ibid., clause 41(1).
45. 19 & 20 Geo. V c. 23, clause 130.
46. 18 & 19 Geo. V c. 45, clauses 39 & 40.
47. Cited in J.R. Edwards, 'The Accounting Profession and Disclosure in Published Reports, 1925–35,' *Accounting and Business Research*, Vol. 6, No. 24 (1976) p. 291.
48. 11 & 12 Geo. VI c. 38.
49. Ibid., clause 127 and schedule 8, clauses 2 to 14.
50. Ibid., clause 161.
51. Ibid., clause 129.
52. 16 Eliz. II c. 81, clause 2.
53. T. Hadden, 'The Control of Company Fraud', *Planning*, Vol. 34, No. 503 (1968) p. 312.
54. The classic work on the development of the Stock Exchange remains Morgan & Thomas, op. cit.
55. Guildhall Library (GHL) Ms 14600, London Stock Exchange, General Purpose Committee Minutes, Vol. 28, p. 97, 26 March 1864.
56. Cottrell, op. cit., pp. 162–4; Hannah, op. cit., pp. 54–5.
57. GHL, ST 122, *Rules & Regulations of the Stock Exchange* (1888) pp. 59–60.
58. W.J. Reader, *A House in the City: A Study of the City and of the Stock Exchange based on the Records of Foster & Braithwaite 1825–1975* (Batsford, 1979) p. 70.
59. GHL, ST 122, op. cit., p. 60.
60. Ibid.
61. GHL, ST 122, *Rules & Regulations of the Stock Exchange* (1906) appendix 26, B10.
62. Ibid. (1929) appendix 35 B.
63. Morgan & Thomas, op. cit., p. 164.
64. GHL, Thomas Skinner, *Stock Exchange Year Book for 1876* (Cassel, Petter & Galpin, 1875) '2nd year of publication'.
65. Cottrell, op. cit., p. 57.
66. Ibid., pp. 57–8.
67. W.A. Thomas, *The Provincial Stock Exchanges* (Cass, 1973); Morgan & Thomas, op. cit., p. 141; Reed, op. cit., pp. 172–82; J.R. Killick & W.A. Thomas, 'The Provincial Stock Exchanges, 1830–70', *Economic History Review*, 2nd ser. Vol. 23, No. 1 (1970).
68. Thomas, op. cit., p. 137.
69. Ibid., p. 138.
70. Ibid., p. 196.
71. Ibid., p. 197.

72. Ibid., p. 198.
73. Ibid., p. 254.
74. William Pilkington's letters to his brother Richard are a good example. Because William was travelling around the country seeking sales but considered himself the senior partner, he created a continual stream of correspondence back to St Helens: T.C. Barker, *The Glassmakers: Pilkington 1826–1976* (Weidenfeld & Nicolson, 1977) pp. 50–2.
75. John Foster, for example, included in one book 'family accounts and accounts relating to the building of the warehouse and the mill': E.M. Sigsworth, *Black Dyke Mills: A History* (Liverpool UP, 1958) p. 138.
76. Examples abound; for example, Huntley and Palmers in 1898 was merely such a conversion, the Palmers who had been partners became directors: T.A.B. Corley, *Quaker Enterprise in Biscuits: Huntley & Palmer of Reading 1822–1972* (Hutchinson, 1972) pp. 151–2.
77. See S.K. Jones, *Two Centuries of Overseas Trading: The Origins and Growth of the Inchcape Group* (Macmillan, 1986) for many good instances.
78. Good examples are the Palmers who gave each partner a particular department to look after: Corley, op. cit., pp. 140–1, as did Crosfields, though their board included non-family members as well: Musson, op. cit., pp. 144–5.
79. Millerson suggests that at least seven such bodies were founded in the 1880s, and another two obtained royal charters although established previously. Of these, four had compulsory examinations by 1892. Several more commenced in the 1890s. G. Millerson, *The Qualifying Associations* (RKP, 1964) pp. 21–5, 124–9 & 159–64.
80. Ibid., appendix 1, column 6 has the titles of journals and their first year of publication.
81. For examples, see W.J. Reader, *Imperical Chemical Industries: A History, Volume one: the Forerunners 1870–1926* (Oxford UP, 1970) p. 220; C. Wilson, 'Management and Policy in Large Scale Enterprise: Lever Brothers and Unilever, 1918–1938' in B.E. Supple (ed.), *Essays in British Business History* (Clarendon, 1977) pp. 131–4; R.A. Church, *Kenricks in Hardware: A Family Business 1791–1966* (David & Charles, 1969) pp. 202–10.
82. M.M. Niven, *Personnel Management 1913–63* (IPM, 1967) pp. 31–7, 90, 107 & 128.
83. M.E. Turner, 'There is No Future for Business History', *Business History*, Vol. 20, No. 2 (1978) pp. 235–9 and Vol. 22, No. 1 (1980) pp. 100–3.

1 Prospectuses

Original purpose

The original aim of a prospectus was, and is, quite simple: to induce the public to buy the securities of a given company. The incentive is the anticipated return the investor may expect via profits distributed in dividends or interest and perhaps capital appreciation of the shares. The prospectus is therefore an advertisement advising potential investors of an opportunity, how and where to apply, and the date by which application should be made. Like any good advertisement, it should encourage the reader to want to apply by painting a glowing portrait of the investment opportunity. It will play up the good points and ignore or paper over the weaknesses and risks. The reader must therefore approach the prospectus with great scepticism; it is not an unbiased source.

The occasions on which prospectuses were issued can be roughly categorized under three headings. The privately circulated prospectus was usually sent out to a hand-picked group who were believed to be likely investors because of some known interest or attribute. Many of the early railway ventures in the UK initially sought promises of capital from local merchants and manufacturers who might benefit from a cheaper, faster form of transport to convey the goods in which they dealt.[1] These chosen individuals would then be sent a copy of the prospectus, probably through the post. Such an operation today is known as a 'private placing'. The conversion of an existing family business into a publicly-quoted company was likely to require a more general appeal. Partly to comply with the Stock Exchange rules, partly to gain a wide dispersion of shares, the prospectus was usually offered to the public at large via advertisements in the financial and trade press. Anyone could obtain a prospectus and apply for a block of shares. Since the business had been in existence for some time, it might be already well known either as a firm or because of its products and this might encourage widespread application. Such operations are variously known as issues, public offerings or offers for sale.

The third occasion on which a prospectus might be issued, again normally to the public, was when a newly formed company required a large amount of capital and was perceived as having an appeal to the general investor because of a current fashion or a particularly high anticipated return. A syndicate, which had carried out an initial investigation and evaluation of the business opportunities, put its findings before the world at large. Many good examples of this were seen in the 1890s when there was a boom in promoting gold mining and precious stone companies in South Africa, Western Australia and New Zealand. Something of a craze had developed for such securities, based on the fabled profitability of a few such enterprises which encouraged the flotation of many over-optimistic and high-risk ventures. It should not be supposed that prospectuses were only created when corporate form became easily available in the nineteenth century. As Dr Newman has shown,[2] many of the earliest joint stock companies such as the East India Company of 1657 and the Royal African Company of 1671 issued prospectuses to the public.

The purpose of raising the money from the public differed in individual cases, but was broadly for two main reasons. Where existing firms were going public, the founding and managing family might wish to put a value on their business by bringing it to the market place; they might have chosen to sell off some of their shareholdings to indulge in a more luxurious life style and had run out of family members or friends who wished to buy shares; after the First World War they may have need to raise cash to pay death duties; alternatively, they may have chosen to invest their capital more widely. The other main motive for issuing a prospectus was to raise capital to allow the initiation of a project, sometimes known as venture capital, or the expansion of an existing firm. Undertakings such as gold mines or steamship companies necessitated heavy investment but imposed a long delay before any return could be anticipated. The prospectus aimed to raise this capital and spread the often quite considerable risk.

The type of security offered by the prospectus varied with time and the reason for going to the market. In the late nineteenth century when many family companies went public, in order to retain control often only debentures or preference shares were offered for sale, the family retaining the equity, for example Lever Bros and Boots the Chemist.[3] The public accepted such securities because they were safer, normally carrying a fixed rate of interest which was cumulative, that is, if not paid in one year it was a prior claim on future years' profits, and the interest took preference over the ordinary shares — the equity.

There was a rough correlation between risk and return in the various types of security offered. Debentures were the least risky as they were secured on the assets of the company and were classed as loan stock. Their interest had to be paid irrespective of profitability, was cumulative and had prior claim over all other forms of capital, but attracted the lowest rate of return. Debenture holders had no rights in the direction of the business except if their interest was not paid. Preference shares were next in order of payment of interest and repayment in the event of liquidation. They too normally paid a fixed rate of interest (though higher than the debenture stock) and the interest was cumulative. They carried some voting rights though usually proportionately less than the ordinary shares. After the Second World War most preference shares lost their voting rights and became little more than another form of loan stock. Today, owners of the ordinary shares, or equity, of a company are the main risk takers and reward earners. However, in the late nineteenth century some companies issued fixed interest, cumulative ordinary shares and made deferred shares the lowest in the pecking order, bearing the greatest risk and, in theory, the greatest reward if the company did well. Generally there would be some difference in the voting rights of the two shares, weighted in favour of the deferred shares. The articles of association (q.v.) of the company should lay down the precise voting rights of each class of share. Deferred shares lost favour early in the twentieth century and ceased to be issued.

The law relating to prospectuses is highly convoluted. Crudely, until 1900 there was little effective legal regulation of what went into prospectuses, although there were numerous attempts to tighten up, for example the 1857 Fraudulent Trustees Act and the 1867 Companies Act. The former made the issue of a fraudulent prospectus a criminal act and the latter required that every contract made by a company or its promoters, directors or trustees should be disclosed in its prospectus, or that prospectus was considered to be fraudulent.[4] These Acts did not significantly restrict unscrupulous company promoters, because of poor drafting in the latter and the inability of shareholders to establish fraud for the former. However, a successful action was brought under the 1867 Act in Twycross vs. Grant in 1877 when Grant was found guilty of issuing a fraudulent prospectus because he failed to disclose contracts between the promoters of the Lisbon Steam Tramway Co and construction contractors.[5] The 1890 Directors' Liability Act made some attempt to remedy the situation by establishing a civil liability on the directors of a company for any untrue statements in a prospectus; but the Act contained such a proliferation of exemption clauses that it was ineffective.[6] The 1900 Companies Act remedied this. It laid down strict requirements on what was to be included in prospectuses and insisted on them being lodged with the Registrar of Joint Stock Companies before issue to the public.[7] The 1929 Companies Act added a further check on prospectuses by requiring that any profit figures in them were certified as correct by the company's auditors.[8] The importance of ensuring prospectuses were accurate was brought home in 1931 when Lord Kylsant, chairman of the Royal Mail Steam Packet Co, was jailed for twelve months for issuing a false one. Although city opinion adjudged him unfairly convicted, the lesson struck home.[9] Further controls over share issues were instituted as a result of the Bodkin Committee of 1936 which led in 1946 to the establishment of the combined Metropolitan and City of London company fraud squad and gave the BoT investigative powers over share dealing and issue.[10]

Sources

The Guildhall Library is a good source of prospectuses for public companies as the Stock Exchange insisted on receiving all such prospectuses in order to monitor the activities of quoted companies and facilitate publication of an annual year book which summarized the financial status of each. The prospectuses were bound alphabetically by year and preserved. These volumes have been deposited with the Guildhall Library and since they are kept on the premises — unlike annual reports which are at an out-station — they can be consulted quickly and easily. They only cover firms seeking capital from the public at large and so do not contain privately circulated prospectuses. The earliest examples date from 1824 but the coverage is patchy until the 1880s after which they are complete. The categories covered are, however, only those included in the *Stock Exchange Year Book*.

In addition to the bound volumes at the Guildhall Library, another useful and very easily accessible source is the press. In order to attract a wide cross-section of investors, companies normally inserted their prospectuses as paid advertisements in both the trade and financial press. Thus the *Grocer, Chemist and Druggist* and *Mining World and Engineering Record* contain prospectuses for companies in their respective fields just as *Bradshaw's Railway Gazette* did in the 'railway mania' of the 1840s. Although the trade press developed in the middle of the nineteenth century, it is unusual to find prospectuses as advertisements until after the 1880s when a boom in company promotions combined with a realization by editors of the useful revenue to be derived from such sources. Some entries in the press contain the whole prospectus, some carry only summarized details and some merely advertise the existence of a full prospectus giving the barest details and the addresses from which they were available. At roughly the same time, the financial press seized the opportunities offered by carrying advertisements for prospectuses, for example the *Money Market Review* of the 1890s, later renamed the *Investors Chronicle*, contains many, as do the *Economist* and *Financial Times*. Even some general-interest newspapers or journals, such as the *Saturday Review* under the proprietorship of the controversial Frank Harris, took advantage of the extra income and touted around the city for such advertising.

Some prospectuses issued to the public are also available in book form. *The Times* issued bound volumes of all the prospectuses which were advertised in its pages from 1891 onwards. The advertisements are arranged in date order of their appearance and each volume contains an alphabetical index of the companies appearing and a summary of the issue details. These are complete reprints of the advertisements which appeared in *The Times* and so have all the strengths and weaknesses of the originals as already discussed. From 1975 Extel, the financial information company, printed its books of *Prospectuses and New Issues*. Like *The Times* volumes, the prospectuses are arranged in date order of issue, several volumes appear each year, and each volume has an alphabetical list of the companies appearing in it. A great strength of the Extel volumes is that they contain the whole prospectus, not simply the advertisement; also their summary tables contain more detail, and are arranged under a number of separate headings allowing easier aggregation of different sorts of issues.

The information they contain

Most prospectuses followed a familiar format which makes them easily recognizable. It also means that they nearly all contain the same type of information. The minimum, even in an advertisement, such as the Dunlop Pneumatic Tyre Company, was: the company name; the amount of capital to be issued and the breakdown into various classes, ordinary, preferred and deferred shares and debentures; the issue price; the location from which prospectuses can be obtained; the date by which applications must be received, the directors (their occupations and addresses), bankers, solicitors, brokers, auditors and registered offices of the company. In addition, the company secretary was always named and, where they existed, the names of any trustees such as for the debenture holders, overseas agents, consultants and correspondents. When an existing company was going public, the vendors were named and often an indication of the amounts of shares they were retaining. This was the basic, factual information required by the Stock Exchange.

The other type of information always included in the full prospectus and sometimes in the advertisements in the press was the piece of purple prose intended to attract the investor and convince him of the future profitability of the venture. This section usually contained a potted history of the company, an appraisal of the market in which it was operating and encouraging descriptions of both the past growth in output and profits and the anticipated future growth. Thus the Humber Company prospectus emphasizes the company's pedigree in terms of cycle manufacture and its past growth in output: 'it has been found quite impossible to keep pace with the orders. . . the Humber factories have been kept running early and late, to endeavour to cope with the demand'. The market for cycles is evaluated: 'cycles are daily becoming more and more a necessity of every household', and future prospects are detailed in glowing terms: 'immediate and exceptional results are guaranteed to this Company'. It will be noted that no firm figures are given for profits. This was not unusual. The prospectus of F. Hopper and Company (another cycle firm) as late as 1907 sought to raise capital without giving any figures for past sales, profits or the firm's current liabilities or assets.[11]

An essential ingredient in the prospectus was the purpose for which the company was formed and the uses to which the capital was to be put. In the

Humber example, the purpose of the company was twofold: to take over the bicycle wholesaling and retailing activities of Messrs Marriott & Cooper and to take over from Humber & Company Limited the sale of all the bicycles which they produced. The capital was required for two distinct but related purposes: to pay Messrs Marriott & Cooper for their business and 'for providing working capital'. Some prospectuses went into details of the manufacturing process presumably to impress the putative investor by its complexity, modernity or sophistication. Some firms also made a great play of their 'unique selling proposition' (USP) as modern marketeers might term it: the quality of the product or service which differentiates it from other like products or services and will thus cause the consumer to want to buy it. In the Humber example, nothing is mentioned about this. The reader is no wiser as to why Humber cycles should be preferred to any other brand of bicycle. Another ploy used by writers of prospectuses, as a means of engendering enthusiasm for their wares, was to use local colour, exotic locations or customs to attract attention. Thus when Bovril sought investors in 1896 it made much of the location from which the raw material came: 'hundreds of miles of the most luxurious pasturage in the world. . . Much of the herbage of the South American *pampa* is known as "alfalfa" and in this country as "lucerne" and it is in reality clover grass of the best quality. . . regularly sown. . . giving no fewer than five or six crops a year.'[12] Ignoring the questions of accuracy and internal consistency, it is obvious that this passage was intended to attract investors by the lush location and the related concept of rich pickings from the investment. Similar techniques were employed in prospectuses for ventures abroad such as gold mines, plantations and even dock and harbour companies: the strange and romantic landscape or peoples were used to attract and give a glamorous image to the investment.

The amount of information contained in prospectuses, and thus their length, has increased enormously over time. Before the First World War a couple of pages might have sufficed, but in the inter-war period double this would have been the minimum required. By the 1960s prospectuses had grown to enormous size and the detail had grown commensurately — ten to fifteen pages being not unusual. This increase in size is explained partly by stricter rules about what prospectuses must contain — both in law and to be acceptable to the Stock Exchange — and partly by the growing sophistication of investors, especially institutional ones, and their battery of tools of analysis to assess one investment against another.

Uses

Because most of the information contained in prospectuses related directly to the internal financial structures of the company involved, the major value of such documents is to the economic and business historian. From the factual material, prospectuses allow an analysis of the relative popularity in different periods of the different types of security — equity, preference shares and debentures. Similarly the denomination of shares can be examined over time, to see if this changed, as is sometimes suggested: in the early nineteenth century large denomination shares — £10 upwards — were the norm but by the end of the century the £1 share had become the usual size. Prospectuses could be used also to calculate the total amount of capital raised from the investing public in any given period, and then an analysis made of the industrial breakdown by type of company. Similarly, changes in the issue price can be analyzed, the amount of premium charged, or if issued at par, and how this changed over time.

However, all of the above uses suffer from a major drawback inherent in this source. Prospectuses are not records of what actually happened. Rather they are statements of intent. There is no guarantee that the company will in fact raise the totals for which it advertises. The prospectus indicates only what it wishes to raise. To ensure accuracy of any analysis of capital formation, it is necessary to check in another source whether the issue was fully subscribed and, if not, whether it was underwritten so that the shares not taken by investors were left in the underwriters' hands. Indeed, an interesting use of prospectuses would be to identify what sort of companies *failed* to attract sufficient investors and, as a result, never commenced business or ceased trading. This would shed light on the fads and fashions of investors and the degree of rationality shown by capital owners.

The researcher should treat the written statement with a similar degree of scepticism. It was intended to entice potential investors into parting with their savings and, although invariably decent, there were many prospectuses that were neither honest nor truthful and only legal by virtue of a lack of effective legislation on such matters until 1900. Thus many over-optimistic claims were made for future profitability, the truth was embroidered, the quality of the product over-stated, the richness of a vein of ore multiplied, or the capacity of a piece of land to carry cattle, rubber trees or tea bushes exaggerated. The user of prospectuses should put no trust in their claims until checked against a quite separate alternative source. An indication of the craftiness of the writers of prospectuses can be gained from two points. Some prospectuses which were for the floating of existing family-owned companies gave no figures of the profits generated over the last few years but contented themselves with very general statements such as 'a rapid growth in profits' or 'marked increase in profitability'. Others gave a set of figures, but made no claim that they had been expertly audited. The sharper city page editors railed against such gross malpractices in the late nineteenth century, but largely to no avail. The other point to be borne in mind is that some of the shadier company promoters of the late nineteenth and early twentieth centuries paid literary hacks large sums of money to misuse their talents for fiction-writing by putting them to work on the drafting of prospectuses. Thus it would be quite wrong to base any analysis solely on the statements of a company prospectus issued before 1900. In the twentieth century, they became progressively more reliable.

In addition to providing a starting point for a range of economic analysis on capital raising, the prospectus could be of some use to the biographer or family historian who suspected an ancestor of being a director of the company. Again it has to be said that the prospectus only states what may happen if the issue is successful. There are many slips between prospectus and subscription; the potential director may find himself off the board if the issue fares badly or may choose not to take up his place on the board. The investigator is better advised to use the return of directors (q.v.) lodged with the Registrar of Joint Stock Companies which stated what actually happened, and by law had to be honest.

Cross-references to other documents

The best sources to use in order to check the prospectus of the company are the papers lodged in Companies House under its registered name and number. The register of directors (q.v.) will confirm if in fact the individuals named on the prospectus did sit on the board and, if so, for how long. Similarly, these returns had to keep the Registrar informed of any changes in capital structure, both quantity and type, so that alterations in share denomination, proportion of capital in debentures, preference or ordinary shares will all appear there and show how successful the company was in its issue. The shareholders' lists (q.v.) are also a useful adjunct as they will show who subscribed for the issue, and thus allow a social and geographical analysis to be made, and also whether the underwriters were left with large blocks of shares indicating public suspicion of the company. Similarly the annual report and accounts (q.v.) will show the profits made, which can be compared with any predictions in the prospectus and show how far the company lived up to expectations.

Works using this source

There are no books or articles which draw solely on this source for it provides only a very partial picture of the total activities of the firm. Additionally, because the prospectus is only an invitation to subscribe capital there is no guarantee that the amount indicated was actually raised as explained in 'Uses' above. The researcher needs to confirm from other sources whether sufficient subscriptions came forward for the issue to proceed to allotment and whether it was underwritten and thus if the prospectus achieved its purpose. Also the existence of a prospectus does not mean that the company named in the document benefited from the capital raised. When a family firm converted to a limited liability company, or an unscrupulous promoter bought a business from its owners and then issued a prospectus to launch it on the public, the additional money raised might go entirely to the family partners or into the pocket of the promoter, not the firm.[13] Prospectuses have been used as evidence of export markets or to show the geographical breakdown of a company's activities,[14] but before 1900 confirmation would be needed from another source.

The example

Humber originated with Thomas Humber, a blacksmith moulder, who began designing and building bicycles at Beeston, Nottingham, in 1868. Humber went into partnership in 1875 with Thomas Rushforth Marriott and Frederick Cooper, both prominent racing cyclists who appear in this prospectus. This lasted until about 1885 when the partnership was dissolved and Marriott and Cooper set up their own firm while Humber went into a new partnership with T. Harrison Lambert, a Nottingham lace bleacher, dyer and finisher. He, it will be noted, in 1896 was a director of Humber & Co Ltd and one of the proposed directors of Humber & Co (Extension) Ltd. In the same year, Humber appointed Martin D. Rucker as manager of their London depot. He was another prominent racing cyclist who went on to become managing director of Humber and appears on this prospectus as putative managing director of Humber & Co (Extension) Ltd.[15]

In 1887 Humber and Co, the partnership, was bought by H.J. Lawson, possibly with the financial backing of E.T. Hooley, both soon to be notorious company promoters of the period, for £125,000, and merged with C.N. Baker's Coventry Cycle Co and the Express Cycle Works of Wolverhampton. In 1895, Hooley and Lawson took advantage of the fashionable mania for all things bicycling to launch Humber as a public company with a capitalization of half a million pounds and Rucker as the managing director.[16] By then Humber was the second largest employer in the UK cycle industry and one of its giants in terms of output and capital.[17] Determined to milk the public while the boom lasted, Hooley then brought out four Humber offshoots in 1896 but 'not one . . . achieved full subscription'.[18] Humber & Co (Extension) was one of these. The ostensible reason for this company was to split manufacturing from selling with the old company concentrating on production and the new firm on marketing, though why these two activities should be better performed in separate firms is not made clear.

Humber then became one of the pawns in Lawson's grandiose plans to monopolize the infant UK motor industry by owning all the relevant patents. Humber began to construct some of the primitive proto-cars, moving its head office to Coventry and closing its works at Beeston in 1905. In 1901, Humber launched a Coatalen-designed, 12 hp, 4-cylinder car selling for £300 'which was the first great popular success of the British industry'.[19] By 1913, Humber 'was the largest producer of cycle cars in Great Britain', known as the Humberette,[20] and was the third largest producer of cars in the UK, surpassed in output only by Ford and Wolseley.[21]

One of the firms which distributed Humber Cars was Rootes Ltd. This firm was started in 1917 by the Rootes brothers, William and Reginald, as a motor distributorship based in Kent. By 1927 it was the largest such firm in the country and integrated backwards into manufacturing to ensure a flow of quality products. Initially Rootes bought a substantial shareholding in Humber and its subsidiaries, Hillman and Commer. By 1932, Rootes held a majority of the shares. Later, Sunbeam and Talbot were added to the group and in the 1950s Thomas Tilling and Singer.[22] In 1964, when Rootes' profitability was slipping, Chrysler of the USA acquired a substantial minority shareholding and in 1966 took control of Rootes, and with it Humber.[23] In the late 1970s when Chrysler was suffering from rising oil prices and a lack of fuel-efficient cars in its home market, it sold its European operation to Peugeot of France.[24]

Notes

1. For example, S.A. Broadbridge, 'The Sources of Railway Share Capital' in M.C. Reed (ed.), *Railways in the Victorian Economy* (David & Charles, 1969).
2. K. Newman, 'Financial Advertising Past and Present', *Three Banks Review*, No. 140 (1983).
3. C. Wilson, *The History of Unilever* (Cassell, 1954) Vol. 1 pp. 46–7; S.D. Chapman, *Jesse Boot of Boots the Chemist* (Hodder & Stoughton, 1974) pp. 129–31.
4. 20 & 21 Vict. c. 54; 30 & 31 Vict. c. 131, clause 38.
5. D.J. Jeremy (ed.), *Dictionary of Business Biography, Vol 2, D–G* (Butterworths, 1984) p. 627.
6. 53 & 54 Vict. c. 64; P.L. Cottrell, *Industrial Finance 1830–1914* (Methuen, 1980) pp. 67–8.
7. 63 & 64 Vict. c. 48, clauses 9 & 10.
8. 19 & 20 Geo. V c. 23, clause 2 of Part II of 4th Schedule.
9. E. Green & M. Moss, *A Business of National Importance* (Methuen, 1982) is the latest and most comprehensive work on this famous case.
10. BPP 1836–7 XV (Cmd 5539); T. Hadden, *Company Law and Capitalism* (Weidenfeld & Nicolson, 1977) pp. 337–8.
11. A.E. Harrison, 'F. Hopper & Co. The Problem of Capital Supply in the Cycle Manufacturing Industry, 1891–1914', *Business History*, Vol. 24, No. 1 (1982) pp. 12 & 13.
12. *Saturday Review*, Vol. 82 (21 Nov. 1896) p. 557.
13. J. Armstrong, 'Hooley and the Bovril Company', *Business History*, Vol 28, No. 1 (1986).
14. R. Munting, 'Agricultural Engineering and European Exports before 1914', *Business History*, Vol. 27, No. 2 (1985) n. 13; S.K. Jones, 'The Decline of British Maritime Enterprise in Australia', *Business History*, Vol. 27, No. 1 (1985) p. 71.
15. A.E. Harrison, 'The Origins and Growth of the UK Cycle Industry to 1900', *Journal of Transport History*, 3rd ser. Vol. 6, No. 1 (1985) pp. 42, 45, 57 & 58.
16. T.R. Nicholson, *The Birth of the British Motor Car 1769–1897* (Macmillan, 1982) pp. 361–3.
17. Harrison, op cit., p. 46; D.W. Thoms & T. Donnelly, *The Motor Car Industry in Coventry since the 1890s* (Croom Helm, 1985) p. 26.
18. A.E. Harrison, 'Joint Stock Company Flotation in the Cycle, Motor Vehicle and Related Industries, 1882–1914', *Business History*, Vol. 23, No. 2 (1981) p. 179.
19. S.B. Saul, 'The Motor Industry in Britain to 1914', *Business History*, Vol. 5, No. 1 (1962) p. 28.
20. K. Richardson, *The British Motor Industry, 1896–1939: A Social and Economic History* (Macmillan, 1977) p. 72.

21. Saul, op. cit., p. 25.
22. Jeremy, op. cit., *Vol. IV* (Butterworths, 1985) p. 936; Thoms & Donnelly, op. cit., pp. 95 & 168.
23. G. Turner, *The Leyland Papers* (Eyre & Spottiswoode, 1971) pp. 83–7.
24. L. Iacocca, *Iacocca: An Autobiography* (Bantam, 1986) p. 198.

The SUBSCRIPTION LIST will be OPENED on TUESDAY, the 31st March, 1896, and will be CLOSED on or before THURSDAY, the 2nd April, 1896.

This Company takes over, as from the 1st March, 1896, the sole right of supplying and dealing in Cycles of all descriptions manufactured by HUMBER & COMPANY, LIMITED, throughout Great Britain and the Colonies; also in France, Germany, Austria, Italy, and many other Foreign Countries, thus acquiring the whole of the wholesale and retail sale trade of HUMBER & COMPANY, LIMITED, of London, Beeston (Notts), Coventry, Wolverhampton, and Paris.

HUMBER & COMPANY, LIMITED, hold the premier position in the Cycle Trade. During the last four years the original £5 Humber Shares rose from £5 to £20. At the end of 1895, when the Capital was re-arranged, the Shareholders received £19 in Shares of £1 each, which Shares are again quoted at a substantial premium.

HUMBER & CO. (EXTENSION)
LIMITED.

(Incorporated under the Companies Acts, 1862 to 1890.)

CAPITAL £200,000,

Divided into 200,000 Shares of £1 each.

The NATIONAL PROVINCIAL BANK OF ENGLAND, Limited, is authorised to received Subscriptions for the above Shares, payable as follows:— 2s. 6d. on Application; 7s. 6d. on Allotment; 5s. One Month after Allotment; 5s. Two Months after Allotment – Total, £1.

DIRECTORS.
° ARTHUR R. MARTEN,
° FREDERICK GODDARD,
° T. HARRISON LAMBERT,
° DUNCAN F. BASDEN,
° CHRISTOPHER N. BAKER,
° MARTIN D. RUCKER, *Managing Director.*
° Director of HUMBER & CO., LIMITED.

BANKERS.
THE NATIONAL PROVINCIAL BANK OF ENGLAND, LTD.,
112 Bishopsgate Street, London, E.C., and Branches.

BROKERS.
Messrs. COATES, SON & CO., 99 Gresham Street, E.C., and Stock Exchange

SOLICITORS.
Messrs. WILSON, BRISTOWS & CARPMAEL, 1 Copthall Buildings, E.C.

AUDITORS.
Messrs. J. R. ELLERMAN & CO., Chartered Accountants,
12 Moorgate Street, E.C.

SECRETARY AND OFFICES.
JAMES T. ALLBUTT, 32 HOLBORN VIADUCT, E.C.

PROSPECTUS.

HUMBER & COMPANY (EXTENSION), LIMITED, has been formed (1) to take over from Humber & Company, Limited, the sole right of supplying both wholesale and retail, in all parts of the world except the United States of America, Russia, Japan, Spain and Portugal, Cycles of all kinds manufactured by Humber & Company, Limited, of London, Beeston (Notts), Coventry, Wolverhampton, and Paris, thus becoming the sole distributing agency for the entire output of the Humber factories; and (2) to facilitate the acquisition by Humber & Company, Limited, of certain rights in the name of "Humber," as mentioned below, the advantage of which will accrue to this Company.

The prosperity of Humber & Company, Limited, has been such that, although season after season, for years past, extensive alterations and additions have been made to the manufactories, it has still been found quite impossible to keep pace with the orders constantly received from nearly every country in the world for Humber machines.

The demand for Humber Cycles is steadily growing, the current turnover to 29th February last being greatly in excess of the previous year. From the orders received the approaching season is likely to prove a record one in prosperity. Throughout the winter months the Humber factories have been kept running early and late, to endeavour to cope with the demand, which is entirely without precedent.

Having regard to the remarkable development and extent of the business, the Directors of Humber & Company, Limited, recently decided to separate the manufacturing department from the wholesale and retail sale department of the business, and this Company has accordingly been formed to carry on the wholesale and retail trade; and thus secures an established profit-earning business. The benefit of all existing Humber Trade contracts and arrangements, with agents and customers, which will not in any way be disturbed, and the show-rooms and depôts in London and Paris, will be transferred to the new Company, which will in future undertake all obligations in connection therewith. By this arrangement, Humber & Company, Limited, will be left free to devote the whole of its capital and resources to increasing its manufacturing capabilities, and making the necessary factory extensions (which have already been commenced), with a view to largely increasing the present output and profits.

As a part of the foregoing arrangement, Humber & Company, Limited, acquires, as hereafter mentioned, the good-will of the business of Messrs. Marriott & Cooper, Cycle Manufacturers, of Coventry and London, together with stock-in-trade, premises, trade marks, and certain rights which they had acquired in the name of "Humber" (they having been formerly partners with Mr. Thomas Humber, whose business was the foundation of Humber & Company, Limited), which enabled them to describe certain machines made by them as "Humber" machines. These rights have been found to give rise to serious inconvenience, especially on the Continent of Europe, and their acquisition by Humber & Company, Limited, will ensure that in future all machines made in this country and sold as "Humber" machines are manufactured by that Company, which cannot fail to be highly advantageous and of great importance to this Company also, having, as it will have, the sole right of supplying and dealing in such machines.

The Directors of Humber & Company, Limited, who are also the Directors of this Company, have made such arrangements as to the price which this Company will pay for machines, &c., and as to the terms and conditions under which it will work, which, while safeguarding the position and profits of Humber & Company, Limited, will, they believe, yield substantial Dividends to the Shareholders in this Company.

The £5 shares of Humber & Company, Limited, with a Capital of £125,000, advanced from £5 2s. in 1891 to £20 in November 1895. For the year ending 31st August, 1895, the Company paid a dividend of 28 per cent. At the end of last year the Company was reconstructed with a Capital of £500,000, divided into 250,000 6 per cent. Preference Shares, and 250,000 Ordinary Shares of £1 each, and the Shareholders received £19 in shares of £1 each in exchange for each original £5 share. Both classes of the new shares are now quoted at a premium.

The Cycle Industry is now generally acknowledged to occupy the first rank amongst the soundest and most prosperous of industrial investments in this country. Owing to their use for business purposes generally and the large number of riders of every class, especially the recent accession of lady riders, cycles are daily becoming more and more a necessity of every household. This Company, starting with the widest, oldest, and highest class connexion amongst cyclists all over the world, will not have to inaugurate a business, but will simply have to continue executing orders which are ready to hand, and which should certainly go on increasing from all parts of the world, the extraordinary demand for machines from France and elsewhere on the Continent being only equalled by the home trade. This being so, immediate and exceptional results are guaranteed to this Company, while the present arrangement will better enable Humber & Company, Limited, to cope with the enormous demand which has arisen.

The Humber sale trade will be taken by this Company as from the 1st March, and all accounts will be adjusted between the two Companies on the footing of the new arrangement as from that date. On the 1st March, 1896, there were orders on hand, unexecuted, for upwards of 12,000 machines, the sale profit on which will accrue to this Company.

The Company Registration Syndicate, Limited, have recently contracted to acquire the business of Messrs. Marriott & Cooper, and to transfer the same, free of cost, to Humber & Company, Limited, in part consideration for the concession of the sole right of purchasing, selling, and dealing in Humber machines, and have agreed, in consideration of £100,000, payable in cash or shares, to transfer all such rights to this Company, and to pay all costs and expenses of and incidental to the formation of the Company down to allotment. The Company thus retains 100,000 Shares available for providing working Capital, and £75,000 out of the first subscription will be so applied.

No part of the Capital has been underwritten.

The following Contracts have been entered into: (1) Letters dated 29th July, 27th July, 11th December, 1895, and 12th February and 25th March, 1895, between Thomas R. Marriott and Frederick Cooper and The Company Registration Syndicate, Limited; (2) dated 23rd September, 1895, between Humber & Company, Limited, of the one part, and Christopher Sydney Oxenburgh of the other part; (3) dated 21st December, 1895, between Christopher Sydney Oxenburgh, of the one part, and The Company Registration Syndicate, Limited, of the other part; (4) dated 27th March, 1896, between Humber & Company, Limited, of the one part, and Humber & Company (Extension), Limited, of the other part; (5) dated 27th March, 1896, between The Company Registration Syndicate, Limited, of the one part, and Humber & Company (Extension), Limited, of the other part.

In addition to the foregoing there are arrangements which have been entered into by The Company Registration Syndicate, Limited, who, as above mentioned, bear the costs and expenses of the formation of the Company, and of this issue, with reference to such expenses, and also to the division of the purchase consideration and profits, which may constitute Contracts within the meaning of Section 38 of the Companies Act, 1867; but the Company is neither a party to nor bound by such Contracts, and there are also various Contracts and Agreements entered into by Humber & Company, Limited, with agents, managers, employés, customers, and other parties, with reference to the sale department of the business which will be taken over by this Company, which are of the usual character, but are too numerous to specify. Subscribers will, therefore, be deemed to have had notice of such Contracts and arrangements, and to accept the particulars furnished in this Prospectus as a sufficient compliance with Section 38 of the Companies Act, 1867.

The Contracts specified above, together with copies of the Memorandum and Articles of Association, can be inspected by intending subscribers at the offices of the Company's Solicitors.

Application for a Stock Exchange quotation will be made in due course.

Prospectuses and Forms of Application for Shares may be obtained from the Bankers, Brokers, Solicitors, and the Offices of the Company.

1. Prospectus of Humber & Co (Extension) of 1896.
Source: Saturday Review, 28 March 1896.

2 Articles of association

Original purpose

Articles of association are at the heart of the joint stock limited liability company for they specify in legal terms the limits and purposes of the company and how its affairs should be conducted. They are, in theory, a tool for the shareholder to use in controlling the directors should they step outside these limits.

The concept of articles of association was introduced in the legislation of 1856–62 which made the adoption of limited liability simple and straightforward.[1] To form a joint stock limited liability company, the initial subscribers sought provisional registration from the Registrar of Joint Stock Companies and among other documents lodged a memorandum of association. This stated briefly the salient facts of the proposed company such as the name, objects and capital structure. To achieve full registration, the Registrar required, *inter alia*, the articles of association. These were bulky items, normally running to over one hundred clauses and fifty sheets of foolscap. Because they were a legal document, articles of association were couched in lawyers' English which today reads rather archaically but was essential at the time to stand up in a court of law. They were written longhand in copperplate in the early nineteenth century but by the end of that century were usually printed as a standard format had begun to be acceptable to many companies, allowing easy production of copies.

Articles of association specified the parameters within which the company had to operate, the rules and regulations concerning its running, and the powers and authority of the directors. Should the directors go beyond those objects laid down in the articles or fail to perform some duty therein specified, they laid themselves open to an action by any of the shareholders. Usually any change to the articles of association required the consent of a majority of the shareholders at a general meeting, and when made were added as 'amendments' at the end of the articles. However, some companies found their articles so irksome after a lengthy period of time that they found it necessary to introduce a whole new set: the Wigan Coal and Iron Company, formed in 1865, registered new articles in 1894.[2]

The 1856 Companies Act introduced by Robert Lowe, then Vice President of the Board of Trade, laid down 'model' regulations for the articles of association in Table B of the Act, and the 1862 Joint Stock Companies Consolidation Act perpetuated this practice by publishing the same model regulations but in Table A.[3] However, neither Act made it mandatory that all companies should adopt these model regulations; rather the model rules only applied by default, that is if the individual company did not specify in its memorandum of association that they did not apply. As a result, one of the earliest returns lodged with the Registrar by many companies is their disclaimer that 'Table B of the 1856 Act (or Table A of the 1862 Act) shall not apply'. So for the whole of the nineteenth century, companies could draw up their articles of association as they chose. The Registrar neither examined or approved them and had no power to enforce any provisions.[4] That said, a large number of companies followed the model regulations of the Acts in drafting their articles, for example the Wigan Coal and Iron Company.[5]

Documents very similar to articles of association can appear under different names, such as a deed of settlement. This was the document submitted to the Registrar under the 1844 Companies Act to obtain joint stock form. Thus from 1844 to 1856 the deed of settlement was the equivalent document to the articles of association, but for joint stock companies with unlimited liability.[6] It was also used until the mid-nineteenth century to try and acquire limited liability for a company without going to the trouble and expense of a crown charter or Act of Parliament. The assets of the company were vested in trustees through a deed of settlement and the shareholders were called co-partners. Careful drafting of the clauses of the deed meant the shares were freely transferable and each shareholder was liable for only a proportionate amount of any liabilities. This device ceased to be necessary after the legislation of 1856–62 made limited liability readily and cheaply available and so fell into disuse.[7] A similar document for unlimited partnerships was known as the 'articles of partnership', a legally binding contract specifying the limits and obligations of the partnership concerned. In some cases the articles of association may be lodged as a very brief and general document and then a 'special resolution' is drawn up and passed which puts the flesh on to the bare bones of the articles. However, whatever title they may lurk under, the articles of association should be easily identified by their length, legal language and item-by-item approach.

When drafted, the intention was that the articles should be sufficiently comprehensive to cover all the areas in which disputes might arise but also be sufficiently broad in their definitions or general in their wording as not to shackle the directors. However, if shareholders felt the articles were too vague or left too much leeway to the directors, they could choose not to invest in the company, so the company strived to achieve a balance. Despite the 1856 and 1862 Acts, there were great variations between the articles of different companies founded at the same time as their promoters sought to create different systems of control. It should also be stressed that articles are not static, fixed for all time at the inception of the company. Quite the contrary: the articles of association of a long-lived company change over time as the directors and shareholders appreciate that they have failed to anticipate a particular contingency or that conditions and rules suitable for the 1890s have become obsolescent by the 1920s or 1960s.

Sources

Because of their importance in defining the boundaries of the business and laying down the ground rules of operation, and because they are a crucial legal document, articles of association for companies in current existence will be carefully preserved among the company's papers, often by the company secretary or in the legal department. An alternative source for current companies is Companies House, or the depository where the oldest files are kept, Pontypridd near Cardiff. From the earliest legislation facilitating the formation of joint stock companies, the 1844 Act, one of the conditions of registration was that a copy of the deed of settlement should be lodged with the Registrar and that all subsequent alterations should be notified to him.[8] (After 1856 the requisite document became known as the articles of association.) Thus by a perusal of the appropriate files the researcher can discover not merely the articles drawn up when the company was formed but also trace when and how alterations were made to this original set of rules. Although the oldest files are not kept at Companies House, they can be brought in from the repository within a week or two after payment of the search fee, currently (1986) £1 per company.

Fortunately it is no more difficult to find the articles of association for those registered companies which have ceased to trade. When they were active, they too were required to lodge copies with the Registrar and when the company ceased to exist the Board of Trade passed the files over to the Public Record Office. They can now be found there under the BT31 and BT41 classifications. There are lists arranged by year and registration number and also alphabetically by company name, so that it is not difficult to locate the file of a given company providing either its name, year of registration or registered number are known. Although the contents of the files have been heavily weeded, this does not seem to have affected either the original articles of association or subsequent amendments. This does not, however, mean that all files contain articles. A surprisingly large proportion of early joint stock companies were virtually abortive — Shannon estimates about one-third of the total[9] — and never got beyond provisional registration. In these cases, articles of association are rarely on the file, as copies were never lodged, the promoters appreciating that they were on to a loser and cutting their losses by ceasing all activities.

The information they contain

Articles of association deal with the whole gamut of activities relating to the running of the company. They state basic information such as the name and registered address of the company, the objects of the company, often in the most general and vague terms in order not to constrain the actions of the directors. They specify the total capital of the company both nominal and actual, how it is broken down by class of share, the numbers and denomination of each type of share and the rights attached to each sort. They contain clauses on calls on shares; regulations about arrears and pre-payments, the rules of transfer of shares, joint shareholdings and deceased shareholders; when and how shares may be forfeit and the conditions under which loans may be entered into and increases made in the capital of the company.

The articles also define types of meetings of shareholders — ordinary, annual and extraordinary — state the frequency with which they should be held and the rules for calling extraordinary meetings in terms of numbers of shareholders or proportion of total shareholding signing the request. The range here could be quite large: Robsons Brewery Co insisted on three-quarters of the shareholding signing a demand for an extraordinary meeting.[10] The articles also lay down the procedure to be adopted at meetings: how the chairman should be determined, quorums, procedure for putting resolutions, when and how an adjournment could be called, methods of voting and who may act as a proxy and the procedure required in that case. These include the provision for guardians of lunatics and idiots to act for their charge. Many companies required only a show of hands at the meeting to carry a resolution and a poll of shareholdings might only be required if at least a given number of shareholders requested it. The articles stipulate the voting rights of different classes of shares, and the votes attached to different tranches of shares, for not all shares carried the same rights and votes were not necessarily directly proportional to shareholdings. One example, the Oakerthorpe Iron and Coal Co (OICC), gave one vote for every share up to ten, one additional vote for every five shares owned between eleven and one hundred, and one additional vote for every ten shares over 101.[11]

Normally a substantial proportion of the articles of association is concerned with the powers and responsibilities of the directors: the number to be appointed, how their remuneration is to be fixed, the qualifications in terms of numbers of shares held, and the conditions which disqualify an individual are all specified. Any director becoming a bankrupt, or holding less than a certain number of shares, or becoming an employee of, or contractor to, the company was automatically debarred from office by the OICC. The method by which directors were to retire, their re-eligibility and method of replacing them were laid down, as were the powers of the shareholders in general meeting to appoint, remove, replace and alter the number of directors. The method of conducting the 'proceedings of directors' was also rigorously specified. Often the guidelines were very broad to give the directors full powers: they 'may meet together for the despatch of business and regulate their meetings as they think fit and determine the quorum necessary'. The question of the chair at meetings, the formation of sub-committees, methods of reaching decisions were all itemized, as was the method of recording decisions. For example, clause 85 of the OICC articles reads:

> The Directors shall cause minutes to be made in books provided for the purpose:
> 1. of all appointments of officers made by the Directors
> 2. of the names of the Directors present at each meeting of Directors and Committees of Directors
> 3. of all orders made by the Directors and Committees of Directors
> 4. of all reports presented to the Directors by the Managing Director
> 5. of all resolutions and proceedings of the meetings of the Company and of the Directors and of the Committees of Directors[12]

Thus if they had survived, which they have not partly because of the relatively short life of the company, the minute books of this company would have been a valuable record of the directors' decisions.

The articles also detailed how and when a dividend might be declared (usually only out of profits and by the directors) and indicated whether the directors were empowered to establish a reserve fund from profits to equalize dividends, meet contingencies or repair and maintain the works. The establishment of such a fund, which might be invested outside the business in gilts or government stock, was not an unusual practice for successful companies in the late nineteenth century, though it tended to fall into disfavour in the 1930s after the trial of Lord Kylsant and his auditor brought secret reserve funds into disapprobation.[13] Another area which received significant attention in any articles was the accounts. The responsibility of the directors to keep 'true accounts' of the 'capital and trade. . . sums of money received and expended. . . credits and liabilities' was delineated, as were the rights of the shareholders to inspect them, receive income and expenditure accounts at the general meeting or not, and a balance sheet either at the same meeting or printed and pre-circulated. The question of auditing the accounts was also dealt with in terms of who was qualified and who not to be an auditor, how they were to be elected and remunerated and the rights of access they had to the various books of the company. The articles usually ended with a set of clauses about the notice to be given for various meetings, a set of definitions and a few general clauses. Thus articles of association contain a mass of detailed information about the ground rules for running a company and the split of power between directors and shareholders.

Uses

Among historians, articles of association are of greatest interest to the business historian. They are essential early reading for the historian of a specific company, for they will explain and amplify many other sources and enable the researcher to determine basic information such as the initial objectives of the company, the amount of capital raised and the type of security offered, the voting rights of each type of share, the amount of information disclosed to the shareholders and the powers and responsibilities of the directors. They also provide a feel for the company's management style — whether it kept shareholders well informed and encouraged them to participate in the direction of the company or preferred to disclose a legal minimum and so hedged the shareholders around that they found it impossible to inspect the books, call meetings or change directors. By bringing together the articles, amendments and special resolutions, the researcher can examine how the company changed in some aspects over time.

The accounting historian will also find articles of association a valuable and fascinating source for they demonstrate the intentions of firms in terms of the types of books kept, the level of disclosure that was proposed, policies on auditors and auditing and the frequency of use of reserve funds. The accounting historian, by studying a random sample of such articles, could arrive at reasonable conclusions as to what was normal current practice and then compare this with the best, as laid down in contemporary textbooks and the rulings handed down by the courts. As well as this static analysis, the researcher could look at the dynamic situation of how accounting and auditing procedures and ideas on disclosure changed over time, as alterations were made to the articles. This would provide an empirical base for some of the theoretical explanations of how and why accounting conventions changed.

The legal historian could also consult the articles of association with due reward. For the articles were legal documents and where directors exceeded or contravened them shareholders could claim the directors to be ultra vires. They provide the legal historian with an insight into the current ideas on rules and regulations, how and why loopholes were perceived and the actions taken to close them. They are worth studying to see how far current actual practice conformed to court rulings on business matters. Although courts in the late nineteenth century were reluctant to become involved in many internal business matters, they did pronounce on fraud, the profits fund and some accounting practices.[14] What is not currently known is the extent to which companies then altered their practice, or the speed with which they made any such alterations. In the twentieth century the courts were even more involved in business matters such as voting rights and prospectuses and so the interaction between court rulings and company practice becomes more immediate. The articles would also be useful in tracing the evolution of company law; in showing to what extent best or average practice was subsequently embodied in legislation, or whether company law was consistently ahead of best practice, or the relative weight of these two extremes.

The management scientist could also profitably use the articles to trace the evolution of control systems, directors' powers, procedures at meetings, voting rights etc. Although there has been much work on some aspects of the development of management science, such as 'scientific management', motivation, the interaction between strategy and structure and aspects of labour relations, many areas have been almost totally neglected. A systematic study of a sample of articles of association would shed light on the evolution of many managerial techniques, ideas and practices.

The great drawback of articles of association is that they tell us almost nothing about the larger issues in society outside of business. Thus the economic, social or political historian would find them a sterile source. If pushed, they might contribute something to a debate on power or authority and the relationship between owner and manager, but they are a narrow source and throw no real light on to the wider screen. Even for the business historian, they are far from being the most exciting source. They say nothing about how the company performed or its policy, but are merely a set of rules containing no information on the actual operations.

Cross-references to other documents

Articles of association provide valuable cross-references to a large number of other documents. They indicate what types of books were to be kept, both for accounting or book-keeping purposes such as ledgers or journals (q.v.), and to record decisions made, for example by the board of directors in the board minute books. They also indicate how frequently meetings are to be held which might be reported in the press or might give rise to minutes being taken and so documents created. They are also very useful when used in conjunction with the shareholders' lists (q.v.) to calculate the voting rights of individual shareholders and thus the degree of influence which large shareholders could exert over the directors. Where they lay down the qualifications of directors and state the grounds on which they must cease to serve, this may help to explain some of the changes in the composition of the board recorded in the register of directors (q.v.).

Works using this source

Like some of the other documents covered in this book, it is highly unlikely that the articles of association of a company would be the sole source of any publication or even the major source. This is because they shed little light on the actual activities of the firm, merely laying down the ground rules for its operation. As such, they make fairly dry reading and apart from a historian interested in the development of the internal management rules of a company are unlikely to give a wide enough spread of information.

Authors have therefore tended to consult them in order to establish who set the rules and how this affected control. Wells used, among other sources, 'articles of co-partnership of William Hollins & Co', 'deed of co-partnership' and a 'supplemental deed to the above' and also the 'deed of dissolution of partnership of William Hollins & Co'. These were the equivalent for a partnership of the memorandum or articles of association in a joint stock company. Also listed among Wells' sources are the 'memorandum and articles of association of William Hollins & Co Ltd' and the 'resolution amending the articles of association of William Hollins & Co (Nottingham) Ltd' showing that the firm evolved from private partnership to limited liability joint stock company.[15] A good example of the use of such documents is to be found in a recent article on the early days of the Norwich Union Life Insurance Society.[16] Ryan uses a copy of the deed of settlement and amendments to the original deed enrolled in Chancery in March 1806 to show how Samuel Bignold, the secretary of the Society, drummed up 'support among local small traders and farmers who were Tories. . . to remove the existing directors and trustees and replace them with members who were prepared to back his plans for expansion'.[17] He was able to do this because, as the 1797 deed of settlement and the 1806 amendment show, he could only be removed from office if shareholders 'voted for his dismissal at two successive general meetings called specifically for that purpose'.[18]

Another use of the memorandum of association is to determine who were the original prime movers of a company and possibly what their motivation was. Stephanie Jones used the memorandum and articles of association of the Australasian United Steam Navigation Co to show that, despite claiming that the shareholders included local men who were also directors of other local shipping companies, the majority of the original proposers were closely connected with the British India Steam Navigation Co which was British owned and registered and that local involvement in the company was negligible.[19] The financing of a subsidiary company can sometimes be deduced from articles of association. Richardson, investigating the Australian Explosives and Chemical Co (AEC), showed from its new articles of association, confirmed in June 1922, that when Nobels reformed the company, appointing its own men as directors and managers, it also increased the loans from the parent company by £86,500.[20] Three years later, as a result of the merger of AEC with a number of other explosives firms, Nobel (Australasia) Ltd was born with a capital of £1.5 million. This information was drawn from clause IV of the memorandum of association of the new company.[21]

The example

The Oakerthorpe Iron and Coal Co was registered as a company in November 1859 and was based in Wingfield, Derbyshire.[22] It was established to buy leasehold property and mineral rights in ironstone and coal at Oakerthorpe near Alfreton and buy furnaces, engines, workings, plant and stock from an existing partnership in order to mine iron ore and coal, smelt iron and manufacture pig and bar iron. It had a nominal capital of £120,000 in £10 shares (high by modern standards but not unusual in the mid-nineteenth century)[23] of which about £74,000 was actually paid up.

The impetus for the establishment of the company came mainly from two families, the Marshalls of Birmingham, who ran the Britannia Carriage Works which constructed rolling stock for the railways and would have an obvious appetite for iron products, and the Worswicks who owned collieries in Leicestershire and provided expertise in operating a mining venture. These two groups contributed over 80 per cent of the capital and therefore had a controlling interest in the company. The remainder of the shares were owned by approximately 53 shareholders whose average holding was about 30 shares each compared to William Worswick's 2730 and Isaac Marshall's holding of 1770 shares. They were therefore small investors with little power over the decision making of the firm. The only other major shareholder was Colonel Richard T. Rowley, who was the Conservative MP for Harwich from 1860 to 1865[24] and held 500 shares.

By 1863 the company was in need of more capital but not finding it. To facilitate the running of the company, the shareholders agreed by special resolution in August 1863 to allow some of the unallotted shares to be issued as preference shares carrying interest of 5 per cent per annum in addition to any dividends declared on the ordinary shares. These shares were then allotted to Mr Worswick and Messrs Marshall 'in repayment of the sums they have respectively advanced up to this date', indicating that the two founding families had been forced to put in more capital than had been raised, and it was anticipated further would be needed because additional preference shares were to be allocated for future sums they 'shall hereafter advance for the purpose of carrying on the business of the company'. All was not well with the Oakerthorpe Iron and Coal Co for by August 1864 the Marshalls held £11,900 of preference shares and Worswick £8000 and a year later these figures had risen to £14,130 and £10, 770 respectively.

The end was not long in coming. In June 1866 the shareholders passed a special resolution winding up the company voluntarily and a local liquidator, William Saunders of Derby, was brought in to settle its affairs. Why the firm ceased trading is not certain. The leniency of company law in not requiring the deposit of documentation with the Registrar of Joint Stock Companies meant no balance sheets or profit and loss accounts were deposited and so it was impossible to gauge its profitability. Two tentative lines of explanation may be advanced. In July 1864, Edwin Marshall died. He had been a founder of the company, his name being the first to appear on the memorandum of association, and a partner in the Britannia Carriage Works. It might have been that he was the driving force behind the company and his passing left it without a strong entrepreneur to keep it going. This may have been compounded if the firm was making no profit and required greater amounts of capital than had been foreseen. Both seem likely from the need to create preference shares. This may have led the shareholders to determine to cut their losses and wind up the company in the hope of recouping some of their capital. The company, therefore, lasted less than seven years, a relatively short existence, and below the average lifespan which Cottrell found for limited companies registered in London in 1860.[25] A small and unsuccessful footnote in the broad sweep of economic growth.

Notes

1. For example, 19 & 20 Vict. c. 47, clauses IX & X.
2. J.R. Edwards & K.M. Webb, 'The Influence of Company Law on Corporate Reporting Procedures, 1865–1929', *Business History*, Vol. 24, No. 3 (1982) p. 260.
3. 19 & 20 Vict. c. 47; 25 & 26 Vict. c. 89.
4. P.L. Cottrell, *Industrial Finance 1830–1914* (Methuen, 1980) p. 60.
5. Edwards & Webb, op. cit., pp. 260 & 272.
6. 7 & 8 Vict. c. 110, clauses 7 & 8.
7. Cottrell, op. cit., p. 40.
8. 7 & 8 Vict. c. 110, clause 7.
9. H.A. Shannon, 'The First Five Thousand Limited Companies and their Duration', *Economic History*, Vol. 2 (1931).
10. BT 41/598/3285.
11. BT 31/435/1677.
12. Ibid.
13. E. Green & M.S. Moss, *A Business of National Importance* (Methuen, 1982) chapters 6 & 7.
14. H.C. Edey & P. Panitpakdi, 'British Company Accounting and the Law, 1844–1900' in A.C. Littleton & B.S. Yamey (eds), *Studies in the History of Accounting* (Sweet & Maxwell, 1956); B.S. Yamey, 'The Case Law Relating to Company Dividends' in W.T. Baxter & S. Davidson, *Studies in Accounting Theory* (Sweet & Maxwell, 1962).
15. F.A. Wells, *Hollins & Viyella: A Business History* (David & Charles, 1968) p. 260.
16. R. Ryan, 'The Early Expansion of the Norwich Union Life Insurance Society 1808–37', *Business History*, Vol. 27, No. 2 (1985).
17. Ibid., p. 174.
18. Ibid., p. 175.
19. S.K. Jones, 'The Decline of British Maritime Enterprise in Australia: The Example of the Australasian United Steam Navigation Company, 1887–1961', *Business History*, Vol. 27, No. 1 (1985) pp. 60–1.
20. P. Richardson, 'Nobels and the Australian Mining Industry', *Business History*, Vol. 26, No. 2 (1984) p. 182.
21. Ibid., p. 185.
22. This section is drawn largely from BT 31/435/1677 in the PRO at Kew.
23. Cottrell, op. cit., p. 81.
24. M. Stenton (ed.), *Who's Who of British Members of Parliament Vol. 1, 1832–1885* (Harvester, 1976) p. 335.
25. Cottrell, op. cit., p. 89: of his sample of companies which actually raised their capital, 50 per cent lasted for 29 years.

Copy Special Resolution of the *Oakerthorpe Iron*

and Coal _____ Company *Limited*

passed at a General Meeting held on the _31st_ day of _July_

18_60_ , and confirmed at a General Meeting held on the

_4th_ day of _September_ 18_60_ .

B. S.

It is resolved that the following Regulations shall from henceforth be the Regulations for the management of the Company in lieu of those contained in the ~~~~ Articles of Association that is to say

--------- Shares ---------

1 The Directors shall have full power to allot, sell, or otherwise dispose of the Shares in the Company which have not been subscribed for and which remain unallotted, in such manner as they shall think best for the interests of the Company and to adopt such measures with a view to the disposition thereof as they shall see fit

2 If several persons are registered as joint holders of any share or shares any one of such persons may give effectual receipts for any dividend payable

2. Selected pages from Copy Special Resolution of the Oakerthorpe Iron and Coal Co Ltd, 31 July 1860.
Source: PRO, BT 31/435/1677.

and Coal _____ Company *Limited*

and confirmed on the ___*4ᵗʰ*___ day of *September* 18 *60*

—Votes of Shareholders—

52 **Every** shareholder shall have one Vote for every share held by him up to ten, he shall have an additional Vote for every five shares held by him beyond the first ten shares up to one hundred, and an additional vote for every ten shares beyond the first hundred shares

53 **If** any Shareholder is a lunatic or idiot he may vote by his Committee Curator bonis or other legal Curator, and if any shareholder is a minor, he may vote by his Guardian, Tutor, or Curator or any one of his Guardians Tutors or Curators if more than one.

54 **If** two or more persons are jointly entitled to a share or shares, the person whose name stands first in the register of shareholders as one of the holders of such share or shares and no other, shall be entitled to vote in respect of the same

55 **No** shareholder shall be entitled to vote at any General Meeting unless all calls due

[*This Sheet may be divided, or may be had in Quires.*]

Copy Special Resolution of the _Oakerthorpe Iron_

passed in General Meeting on the _31st_ day of _July_ 18_60_

of the Company in general meeting declare a dividend to be paid to the Shareholders in proportion to their shares. –

88 No dividend shall be payable except out of the profits arising from the business of the Company.

89 The Directors may before recommending any dividend set aside out of the profits of the Company such sum as they think proper as a reserved fund to meet contingencies or for equalizing dividends or for repairing or maintaining the works connected with the business of the Company or any part thereof and the Directors may invest the sum so set apart as a reserved fund upon such securities as they may select. –

90 The Directors may deduct from the dividends payable to any shareholder all such sums of money as may be due from him to the Company on account of calls or otherwise. –

36

2. Selected pages from Copy Special Resolution of the Oakerthorpe Iron and Coal Co Ltd, 31 July 1860.
Source: PRO, BT 31/435/1677.

and coal   Company *Limited*

and confirmed on the ___11th___ day of ___September___ 1860

91 **Notice** of any dividend that may have been declared shall be given to each shareholder in manner hereinafter mentioned and all dividends unclaimed for three years after having been declared may be forfeited by the Directors for the benefit of the Company. —

92 **No** dividend shall bear interest as against the Company.

Accounts

93 **The** Directors shall cause true accounts to be kept —

Of the capital and trade of the Company

Of the sums of money received and expended by the Company and the matter in respect of which such receipt and expenditure takes place and

Of the credits and liabilities of the Company

94 **The** books of account shall be kept

3   Board minute books

Original purpose

The requirement to keep minutes of the meetings of the board of directors of a company was enacted by the 1908 Companies Act[1] and thus until that date there was no legal necessity for companies to keep such books. However, in both the 1844 Act, which opened the path to company formation, and the 1856 Act, the model regulations enshrined respectively in 'schedule A' and 'table B' stipulated that clauses to this effect ought to be included in a company's articles of association[2] but were not compulsory. Thus the law before 1908 strongly encouraged the keeping of such a document and where a company failed to register separate articles these model articles were deemed to apply and thus had the force of law. Although company law did not require the keeping of board minute books until after 1908, this should not be taken to mean that very few were created before that date or that the reason for the legislative enactment was to compel reluctant companies to keep such records. On the contrary, most joint stock companies wrote into their articles of association that regular meetings of the board should take place, and the minutes of each meeting should be kept and duly signed. The reason for legislative action was because most companies already kept such documentation, thus codifying current best practice and bringing the minority of more casually run companies into line.

Thus board minute books in the nineteenth century were kept as a form of self-imposed rule determined by each firm at its formation. They were kept so that the directors of a firm could maintain a permanent record of decisions made. This would prove valuable in the event of subsequent disputes. In some cases these books were also available to the officers of the business to aid them in the execution of the policy laid down by the board of directors. Sometimes the board minute books were also open for the inspection of the shareholders. Although the various Companies Acts encouraged firms to make their books available to shareholders, there was always the overriding caveat that this was subject to what was laid down in the deed of settlement or articles of association, so that the company could choose to prevent the owners from examining the board minute books.

Since the law laid down no requirements until 1908, it was left to the individual company to determine the regularity of board meetings, rules on the quorum, the procedure and format of the meeting, and thus there was no standard set of procedures. Rather each company laid down in its articles or deed the rules it chose, or in some cases laid down no rules at all on these matters. For example, the Borneo Company formed in 1856 defined a board meeting as 'any Board of Two or more Directors, and any extraordinary Board of Directors, duly convened, at which Two or more Directors shall be present, shall be a Board of Directors for all purposes'. Ordinary meetings of directors were held weekly at the head office, with extraordinary meetings at two days' notice, with a procedure determined in advance by the board. Issues were decided according to the majority of votes cast, with the chairman having the casting vote and 'minutes of the Attendance and proceedings of Directors at every Board of Directors shall be entered and signed by the Chairman of such meeting, and reported at the next General Meeting'.[3]

Absent directors could consult the minutes of meetings that they had missed to catch up on events; active directors could note persistent non-attending colleagues which might lead them to argue that the absentees should be required to quit the board. Reference to the minutes aided continuity of decision making and therefore policy made by the directors. This was especially true when there was a rapid turnover of directors or when there was a rotating attendance and no hard core of regular attenders. Small firms had less need for detailed minutes for there might be only a handful of directors. However, in large firms with a substantial capital base the directors could be held accountable to a great number of shareholders who might challenge the thinking behind their decisions at annual general meetings.[4] In these cases, board minute books might be a useful aide memoire not merely of the decisions made but also why they were made.

It needs to be said that board minute books were only created in joint stock companies, for the concept of a board of directors only applies to this type of business. Where the firm was a partnership, the directors' role would be performed by the partners and the equivalent record to the board minute books would be the partners' books or private papers.

Sources

Minute books were likely to be preserved as they recorded high-level strategic decisions that laid down policy for the future: thus they were often consulted and still relevant many years after they had first been compiled. As there was no legal necessity to lodge copies of board minutes with any government agency, such as the Board of Trade, where they survive this source is to be found in the offices of companies, or in local repositories or county record offices which hold business records. As in the case of registers of members, board minutes of subsidiaries are usually kept at the head office of the appropriate holding company. Similarly, they are often to be found in a company secretary's private store, rather than in the archives of the company generally. Again, as key documents in the life of a firm, their survival rate is good and a continuous series can be found for many firms. In some cases, a collection of board minute books is the *only* item remaining of a particular firm within the company,[5] although the usual publicly deposited records, such as prospectuses, articles of association and balance sheets, will survive outside the company. If wishing to keep only a minimum of documents, a company secretary could argue that registers of members, reports and accounts, articles of association, prospectuses, registers of directors and secretaries, registers of charges on the company's property and registers of directors' shareholdings had to be filed by law. Thus, if copies of some company documents could be found elsewhere, they could be disposed of at head office. The board minutes, of which the company held the only copy, needed to be kept for reference. Certainly currently registered companies kept their board minutes at head office — they were sent to record offices or repositories only in the case of defunct firms.

Thus the researcher seeking the board minute books of a live company would be well advised to approach the company first. For defunct companies and for some live companies, both the BAC and NRA[6] may be able to ascertain whether these documents survive, if they have a listing of the records of the particular company. The caveat applies of course that these books will only ever have existed in a joint stock company; they do not occur when a firm is or was a partnership.

The information they contain

Board minute books recorded the place of the meeting — usually the registered office of the company — and stated the firm's official name and form. The full names of the directors present were listed, often with their titles or areas of special responsibility, and sometimes included apologies for absence from those unable to attend. The director chosen to act as chairman at each meeting was always identified, and his signature usually appears at the end of each set of minutes, as in the example. The first board minute kept by a firm often recorded the number of shareholders, the amount paid up on each share, and the total capital of the company; it also recorded the appointment of directors and key personnel in the firm, such as the company secretary, and decided who was to act as the company's auditors, bankers and solicitors. All this information also had to appear on the prospectus, by law after 1900, by custom previous to this.[7]

As records of the meetings of directors and their decisions, board minute books can give a more detailed picture of the day-to-day running of a firm than, for example, the minutes of annual general meetings which tended to ratify decisions already taken, and present accounts, summarize activities and changes in the firm without debate. Meetings where shareholders were present tended to be tailored for their consumption and intended to maintain their confidence in a firm, whilst in the board minute books, a fuller and more accurate statement of decisions may be found. However, although board minute books are meant as a record of decisions made, the quality of information given describing the debates which led up to these conclusions varies enormously. This can be frustrating to the researcher, especially in trying to track down the originator of company policy. Board decisions are presented as the results of the deliberations of the board as a whole, rather than individual directors. Some board minute books record each meeting in a few lines, listing those present and the briefest indication of the practical results. Others were written up at great length, detailing individual contributions to the discussions, with comments on the firm's results and progress. Many are a combination of the two. In recording the persons present at each meeting, a sharp distinction was usually made between those taking an active part (listed as 'present') and any outsiders, such as the secretary taking the minutes, the firm's solicitors and accountants, acting in an advisory capacity who were referred to as 'in attendance'.

Although the agenda for each board meeting was often kept separately in another volume, or was issued as a separate sheet to each director before the meeting, or put on their desks at its commencement, many minute books include a list of headings to be discussed after listing those present. Often, each item discussed is given a separate subject heading, usually in the margin. These headings were sometimes listed in an index in the front or back of the book, a practice of great value to researchers. Again, they may do no more than summarize the main points in the debate and refer to other documents for further explanation, such as reports and correspondence. Frustratingly, the board minute books can indicate the erstwhile existence of potentially useful records which have since disappeared or been destroyed. An exception may be found when special 'board papers' were prepared, reporting details of special ventures or proposals, which were bound into the board minutes.

Overall, the general impression to be gained from working on this source is that most companies operating in the nineteenth and early twentieth centuries kept quite detailed minutes, whilst later twentieth-century minute books, particularly of small companies, are generally scanty and uninformative. As a record of the meetings of directors rather than the lower echelons of a firm, such as its regional managers, agents or branch managers, board minute books cannot provide minute detail, but are vital in an understanding of the corporate structure and strategy of a company, and the changes in this over time.

The example quoted, the first of this firm as a limited company, includes details of this incorporation, the directors, secretary, registered office, seal and lists the holders of the subscribers' shares. These minutes also discuss agreements entered into by the company and the appointment of bankers and auditors. Some board minute books also make specific reference, especially in a first meeting, to the persons empowered to sign cheques on behalf of the company and whether any powers of attorney have been created, and include appendices noting the directorships and partnerships in other companies of the firm's directors. The 1929 Companies Act required such a declaration: sometimes this was recorded in the minutes and sometimes in separate volumes.[8] At their fullest, board minute books are a fascinating record of high-level decision making; at their briefest, they are a frustrating glimpse of the menu with neither sight nor smell of the dishes there displayed.

Uses

For the writer of a company history, the board minute books serve as an essential starting point, for they provide an account of the development of the life of a company, its activities and the names of its directors. They usually give a basic outline of the legal and financial aspects of a firm in brief terms, serving as an introduction to other documents to which they refer. As the directors considered and discussed the main aspects of the company's activities, they provided a record of its performance over its life, at regular intervals, with special meetings held at times of particular crisis.

The researcher can identify the key personnel in a company from this source, together with the length of their service and their impact on the running of the company. However, not all directors would have attended all the meetings and a full list may usually be found in the register of directors. It is important to make the distinction between the passive, non-executive directors and the active, executive ones. Many companies gave directorships to especially large shareholders or to family members (in the case of family-dominated firms) who were not regarded as vital in decision-making processes. The large boards tended to be associated with those companies which had grown by merger or amalgamation whereas in the family firm which had been converted from a partnership the distinction between executive and non-executive does not really exist, the partners becoming the directors.

By indicating the registered office of a firm as the place of the meeting, the board minute books could give a lead into the whereabouts of other documents: often a company moved offices and although board minutes would have moved with it, some less vital records may have been left behind, to moulder in the cellar of a disused building. The statement of the company's official name and title can also be useful, especially when it changed frequently, incorporating other firms, shedding associations, or adopting a different corporate structure, such as becoming a group of companies. In recording the appointment of directors, the company secretary, bankers, auditors, solicitors, agents, representatives and other advisers, the board minute books can identify other firms having a bearing on the company in question, and thus add to the avenues of enquiry open to the researcher.

Board minute books can also be useful to the genealogist and biographer interested in a particular director — the minutes can indicate his importance in a company, his relationship with other directors, his date of appointment, and who proposed and seconded his selection. Where the board minute books contain details of the directors' other holdings, this can also be important to the biographer as a clue to other sources to be investigated which will indicate the overall wealth of the director and the ramifications of his business involvement.[9] They are also vital in explaining why directors left a board, and often refer to appointments and redundancies. Employees and managers were sometimes mentioned mainly when there were problems or special consideration was needed such as a breach of the rules requiring disciplinary action.

Board minute books as a source can have their limitations. In offering only a brief summary of discussions, they can over-simplify the story of how and why a firm acted as it did, and omit vital information. This was occasionally lodged in separate files or books but not copied in, and the researcher should enquire further to locate items briefly referred to in this source. In following a particular development through the minute books it is often the case that the final decision on a subject was delayed and postponed constantly. In this respect, however, the minute books are reflecting the dilatoriness and procrastination which afflicted (and continues to afflict) many directors! The sheer volume of the board minute books can be off-putting, for if there is a good run they can amount to dozens of volumes. Although using them is often eased by the index, the method of drawing this up can be eccentric and requires a degree of lateral thinking on the part of the researcher to extract all the relevant information on a particular topic.

The board minute books are vital for a study of the firm from the aspect of corporate strategy or business policy. Given current interest in how strategic decisions are made in industry, historical case studies can be of great interest, such as that on three steel companies in the inter-war period by Jonathan Boswell.[10] The study of business policy needs real-life examples from which generalizations may be made and lessons learnt, and the board minute books are essential for such a reconstruction. The researcher in architectural history or the history of design will also find material of relevance in some board minute books. For when decisions had to be made on new buildings, the board were involved in choosing sites, deciding on architects and approving designs. Sometimes their reasons for preferring a particular plan or architect will be given as well. Similarly, when major refurbishment of fittings, fixtures or interior decorations were planned, the board would be closely involved.

In summary, the use of this source is based on its three main functions: to record progress reports; to record policy decisions made; and to record the sanctioning of programmes resulting from these decisions, such as giving permission for investment projects, the appointment of key staff, and changes in agencies and areas of activity. The central role of these meetings resulted from their control of the purse-strings of a company: they considered the implications of the annual results and the bearing this had on authorizing future expenditure. Cutting across departments in a firm and looking at a company as a whole, board minutes are most useful in providing an overview of a company's development.

Cross-references to other documents

As previously indicated, the mention of other documentation in a firm's board minute books makes them of particular value, especially when they include transcribed material from other records which have since been lost. For example, details of the take-up of shares were often recorded, especially in the early days of a company, and special shares given to trusted employees like the company secretary, which were not subject to transfer notices, were mentioned. Thus board minute books can be used in conjunction with registers of members for details of share transactions. The statement of directors at each meeting can be augmented by the firm's register of directors, which would give more details of their addresses, occupations and length of time serving as a director. Often shareholdings of directors were recorded in the board minute books, at the request of other directors and after 1929 as a stipulation of the Companies Act of that year.[11] These interests might impinge on their decision making and needed to be known in advance, so that any bias was made explicit.

Agenda books of board meetings can provide a 'contents page' to the main board minute books, helping the researcher interested in a particular aspect of a firm's activities. If lost, agendas can be reconstructed from the full minutes. Changes in a firm's articles of association or memoranda and the issue of prospectuses were always discussed at board meetings, and thus the minutes can help in understanding the background to the changes in a firm's corporate or financial structure and aims, such as an increase in share capital, amalgamation with another firm or a change in activities.

The board minute books may also refer to agency agreements, with the amount paid to agents or received (if the company in question is to act as agent for another firm), giving the reasons behind the decision. This also applies to the appointment of bankers, solicitors and auditors. The company's premises, its offices and land holdings are often referred to in the minute books, which mention purchases and sales of importance to the company. Similarly, board minute books may be studied in conjunction with ledgers of investments made by the company, in bonds, stocks and shares in other companies and in capital goods. The existence of branch records may also be mentioned in the minute books, together with reports on specific projects. Sometimes registers of seals were kept, specifying by whom and when they were employed. This question was often first raised at board meetings.

Reports and accounts, with returns of profit and loss, can also be augmented by the board minutes, which often include discussions of the rate of dividend to be announced and the general performance of the company. Reference has already been made to the use of this source in supplementing staff records, by mentioning appointments and redundancies, changes in staffing policy and problems of discipline or fraud. Discussions are likely to be much freer and fuller in the board than would be allowed either in the chairman's statement or at annual general meetings.

Works using this source

Most business histories rely heavily on board minute books to explain the development of particular companies, in analysing decision making and major policy changes, as well as to provide a solid basic narrative of the principal events in their history. An interesting example is Church and Miller's article on the British motor industry between the wars.[12] The minute books of the Austin Motor Company at Longbridge, Birmingham, were used extensively, as well as those held in the Ford Archives, at Detroit. T.C. Barker's contribution to the same collection uses board minutes to analyse how the inventor of the float process, Alastair Pilkington, was appointed, despite being a member of an obscure and distant branch of the family. As a result of this decision, 'after considerable discussion, the board agreed that in principle, they were prepared to open the door wider to really promising candidates'. These minutes provide a detailed account of the success and failure of the many experiments that were eventually to culminate in this vital technical breakthrough.[13] B.W.E. Alford used board minute books in examining the reaction of the directors of the Imperial Tobacco Company to the threatened invasion of the UK tobacco market by the American Tobacco Company in 1901. They reveal that the directors had no long-term strategy to meet this threat but rather reacted by a rapid and poorly considered merger.[14]

Professor Checkland drew on the board minute books of the Tharsis Company when compiling his masterly work on this important Glasgow-based firm which extracted pyrites, rich in iron, copper and sulphur, from the Huelva province of Spain. He was fortunate in having a complete run of these books from the formation of the company in 1866.[15] Scott was similarly lucky in being able to draw on an unbroken series of 'the company's minute books from its foundation as a limited company to the present day' in writing his history of Siemens which pioneered the construction and laying of transatlantic telegraph cables.[16] Wells, in his history of the textile group Hollins and Viyella, explained some of the weaknesses of the minute books he drew on. 'There are no minute books until the conversion of the partnership into a joint stock company in 1882. From this time board meetings are regularly reported, but often less fully than one would wish: in the period of the private company decisions are recorded, but little is recorded of the decision-making process. However in the 1920s the board minutes became much fuller, and they are supplemented to an increasing extent by the minutes of various committees.'[17] This is a good example of the value of board minute books at their best and the frustration they can cause when at their minimalist.

The example

Gray, Mackenzie & Company was formed in 1869 in Basra to provide an agency service for the British India steamers in the Persian Gulf. This service originated in 1862 following the award of the Persian Gulf Mail Contract to Sir William Mackinnon. A related firm, Gray, Paul & Company, was based at Bushire and further branches were opened along the Persian Gulf at Bahrain, Kuwait and Dubai. Many of these ports in their early days were little more than open roadsteads and problems of accommodating staff and establishing communications are discussed in the board minute books. Shipping agency work continued to be the backbone of the firm but with the Middle Eastern oil boom it diversified into engineering, ship repair, insurance and lighterage and trading in dates, grain, wool as well as importing consumer goods.

Gray, Mackenzie operated jointly with Lynch Brothers as the Mesopotamia Persia Corporation Ltd during the 1920s, but abandoned this organisation, returning to separate status in 1936–7. It was then launched as a limited company.[18] The firm's first board meeting, the minutes of which are reproduced here, refer to the ending of this agreement with Lynch Bros. These minutes are particularly interesting for the detailed reference to the appointment of bankers to the firm, in Britain and in the Middle East, and the requirements of the firm in the discounting of bills, promissory notes and acceptances. In this respect the board minutes are useful in providing details of the financial and corporate arrangements of this particular company. Overseas trading businesses, unlike those operating in one country, faced remittance and exchange problems which require attention in compiling their histories. Sound financial arrangements were vital for a firm that was to play an important part in the development of the oil industry of the region.

Notes

1. 8 Edw. 7 c. 69, clause 71.
2. 7 & 8 Vict. c. 110, schedule A, clauses 16 & 21; 19 & 20 Vict. c. 47, table B, clause 61.
3. Articles of association of the Borneo Company, Inchcape archives, BCL 1/1 (1244).
4. Such as the case of the Royal Mail Group: E. Green & M. Moss, *A Business of National Importance: The Royal Mail Shipping Group, 1902–1937* (Methuen, 1982) pp. 137–8.
5. For example, many London businesses which have deposited their records with the Guildhall Library still retain their minute books.
6. See 'Useful addresses'.
7. 63 & 64 Vict. c. 48, clause 10(1).
8. 19 & 20 Geo. V c. 25, schedule 4, part 2, clause 2.

9. R.P.T. Davenport-Hines, *Dudley Docker: The Life and Times of a Trade Warrior* (Cambridge UP, 1984) p. 266, n. 71.

10. J.S. Boswell, *Business Policies in the Making: Three Steel Companies Considered* (Allen & Unwin, 1983).

11. See note 8 above.

12. R. Church & M. Miller, 'The Big Three: Competition, Management and Marketing in the British Motor Industry, 1922–1939' in B.E. Supple, *Essays in British Business History* (Oxford UP, 1977).

13. T.C. Barker, 'Business Implications of Technical Developments in the Glass Industry, 1945–1965' in Supple, op. cit.

14. B.W.E. Alford, 'Penny Cigarettes, Oligopoly, and Entrepreneurship in the UK Tobacco Industry in the late-Nineteenth Century' in Supple, op. cit.

15. S.G. Checkland, *The Mines of Tharsis* (Allen & Unwin, 1967) p. 278.

16. J.D. Scott, *Siemens Brothers 1858–1958* (Weidenfeld & Nicolson, 1958) p. 268.

17. F.A. Wells, *Hollins & Viyella: A Business History* (David & Charles, 1968) p. 13.

18. S.K. Jones, 'British India Steamers and the Trade of the Persian Gulf, 1862–1914, *The Great Circle*, Vol. 7, No. 1 (1985) pp. 23–44 and *Two Centuries of Overseas Trading* (Macmillan, 1986).

Minutes of the first Board

Meeting of Energy Exchanges & Company
Limited held at 122 Leadenhall Street,
London EC3, at 3:15 pm on Monday
11th January, 1937.

Present   W.A. Buchanan (in the chair)
          H.H. Matlock
          [H.] H. Taylor

In attendance   J. Baden, Secretary (pro tem)
                H.H. Wynne of Messrs. William &c.

Incorporation   The Secretary reported
                that the Company had been
                duly incorporated on 5 January
                1937, and that he had received
                the Certificate of Incorporation
                from the Solicitor.

Directors   The Secretary produced
                the appointment signed by the Solicitor
                to the Memorandum and Articles
                of Association appointing William
                Alexander Buchanan, Henry Hugh
                Matlock and John Herbert Taylor the
                first Directors of the Company

Secretary   It was resolved that Mr P. Baden
                be and is so hereby appointed
                Secretary of the Company

Registered   It was resolved that the
Office   registered office of the Company be
                at 122, Leadenhall Street, London,
                EC3

Seal   It was resolved that the Seal
                produced be affixed to the Common
                Seal of the Company and that an
                impression of the seal but be
                made upon that minute

                It was further resolved that
                one key of the Seal be kept by
                Mr W.A. Buchanan and one by
                Mr P. Baden, the Secretary

Subscribers'   It was resolved that William
Shares   Alexander one of the Subscribers to
                the Company's Memorandum and
                Articles of Association be placed upon
                the Register as the holder of the Ordinary
                share number B.1. and that Henry
                Baden the other Subscriber to the
                Company's memorandum and
                Articles of Association be placed upon
                the Register as holder of Ordinary
                share number B2. and that the
                said

3. Minutes of the first board meeting of Gray, Mackenzie & Co Ltd, 18 January 1937.
Source: Inchcape plc archives.

the said bank be and they are hereby authorised:—

1/ To honour and comply with all Cheques Drafts Bills Promissory Notes Acceptances negotiable instruments and orders expressed to be drawn accepted made or given on behalf of this Company at any time or times whether the banking account or accounts of this Company are overdrawn by any payment of or in relation thereto or are in credit or otherwise and

2/ To honour and comply with all instructions to deliver or dispose of any securities or documents or property held by the Bank on behalf of this Company.

Provided any such Cheques Drafts Bills Promissory Notes Acceptances negotiable instruments and orders and instructions are signed by two Directors or one Director and countersigned by the Secretary.

3. To treat all [illegible] Notes and Acceptances [illegible] endorsed on behalf of [illegible] Company and to discount or otherwise deal with them provided such endorsements purport to be signed by one Director or the Secretary.

-5-

It was further resolved that the Imperial Bank of Iran be appointed Bankers of the Company in Iraq and Iran and that they be requested to open accounts in the name of the Company at their Branches at Busreh, Bushire, Khorramshahr and Ahwaz and such other places as J.A. Armour and W. Spence may jointly direct and that the said bank be and they are hereby authorised:-

1/ To honour and comply with all Cheques Drafts Bills Promissory Notes Acceptances negotiable instruments or orders expressed to be drawn accepted made or given on behalf of this Company at any time or times whether the banking account or accounts of this Company are overdrawn by any payment of or in relation thereto or are in credit or otherwise and [illegible] to honour and comply with all instructions to deliver or dispose of any securities or documents or property held by the bank on behalf of the Company.

Provided any such Cheques Drafts Bills Promissory Notes Acceptances negotiable instruments orders and instructions are signed by J.A. Armour or W. Spence or by such person or persons as J.A. Armour and

-6-

3. Minutes of the first board meeting of Gray, Mackenzie & Co Ltd, 18 January 1937.
Source: Inchcape plc archives.

4 Letter books

Original purpose

In the days before the typewriter and photo-copier, a normal form of employment in business was as a clerk, one of whose jobs was to copy outgoing letters in a rounded copperplate hand into the out letter book. This acted as the file copy of letters sent out to suppliers, customers, employees in other locations etc. Its function then was identical to its function now: to serve as a reminder of what was said, when it was sent and, if necessary, to act as evidence in a court of law to back up a claim. In addition to serving as an aid to the memory of the writer, the retention of out letters enabled superiors to check on the decisions and actions of subordinates. The board or managers could check whether queries and problems were dealt with promptly and whether officers displayed sound judgement on operational and policy matters. When an employee retired or resigned, the presence of letter books enabled his replacement to pick up the threads of the business more readily.

The obverse of the out letter book was the in letter book, serving exactly similar purposes but recording the letters received from suppliers, customers or employees. Usually the incoming letters would not go into the book until they had been dealt with or answered, and often a handwritten note to this effect will be found somewhere on the letter. The arrival of the typewriter and carbon paper in the very late nineteenth century certainly eased the workload of the clerks and made the job of research into company history much easier except that after some time these carbon copies begin to fade, taxing both the researcher's eyesight and ingenuity. From this time onward, the copies of outward-bound letters tend to be carbon copies or flimsies of the originals. The advent of the telephone as a normal tool of business from the late nineteenth century onwards had the effect of reducing the amount of correspondence generated, as some matters were discussed over the phone and not consigned to paper. Fortunately these were likely to be the more trivial; most major decisions or agreements still required confirmation in writing.

The volume of correspondence created by a business increased with its distance from its suppliers or customers, or the head office from its main works. UK-based companies with activities abroad — such as the Ashanti Goldfields Corporation example — created a much greater volume of correspondence than companies with mainly local connections. There was much less scope for verbal reporting and direct observation, so much more had to be committed to paper. Although this chapter is headed 'Letter books', it should be appreciated that some firms retained their correspondence in loose files, or in boxes, or even bound up in bundles by string or ribbon. What is said in this chapter applies equally well to such documents even though not strictly entitled to the description 'letter book'.

Sources

Letter books were not required to be kept by law, and were never intended to be circulated to shareholders or for external examination. They were essentially internal working documents and records. As such they were kept by the firm in its office until they had outlived their immediate usefulness. Their survival and destination then depended on the record retention policy of the firm. Some kept them in their archive, some were destroyed, some deposited with suitable local public repositories. Thus the probability of the letter books of any individual firm surviving are fairly slim; if the company survives, then the best start is to approach it to see if it has retained the volumes; similarly if the particular company being researched has been taken over or merged into a larger group, it is possible that the head office of that group collected the records together. If an approach to the surviving company proves abortive, or if the company has ceased to exist, there are two routes to try next. The Business Archives Council maintains a card index by company name of business records and their location, and since it has carried out numerous surveys such as of banking records[1] and 1000 of the first registered companies,[2] it may know if the letter books survive. Another useful finding aid is the National Register of Archives, maintained by the Historical Manuscript Commission (see 'Useful addresses'). It has a series of trade books, arranged by company name and type of activity, which record business deposits and their location.

It has to be said that the chances of letter books surviving for an individual company are not good: war, fire, take-overs and recent barbarism have taken a heavy toll. This is particularly true where incoming letters were not bound up but were bundled together with string or ribbon: the lack of hard covers made them physically more vulnerable and perhaps less worth preserving in the eyes of some record keepers. Where the letters or letter books constitute a major collection, the institution which holds them may prepare its own listing[3] and it is worth consulting the various guides to collections of business records in the Bibliography.

The information they contain

At their best, letter books are a superb source containing a vast array of different types of information. They may contain letters to suppliers giving details of raw materials and components ordered, and to customers explaining delays or confirming deliveries. In the specific example, since Ashanti Goldfields Corporation was a London-based company whose only active sites were in the Gold Coast Colony, there was a regular correspondence between the board of directors, via the company secretary in London, and the managers in charge of operations in Obuasi, Kumasi and other mines. The letters, both in and out, were bound up in head office and for the period 1897 (the establishment of the company) to 1940 they fill 60 volumes! Their range of topics is enormous. There is much material on technical matters, such as methods of mining, techniques of stamping the ore and extracting the gold, the richness of the ore, the size of the veins, problems of drainage and conversely finding sufficient water supply for the stamping mills. In the example, the accumulation of tailings — the waste ore after initial refining — is a problem solved by physical female labour rather than any sophisticated capital equipment; the need to sink a sump at the Ashanti shaft in order to drain the works is mentioned, as is the necessity of fresh timbering and clearing fallen soil at Mount Cade.[4].

Related to this is information on the capital equipment that is being used, the source of supply and requirements for spare parts, the reliability and performance of these engines, pumps and mills. There is much discussion of the relative worth of various suppliers, and when machines fail or an individual supplier becomes tardy in delivery, expensive or just 'difficult', a new one is sought. In the example, 'Points and Crossings' are urgently needed because the Corporation operates its own railway to move the ore. It is not only the capital equipment which receives mention in the letter books. The vast range of goods necessary to sustain a British way of life for the expatriate staff had to be shipped out and gave rise to comments on whisky tasting of sea water; London giving preference to certain brands of mineral waters because directors had an interest in the company; and the relative efficacy and price of different sorts of dynamite and gelagnite or, as in the example, the economy of buying quality brands of 'spirits and medical comforts' in the UK and shipping them direct to the mine.

Labour relations are also dealt with exhaustively, though much more is written on the expatriate white staff than the native black workers. A great deal of time is taken up with rates of pay, the proportion of salary to be paid in London and the proportion to be drawn locally. Overtime payments prove vexatious to the board which takes the surprisingly advanced view that it is better to have a third man than two doing substantial amounts of overtime. There is correspondence about individual miners, whether they should be re-employed when their contract expires or whether their work has been so poor as to justify paying them off. Requests from the mines for specific sorts of skilled labour such as enginemen, pumpmen, and replies from London that they are trying South Wales or Bristol or the Tavistock area for suitable people are another regular ingredient. The health of the expatriate staff is another frequent topic, as in the example, where the cause of fever is dismissed cavalierly and over-simply as 'sun'. The references to the native labour occupy much less space in the letters but even so they give an impression of the problems. There are letters about the numbers employed — 3000 were on the payroll in the early days — whether they should be equipped with uniforms at company expense, problems of housing, the amount of subsidy paid by the company on rice that it brought in to feed them; problems of natives stealing 'amalgam' — the ore when it had been crushed and made into a paste — for the gold it contained, and of native carriers stealing money when it was en route from the coast to the mines. The latter complete with depositions from Hausa police escorts and the sentence handed down by the Assistant District Commissioner.

Finally, there is much in the letter books relating to the financial side. The amount of bullion shipped from the mines, their working expenses and how they are made up, the price of commodities 'on the coast' compared to bought in London, and measures taken to economize on costs at the mines. From the London end there is information on movements in the share price, comments on how the shareholders are reacting and reports of comments made by brokers, as well as long and involved letters on overdrafts, total outgoings, the cost of the London Office and regular exhortations to keep down expenditure at the mines. It is clear that when they survive, letter books contain a great amount of information on a multitude of subjects. Because they were never originally intended to be seen generally by outsiders, they are frank and lively and give an accurate and undoctored view of the firm's activities and motivations.

Uses

Because letter books cover the whole range of the firm's activities, they can provide material on a very wide spread of activities and thus are potentially of value across a spectrum of disciplines. As Professor Payne has said, 'letter books and incoming letters are most fruitful in providing descriptive information, for putting flesh on the bare statistical bones',[5] and they are among Professor Mathias's three 'most important documents of all'.[6] This potential value is much enhanced when they are indexed, which is not unusual. Normally the indexes are done for each volume, so a researcher wishing to delve into a specific topic may still face a time-consuming task. The strength of letters is that they are easily understood, showing the routine activities of a business, the nature of the decision-making process and the roles of different personalities. They are absolutely invaluable to anyone investigating the history of a specific company, for the light they throw on the firm's activities and personnel; more importantly, the reasoning of the directors may be given so explaining why certain policies or actions were adopted. They are similarly valuable for research on firms that might have had relationships with the originator firm. In the Ashanti example, anyone looking into Nobels, the dynamite firm, or manufacturers of pumps, mills or crushers would find germane material.

Letter books can also be of great value to the family historian, where an ancestor is believed to have served in the company's employ. There is much detail on individuals including dates of recruitment and discharge, sailing routes, payment, the place from which workers were recruited, illnesses from which they suffered, and too frequently the occasional death in harness at the mines with the resident doctor's report on date and cause. Thus if a relative is believed to have been in a company's service or been in a particular industry or part of the world, it may well be worth trying the company's letter books. Labour history is another field which would benefit from the use of company letter books for they contain much material on employees both as individuals and as a group. To date, not much use has been made of them for this purpose, but the detail they contain on wage rates, grading, other benefits, both financial and non-monetary, enhance our view of labour conditions. At a higher level they also shed light upon the attitudes of the directors towards employees, whether they demonstrated paternalistic or exploitative policies; the attitude of the Ashanti directors towards overtime working might be seen as indicative or a benevolent policy towards labour linked with a practical understanding of the effects of fatigue from over-long hours in reducing efficiency and output.

The historian of science and technology will also find company letter books of value. They are likely to give insights into the uses companies made of machinery; the practical problems associated with particular types of equipment and how they were overcome; the speed of diffusion of new technologies and whether there was a bias in the types of firm or industry that adopted them first; the degree to which technical changes were stimulated by existing inadequacies in processes and machines, and how far the solutions were provided on the spot and fed back to manufacturers. From the letter books of some companies it is possible to glean a great deal of material on colonial or diplomatic history. In the example of the Ashanti Goldfield Corporation, there is material on the relationship with the natives, the amount of local employment that was created and the input into the local economy via wages, goods bought locally, dues, rents or considerations paid to the original inhabitants for use of land, water or rights of way. The role of the company in local development can be examined. Did it encourage facilities for the local inhabitants in hospitals, schools etc; was it involved in improving transport facilities, even if initially to get its supplies in from the coast and its products out?

Was it motivated by self-interest alone, or did it perceive some form of duty or moral obligation towards the less-developed countries and so count among the more enlightened firms?

Finally, a bizarre and perhaps atypical use, not quite confined to Ashanti is for anyone studying the development of codes and ciphers. This arose partly from the company's concern for secrecy and partly from economy, for the company sent and received all its telegrams to and from the mines in a complicated code. Economy was achieved because telegrams were charged by the word, and the company devised an elaborate system of single words, with variable prefixes and suffixes, to indicate different quantities, persons etc.; thus one code word on a telegram conveyed a whole phrase. The desire for secrecy went beyond the normal Victorian concern for trade secrets and fear of competitors learning something to their advantage, for the price of Ashanti's shares, in common with most mining companies, was very volatile and reacted sharply to the quantity of gold refined and ore crushed. Thus any breakdown of plant, deviation or fault in the ore body, or water shortage for the workings, if clearly transmitted and passed on by a sharp telegraph clerk, could have had a drastic effect on share prices. The directors preferred to be the first to know.

Cross-references to other documents

The great value of the letter books, where they survive, is that they can often provide explanations of and motives for decisions, financial results and policies discovered in other documents of the company. For example, a fairly bland statement in the chairman's speech (q.v.) to the shareholders about a delay in commencing milling and stamping of ore from one mine can be traced in the letter books to late delivery of essential machinery which had to be shipped out from England. Similarly, the profit and loss or balance sheet (q.v.) may indicate a rise in profits, but with no explanation: from the letter books and decoded telegrams it is possible to see that more ore has been extracted and processed and hence more bullion produced and sold to Messrs Rothschild and how this had been achieved.

Again many of the decisions made by the board of directors and recorded in the board minute books (q.v.) will become more comprehensible from perusal of the letter books which will contain greater detail and informality. The source of an issue may lie in the letter books, as a problem is raised by one of the managers at the mines. While the board minute book may contain only the outline of the problem and the decision handed down, the letter from the company secretary to the mines manager may well give some of the thinking behind the decision.

Finally, of course, the letter books can be used to confirm facts, causes and ideas which start from other business documents. The letter books will reinforce and support information on premises, staff records and most other documents since they can cover the whole gamut of business activities.

Works using this source

As with a number of other documents, it is most unlikely that a book would be written using only letter books, or files of correspondence, for the whole essence of writing a company or industry history is to use numerous sources to cross-check references, seek alternative explanations and allow one document to explain facts found in another. This is particularly true of business documents because the specialized nature of some of the individual types causes them to have very partial information or to have an element of bias in them. In many ways, letter books are among the least biased sources for many were not intended to be read by anyone outside the firm and thus can be frank and honest. Additionally, because they roam over the whole gamut of the business, they may throw light on a wide range of the firm's activities. Thus where they survive they are a very important raw material in the construction of a business history. Rhodes Boyson, writing the history of the Manchester cotton firm of Ashworth, draws on a whole range of correspondence to and from several of the Ashworth dynasty now located in various archives.[7]

In a similar vein but for a more modern period, a twentieth-century textile magnate writing the history of his firm said 'the most illuminating information comes from my voluminous correspondence with Rolf and Ingo, my brothers. Sharing the management of our English and Czechoslovak factories, Rolf and I alternated between the two countries, writing to each other almost daily . . . I have thousands of confidential letters exchanged between the three of us.'[8] For an earlier period, a historian of the nineteenth-century rubber industry drew on the correspondence of George Spencer, a rubber merchant and inventor, stored amongst his papers in numerous tin trunks. He found 'letters . . . to and from manufacturers of component parts provided an insight into the firm's business tactics from the supply side; letter books . . . made possible a study of pricing policy; letters from commission agents and travellers revealed the evolution and work of the firm's marketing organisation'.[9] The extent of this class of record can be perceived: 'Many thousands of incoming letters from agents, customers, and manufacturers . . . Ten letter books containing copies of outgoing letters' from approximately 1867 to 1890.[10] Correspondence was obviously vital evidence in writing this fascinating study.

Correspondence also formed the major source for an article on a classic firm of the industrial revolution. Cartwright is one of the great names in the textile industry of the late eighteenth century and, when explaining why a particular woollen mill was established by Major John Cartwright and why it failed to do particularly well despite being out of a good stable, Chaloner and Marshall drew heavily on the correspondence between Cartwright and the Birmingham-based, steam engine manufacturing firm of Boulton and Watt.[11] This correspondence has been carefully preserved in the Birmingham Reference Library and showed that Cartwright discussed the use of one of Watt's improved steam engines in his mill in Nottinghamshire to drive the machinery for spinning and weaving woollen cloth. Despite using the most up-to-date technology, the mill was not wildly successful, perhaps because Cartwright was too concerned to further his political ambitions. The survival of the files of letters was crucial to writing this article.

A trawl through a recent volume of the journal *Business History* reveals that correspondence was used quite frequently in the construction of these articles. For example, the history of a British merchant trading in Japan in the nineteenth century draws heavily on the correspondence between the merchant and various other agents, traders and customers mostly now in the Jardine Matheson Archive.[12] An article on the relationship between Nobels, which pioneered the production of dynamite for peaceful purposes, and the Australian mining companies in the early twentieth century also draws on files of 'correspondence outward and general correspondence' among the records of the Broken Hill South Co Ltd held in the Melbourne University archives.[13] A paper on the pharmaceutical industry in the same period uses a letter book among the Evans Papers held in the Glaxo archives *inter alia* to examine and explain the differences in attitude to, and practice in, research and development of firms in Germany, USA and Britain and so explain Germany's immense lead in the invention, manufacture and marketing of pharmaceuticals before the First World War.[14]

Collections of letters which at first sight seem of little relevance to the business historian because they were originated by a primarily political figure can, on closer examination, yield a rich harvest. A good example of this is the Salisbury papers which primarily deal with the political activities of this great Conservative, late-Victorian prime minister. However, before he became either premier or marquess he was involved in business activities and, as Professor Barker has shown, became chairman of the Great Eastern Railway for four years from 1868 to 1872.[15] Salisbury was spotted in Parliament as potential board material by Edward Watkin who, as well as being a Liberal MP, was chairman of both the Manchester Sheffield and Lincolnshire Railway and the South Eastern. When the Great Eastern got into financial difficulties in 1867, Watkin was offered the chair of the Great Eastern board but declined and persuaded Salisbury to take it instead. Barker uses a whole range of letters in the Salisbury papers, from Watkin to Salisbury and vice versa, from Samuel Swarbrick, chief executive of the Great Eastern, to Salisbury, and correspondence with other members of the board, to show how Salisbury was persuaded to take the appointment, how he learnt the basics of railway operation and led the Great Eastern's return to financial safety.

Letter books have often provided the main basis for articles. Those of Owen Owens and Sons, Manchester cotton merchants in the early nineteenth century, were a major source for an article on the highly elastic demand schedule of this firm.[16] The firm drew up the quantities of American cotton it was prepared to purchase at different price levels. There were great variations in quantity demanded for relatively small changes in the price, demonstrating highly price-elastic demand. The same firm used similar techniques in the 1830s when buying American flour and wheat. The letter books of William Jenkins, general manager of the Consett Iron Co in the last quarter of the nineteenth century, were the most important explanatory source used by Richardson and Bass when analysing this company's high level of profits in a period of 'industrial retardation' or 'great depression' as it has been commonly described.[17] From this correspondence they showed how the firm switched from rail rolling to iron plates and later to steel plates just as railway demand was tapering off but shipbuilding was booming; how the manager kept full order books for long periods ahead, kept careful watch on the movement of prices in different segments of the iron market; and how the firm enjoyed favourable raw material prices through owning its own local coal mines and taking a part share in a company to work iron ore resources in Bilbao, Spain.

Where they survive, letter books or files or correspondence have been extensively used both for books and articles as a detailed, voluminous and revealing source.

The example

The Ashanti Goldfields Corporation (AGC) was formally registered as a limited liability company in London on 25 May 1897. It was formed to acquire the interest of the Cote d'Or Co Ltd which received 50,000 fully paid up £1 shares in payment. This syndicate appears to have done the initial work in obtaining the concession to exploit the gold potential from the Adansi, chiefs of the Obuasi area. In addition, they issued another 66,000 shares at par with 5/- paid, the total amount not being called up until 1899. From 1898 more shares were issued but excitement over the prospects of good returns was so high that 9346 were issued at a premium of £1 per share, and in December 1899 another 10,000 shares were issued at a premium of 45/- per share. The initial chairman of the Corporation was Frederick Gordon who had founded a chain of hotels and was the chairman and main shareholder of that business. He remained chairman of AGC until his death in 1904 in Monte Carlo when Viscount Duncannon, founding deputy chairman, succeeded him. The managing director was Edward Arthur Cade who received a salary of £1000 per annum plus a share of the profits. The Corporation had an interesting profit-sharing scheme for the directors. Under clause 72 of their articles of association, once a dividence of 15 per cent had been paid on the equity, the directors were entitled to share 10 per cent of the additional net profits between them; Cade received 30 per cent of this bonus and each of the other four directors 17½ per cent.

Ashanti's main business was the mining, refining and export of gold from West Africa, in what is now Ghana, appropriately called the Gold Coast in colonial days. This required a great deal of capital investment in the locality and, before the advent of air transport or direct telephonic links, involved writing large numbers of letters from both ends of the split-site operation. The majority of the gold was sold to N.M. Rothschild & Son in London who set the weekly gold price. Some idea of the returns from Ashanti can be gained by the amounts of gold sold to Rothschilds. From 1910 to 1918, this averaged over £460,000 per annum, the dividends paid averaged over 75 per cent per annum and the directors shared £2250 in fees and over £2000 per annum in commissions. As well as the industrial investment, Ashanti had to provide most of the social and economic infrastructure, building houses and hospitals, developing forests for timber to shore up workings and even publishing a newspaper, the *New Ashanti Times*. In 1927, Ashanti bought out New Bibiani Ltd which operated goldfields in the same area.[18]

In 1968 Lonrho, under the chairmanship of 'Tiny' Rowlands, took over Ashanti by giving Ashanti Goldfield Corporation shareholders a mixture of convertible loan stock and equity in Lonrho. In the following year, the Ghanaian government with the cooperation of Lonrho acquired a 20 per cent shareholding in AGC with an option on another 20 per cent at £1 per share. In return, the lease on the Obuasi concession was extended to the year 2009. In 1972 the regime of Colonel Acheampong unilaterally took over 55 per cent of AGC's assets and African directors predominated on the board. Talks about compensation dragged on for some years but effectively AGC became a state-owned corporation.[19]

Notes

1. L.S. Pressnell & M.J. Orbell, *A Guide to the Historical Records of British Banking* (Gower, 1985).
2. L. Richmond & B. Stockford, *Company Archives: The Survey of the Records of 1,000 of the First Registered Companies in England and Wales* (Gower, 1986).
3. For example M. Elas (ed.), *Iron in the Making: Dowlais Iron Company Letters 1782–1860* (Glamorgan County Records Committee & Guest Keen Iron & Steel Co, 1960); A.E. Lumb (comp.), *A Catalogue of the James Nasmyth Collection* (Eccles Public Library, 1958).
4. Guildhall Library, MS 14171.
5. P.L. Payne, 'Business Archives and Economic History: The Case for Regional Studies', *Archives*, Vol. 6, No. 29 (1963) p. 28.
6. P. Mathias, 'Historical Records of the Brewing Industry', *Archives*, Vol. 7, No. 33 (1965) p. 10.
7. R. Boyson, *The Ashworth Cotton Enteprise: The Rise and Fall of a Family Firm, 1818–80* (Oxford UP, 1970) pp. 260–1.
8. E.W. Pasold, *Ladybird, Ladybird: A Story of Private Enterprise* (Manchester UP, 1977) pp. xii–xiii.
9. P.L. Payne, *Rubber and Railways in the Nineteenth Century* (Liverpool UP, 1961) pp. vii–viii.
10. Ibid., p. 231.
11. W.H. Chaloner & J.D. Marshall, 'Major John Cartwright and the Revolution Mill, East Retford, Nottinghamshire, 1788–1806' in N.B. Harte & K.G. Ponting (eds), *Textile History and Economic History: Essays in Honour of Miss Julia de Lacey Mann* (Manchester UP, 1973).
12. S. Sugiyama, 'Thomas B. Glover: A British Merchant in Japan, 1861–70', *Business History*, Vol. 26, No. 2 (1984).

13. P. Richardson, 'Nobels and the Australian Mining Industry, 1907–25', *Business History*, Vol. 26, No. 2 (1984).
14. J. Liebenau, 'Industrial R & D in Pharmaceutical Firms in the Early Twentieth Century', *Business History*, Vol. 26, No. 3 (1984).
15. T.C. Barker, 'Lord Salisbury: Chairman of the Great Eastern Railway, 1868–72' in S. Marriner (ed.), *Business and Businessmen: Studies in Business, Economic and Accounting History* (Liverpool UP, 1978).
16. B.W. Clapp, 'A Manchester Merchant and His Schedule of Supply and Demand', *Economica*, new ser. Vol. 29, No. 114 (1962).
17. H.W. Richardson & J.M. Bass, 'The Profitability of Consett Iron Company before 1914', *Business History*, Vol. 7, No. 2 (1965).
18. This draws heavily on Guildhall Library, Mss 14, 164 to 14, 172.
19. S. Cronje, M. Ling & G. Cronje, *Lonrho: Portrait of a Multinational* (Penguin, 1976) pp. 54—61 & 63–6.

Ashanti Goldfields Corporation, Limited.

OBUASSI,
VIA CAPE COAST CASTLE,
WEST AFRICA.

London Office:
6, SOUTHAMPTON STREET,
HOLBORN, W.C.

1st. March 1902. *190*

To The Directors,

    Ashanti Goldfields Corporation Ltd.,

      London, W.C.

Gentlemen,

      I enclose orders Nos. 265, 267 & 268.

<u>Points and Crossings</u> On October 11th last we ordered these
on order No. 583. None have yet arrived and we are badly in
want of them. These things are always kept in stock, and such
a small order can be supplied at once. We can of course make
them here (as we have been compelled to do) but when you
take into consideration the cost of labour, materials &c in
Ashanti you can easily calculate the excessive cost of, after
all, an inferior made article. We have not the appliances or
tools to execute a neat and efficient job, and therefore the
less done on the Mine in making such things the better.

<u>Spirits, Medical Comforts &c.</u>   I also enclose an order
from the Corporations Commissariat Officer (after consultation
with the Doctor). I may add that I had a conversation with
Mr. Daw as to the above and suggested that all drinkables &c.
should be sent from home, and thus save intermediate profits.
Mr. Daw fully agreed with me, and said to order what the
Commissariat Officer and Doctor mentioned. You are well aware
of the <u>high prices</u> charged for perhaps <u>inferior brands</u> by the
firms on the Coast. As the Corporation can save all intermediate
profits and charges, and as a <u>good article</u> costs no more for
freight, landing charges and inland Transport. It is certainly
advisable to have the best quality and then less should suffice.

<u>Lagos & Lokoya.</u>   We are informed that both these Steamers have
been lost. As this Corporation I am informed has cargo on
each of these boats, it will be necessary to at once replace

4. Letter to head office of Ashanti Goldfields Corporation Ltd, 1 March 1902.
Source: Guildhall Library, London Mss 14,171, pp. 319–21.

what has been lost. The invoice No. of the Lokaya's goods is
No. 236, of December 25th. 02.

Andrew Simpson. This man has been tried by a Magistrate in
Kumassi and sentenced to six months imprisonment with hard
labour. The Acting Chief Commissioner (Francis Henderson Esqr.)
in writing me remarked "This is a light sentence for an offence
of this nature". But when sending up the prisoner I did not
press for a severe sentence.

Accounts. These Mr. Ramonson has checked, and he has by my
instructions signed a certificate to that effect. I may however
mention that all the periods referred to were prior to Mr.
Ramonson returning to Obuassi, and consequently others must
explain the matter.

Clean Up. The Obuassi Mill has been stopped to-day for the
monthly "clean-up", and on the 4th. inst., the result will
be cabled to London. I may mention that the two old Tailings
pits have been filled up with Tailings and as no more will
run by gravitation I am working and then cleaning out
alternate pits, Women carrying out the Tailings and depositing
them conveniently for future transport and treatment by
Cyanide process. While they are thus emptying out one pit the
Tailings are running into the other. This is cheaper than
erecting a tailings wheel for elevating and discharging the
tailings at a higher level. The Battery being old and practically
worn out, and inexpensive substitute (as Women carriers) is
more desirable.

Mine.   The "Sump" at the Ashanti Shaft is being sunk to one
side of the Shaft and the Steam Pump will be used in it so as
to drain that level of all water, and sinking continued in it.
Until quite recently, owing to the continual break-down of
the small Pump in the Shaft, both the Shaft and the drive
leading from it were "drowned out", and no mining work could
be done. Now we have recommenced driving on the level but no
ore of any value is as yet shewing on the face of the drive,
only a few stringers containing a small quantity of gold, but
these are doubtless fore-runners of a reef near by.

4. Letter to head office of Ashanti Goldfields Corporation Ltd, 1 March 1902.
Source: Guildhall Library, London Mss 14,171, pp. 319–21.

WINDER. In Cox's winze, No.2. level. we are now working on a good lode some six feet wide and of payable quality.

Mount Cade. Work is being recommenced here. The level, as might have been expected, has "come together" during the time no work has been done there. Fresh Timbering will be necessary in the level and the ground fallen in will have to be removed then fresh progress can be made in developing that portion of the Corporations property. Captain James and a few natives are repairing the level at Mount Cade.

The General Health of this camp is good, a few cases ...... being the principle malady owing principally, I think, ... effects of "Sun". The men cannot be too careful in this ...... are careless in spite of warnings. Dr. Mc- ...... laid up with a slight attack of Fever. I ...... admit the above in his case, ... same in all instances, viz., temporally

I am, Gentlemen,

Yours faithfully,

p. pro ASHANTI GOLDFIELDS CORPORATION L.

N. J. Suckling

GENERAL SUPERINTENDENT

5 The chairman's statement

Original purpose

As explained in the Introduction, the earliest company legislation insisted that an annual balance sheet was sent out to all shareholders a fortnight before each general meeting. Although this requirement was downgraded in the 1856–62 Acts so that it had the status of a strong recommendation or applied by default if no other provision was made, many companies continued the practice. In the late nineteenth century some companies began to send a brief covering letter with the balance sheet. In the early twentieth century this became formalized for in the 1908 Companies Act the model regulations in Table A laid down that the balance sheet, both when sent out and when presented to the meeting, be 'accompanied by a report of the directors as to the state of the company's affairs and the recommended dividend and the amount proposed to carry to a reserve fund'.[1]

In as much as the model regulations were adopted by companies, either by choice or by default, it became normal practice for the balance sheet to be accompanied by a brief statement from the chairman of the board of directors drawing attention to one or two salient points of the company's activities in the last twelve months. These few sentences were often no more than a formality, the main presentation of the company's performance being made at the annual general meeting or ordinary general meeting when the chairman made a long speech. In the days before radio and television, much more emphasis was placed on oratory and the public meeting; the shareholders expected their chairman to give an in-depth appraisal of the company, be willing to answer questions, move the adoption of the accounts and propose the re-election of any retiring directors. The legal position of the chairman's report was clarified in 1928 when the Companies Act of that year moved the requirement for such a report from the model regulations appended to the 1908 Act into the body of the 1928 Act.[2] This meant that it was now compulsory for all registered companies, except private ones, to create and circulate such a document. There was no longer any discretion granted to choose to adopt such a practice. This compulsion was continued by the consolidating Act of 1929.[3] However, the printed reports could still be pretty skimpy. Thus until the Second World War the real chairman's statement was usually made orally in person at the annual general meeting to the gathered shareholders. It was only from the Second World War, which made travelling to the meeting, often held in London, much more difficult, that it began to be printed and circulated beforehand and the chairman's oratorical skills became less important.[4] Thus one major reason for the introduction and widespread use of a chairman's speech was to comply with best practice or, later, the requirements of company law.

The thinking behind this stipulation was the common theme that shareholders had the right to information about the company since they nominally owned it. Insisting the directors disclose the main financial results was supposed to make it more difficult for them to indulge in sharp business practice, and providing a forum for shareholders to ask questions gave them a formal opportunity to acquaint themselves as to whether the directors were acting in the best interests of the company. These twin provisions were perceived as sufficient to keep a board on its toes. All chairman's statements are also in part a public relations exercise trying to portray the company in the best possible light and so ensure the continued support of the shareholders and the approbation of 'the City', and hence maintain share price and ease future funding. In this role it is likely to be a less unbiased source, tending to view the company's activities through rose-coloured spectacles.

In more recent times the chairman's speech has been used as a signalling device:[5] to the workers, perhaps for the need to keep down wage demands or the problem of looming over-capacity which may lead to redundancy; to the government of the hardship caused by particular tax provisions, as in the Bovril example, or of the board's desire for changes in government policies. As such, the chairman's speech can be of wider importance than merely to the shareholders. A good example is Sir Edward Holden who used the occasion of his annual address as chairman of the Midland Bank as a platform for his views on financial policy advocating, *inter alia*, the creation of an English equivalent to the Federal Reserve, the build-up of gold reserves by the English clearing banks, and the creation of a gold-based 'war chest' prior to the Great War.[6].

The chairman's statement is sometimes also known as the 'report of the board of directors' which it officially is, and the chairman delivers it by virtue of his role as spokesman for the board. The remarks made here about the chairman's speech can equally apply to the report of the board of directors.

Sources

In the early days of the joint stock company when the railway firm was the most normal example in the 1840s and 1850s, the chairman's statement was printed in various specialist trade papers and journals such as the *Railway Times* and the *Railway Magazine*.[7] In addition, from the 1850s some daily newspapers such as *The Times* and *Morning Chronicle* began to summarize the main points of the chairman's statement, though they rarely gave the speech in full. By the last decades of the nineteenth century the quality press, such as *The Times* and *Financial Times*, were regularly carrying full reports of the chairman's statement of the larger public companies, and usually they charged the company for the privilege; indeed, some newspapers made this a major source of revenue.[8] This was normal practice until the Second World War when, for the reasons previously stated, the chairmen ceased making their speeches in person and began having them written and pre-circulated with the accounts. This meant there was no longer the need for verbatim newspaper reports.

Thus for the period say 1880 to 1940, for most of the larger public companies the chairman's speech can be found in either the quality newspapers or the trade press relevant to the industry. The newspaper section of the British Library, currently at Colindale in north London, carries the most comprehensive stock which is available in paper form, as distinct from on microfilm. In addition, the minute books of the board of directors of some companies contain the chairman's speech more or less verbatim.[9] This obviously depends on the survival and successful location of such company minute books. The Guildhall Library in the City of London is another excellent source, for the Stock Exchange insisted on receiving a copy of all documents sent out to shareholders, from which it compiled the abstracts included in the annual *Stock Exchange Year Book*. Fortunately the Stock Exchange preserved this body of records, and recently handed them over to the Guildhall Library where they may, with sufficient notice, be inspected. The volumes contain both the skeletal statements sent out with the accounts and the longer versions where companies were more informative. Occasionally there are also reprints from the press of their reports of the chairman's speech, when these have been circulated by the company to the shareholders. The earliest of these reports held by the Guildhall Library date from about 1869; they are fragmentary until about 1880 but virtually complete thereafter.

For the period from the Second World War onward, companies are more likely to have retained the printed copies of their chairman's statements and the City Business Library, part of the City of London Library, contains a good selection of more recent company statements. *The Times* published a series of annual volumes called *Through the Chairman's Eyes* from 1949 which were a compilation of views culled from chairmen's statements. Their drawback is that they do not reproduce any full statements, only selected extracts; also, only some of the later volumes have an index to the companies from which these extracts have been taken, or a subject index, and few even have a personal index to the chairmen quoted. They are therefore an incomplete and awkward source. The student of a particular firm is better advised to go direct to the company report; the volumes may be of use for a broader study of a particular industry or economic problem area.

All of the above of course only applies to companies which are publicly quoted on the Stock Exchange. It is much more difficult to track down chairman's statements for the private company. The best two sources are the company itself, if it still survives, and the papers of any known major shareholders, if deposited at a public repository, which may contain copies of the chairman's statement. The best starting point for the latter is the files of the National Register of Archives at the Historical Manuscripts Commission. A major drawback for many private companies is that the number of shareholders was so small that often no formal statement was made, or when made was not printed or circulated.

The information they contain

Although it is dangerous to generalize, for some chairmen's statements will contain much detailed information while others will give only the bare bones of the year's activity, there are a number of areas which are usually covered. Some of this information is of relevance only to the development of the specific firm but some may also shed light on general trends in the industry or have significance outside the individual company. However, the public relations function of the chairman's statement should be borne in mind. It may be very bland, self-congratulatory and even deceitful. It is not likely to reveal major mistakes or losses unless absolutely necessary because of repercussions on the profit figures, and wherever possible any downturns of profitability will be blamed on factors external to the firm and beyond the control of the directors rather than on any internal mismanagement. So they need to be read very carefully and with a degree of scepticism.

There is usually a statement of any changes that have been made in the composition of the board of directors. If a director has retired, resigned or died in harness, this is usually reported and it was legally required that any replacement appointed by the board be approved by the general meeting. Hence in the example from Bovril, the second paragraph reports the death of the Duke of Atholl, the vice chairman of the company. There appears to be no replacement, perhaps because of the unusual circumstances of the war. Normally there is some brief appreciation of the existing director, which may contain biographical material; thus we learn that Atholl was Scottish, an MP, presumably before elevation to the peerage, a soldier, and on the board of Bovril for fifteen years.

Another regular inclusion in the chairman's statement is a commentary on the accounts submitted to the shareholders. This provides some explanation of otherwise inscrutable figures in the balance sheet and may give some idea of overall business conditions which have affected the specific firm. In the example, we learn that as a result of the war, provision for taxation has been increased and problems have arisen in getting debtors to pay up. Other examples talk about movements in raw material prices, the impact of strikes, or increases in wages which have had to be borne.

A third area usually requiring explanation was any strategic change in the nature of the products, the market served, the structure or organization of the company, and changes in sources of raw materials or components. In the example, because of the restricting nature of the war economy, there are no innovative developments, so the chairman contents himself with discussion of methods of distribution to ensure equity and the need for three-shift working, giving an indication of the wide range of industries which may be considered war-related. Negative points may be informative as well: the chairman is proud of this company's record in *not* raising the price of the product in wartime despite general inflation; it is interesting to speculate how this could have been squared with remaining profitable. Clues may lie in the pre-war level of profits, and the excess profits tax mentioned.

Quite commonly there are reflections on events of general, interest occurring external to the firm. Thus in the example we learn something of government policy for war finance, in terms of increased taxation; the diet of the nation in wartime: although meals may be monotonous, the introduction of rationing has allowed the government to introduce a food policy which has led to significant improvements in the general level of nutrition; and also entrepreneurial attitudes towards high rates of tax — the chairman forgoing his salary which was to be paid net of tax to him but at a high cost to the company. Similarly, some of the early joint stock bank statements give a detailed appreciation of the local economy in which the bank operated.

In the more modern examples there is usually some mention of significant changes in the firm's staff. This information is rare indeed in nineteenth-century examples, except where individual firms had a particular commitment to good labour relations or employee welfare, but more common after the first third of the twentieth century. In the Bovril example, the material is kept at a superficial level — a mention of teamwork and then a list of employees earning long-serving awards. Finally, some chairman's statements also have a report of the questions put by shareholders to the chairman and the answers given. These can be extremely informative: not only do they give an insight into the degree of shareholder involvement, but also focus on the difficulties faced by the company in the previous year which the chairman may have tried to skate over. For example, the 1891 AGM of the Buenos Aires Water Supply and Drainage Company threw up some very probing questions as the company had been a major cause of the illiquidity of the merchant bankers, Baring Brothers, in 1890 which had given rise to the financial crisis of that year.

Uses

Although they need to be read with a certain amount of scepticism because the chairman was unlikely to give an unbiased view of the year's proceedings, they can shed light on a surprisingly wide range of topics and so are potentially useful to an assortment of researchers. For instance, biographers of great men, whether primarily businessmen or more famous in other spheres, if they know or believe their subject to have been a director in any given company can check through the pertinent chairman's statement to see if the director is mentioned. The minimum information that will be given is when he joined the board and left it, but there may be more meaty material that will confirm other sources or give clues which can be pursued in other documents. In the Bovril example, a biographer of the Duke of Atholl could follow up his army career or his parliamentary activities via various well-known sources such as *Hansard*.

Genealogists are able to use the chairman's statement in a similar way to the biographer. If an ancestor was known to have been a director of a particular firm, then a quick search would repay the effort by providing at least some details. In theory, if an ancestor was known to have been an employee, there might be some mileage in scanning the chairman's statement for a reference but, in practice, the probability of an individual employee being mentioned before the Second World War are so slight as to be negligible. The only real point for the family historian of reading through the chairman's speech is when the relative is *known* to have worked for the firm as some general remarks may be made on labour relations, working conditions or wage rates which will give a general idea of the conditions of life of the predecessor. This sort of information is also of value to the labour historian both as an indication of the conditions in a particular firm or industry and, if enough examples can be found, to construct generalizations about labour relations in a specific period or sector of the economy and the attitudes of the owners and managers towards their labour force.

When the chairman did not confine himself to the activities of his firm alone but also commented, as they were apt to, on general business conditions, or reflected upon the impact of government measures on the company, the economic and social historian will find material of value. Three areas may be identified: the attitude of the board to changes in legislation or business conditions; the perceived impact of those changes upon the particular firm; the actual impact of those alterations in the external environment. In the Bovril example there is mention of increased government taxation. The attitude towards it which permeated the speech is fairly hostile: 'I do not think there ever was any suggestion that Excess Profits Tax was an equitable scheme' and rather cynical: 'No doubt the standard years selected . . . in their wisdom . . . by the Inland Revenue . . . would provide the largest possible revenue.' Its impact was seen as negating the desire of the firm to make any improvements in their performance, and in fact this may also explain the 'proud' announcement that the price of the product had been held constant despite rising costs. Any price increase would have increased profits which would have been totally taken in tax.

Finally, that *rara avis* the historian of accounting theory and practice will find some goodies in the section of a chairman's statement which relates to the financial results. The chairman may indicate the current practice of the firm on some aspect of financial control; in the Bovril case there is mention of depreciation policy, the transfer of some profits to reserves and provision for taxation. When there are issues currently taxing the accounting profession, the chairman may comment not only on his own firm's practice but also his board's attitude towards the issue, so providing material for an attitudinal survey.

Cross-references to other documents

Quite obviously the chairman's statement, whether spoken or written, was not meant to be freestanding, but was to be taken in conjunction with the accounts (q.v.) which were circulated, and indeed some sections of the statement will make no sense without the accompanying balance sheet. The statement may explain some of the changes in the financial figures but the actual accounts will be needed to provide the raw data which is being discussed. Similarly, the chairman's statement may indicate changes in the board of directors during the past year. This can be confirmed, and precise dates assigned, by reference to the returns of directors (q.v.) which had to be lodged with the Registrar of Joint Stock Companies and should be available from Companies House.

The minute books of the board of directors (q.v.) of the particular company, when they survive, are also an invaluable adjunct to the chairman's statement; the minutes may well give an indication of the reasoning which lay behind some of the decisions reported at the AGM. A bland statement about reserves or dividend may conceal significant differences of opinion within the board, and some of that debate *may* come out in the minute books but will not appear in the chairman's statement which will present a united front to the shareholders. The trade press will complement the chairman's statement; the latter may be printed in the former and again some commentary may occur on the company's performance in the relevant journals, which will amplify or explain the chairman's remarks.

Works using this source

Like a number of other documents discussed in this book, the chairman's speech is most unlikely to be the sole source for any publication. Because of its public relations role it is likely to omit, or put the best gloss on, any less than successful operations or decisions and as such must be treated as a biased source. It is also unlikely to be detailed enough to act as even the major source for any book or article, dealing as it often did with general trends in the business and needing to be confirmed and amplified by other records.

This said, chairmen's speeches are a useful supplementary source for any business history. Wells, writing the recent history of Hollins, which commenced in the late eighteenth century spinning and weaving wool and cotton mixtures and merged with Viyella in 1961, used 'reports of the chairman's address at annual general meetings of shareholders of William Hollins & Co 1919–60' and similarly those of Viyella International from 1961–6.[10] Richardson, discussing the relationship between Nobels, the firm which introduced dynamite, and the Australian mining industry in the late nineteenth and early twentieth centuries, uses reports of the chairman's speeches of the Nobel Dynamite Trust now in the ICI archives to show that the presence of an Australian-owned explosives company, Australian Explosive & Chemical Co, menaced the European-based companies even when AEC agreed to adhere to the pricing agreements drawn up by the European cartel, thus eliminating price competition. This threat would have been exacerbated if the Australian government had introduced tariffs on imported explosives. In order to remove this danger, the Europeans acquired ownership of the share capital in 1897.[11] Later in the same article, Richardson uses the speech of Sir David Harris, chairman of De Beers Consolidated Mines Ltd, at the annual general meeting of 1917 to show how prices of dynamite dropped dramatically in the Australian market as a result of the Cape Explosives Works Ltd of South Africa being invited to tender to supply Australian mining companies with their requirements, so breaking the European monopoly.[12] Professor Checkland, when writing the history of the Tharsis Sulphur and Copper Co, which was founded in 1866 in Glasgow to work the pyrites deposits of Huelva province in Spain by, among others, Charles Tennant the great Scottish chemical entrepreneur, drew on the directors' annual reports of the company which survived from 1867 in the archives of the firm.[13]

Some continental countries created similar documents as in the UK. In France it was normal for companies to hold annual general meetings and for there to be either a report or an address made to that meeting. A good example of an article using such reports is that by Francois Crouzet on the Fives-Lille engineering company.[14] The paper was 'mostly based on the annual reports to shareholders' meetings from 1867 onwards'.[15] They were used to show that this large engineering firm located in northern France suffered a sharp drop in sales and profits in the period 1875–1900 through having concentrated on railway locomotives and equipment when orders from the large French railway companies were in decline and very irregular. The company was unable to diversify successfully into public works and overseas markets and only revived after 1904 when orders for railway equipment for the home market picked up. Crouzet used the accounts to tabulate sales and profits figures and the reports to the shareholders to show the cause of movements in the statistics and the stratagems used by the directors to seek alternative sources of profits.

The example

Bovril was invented by John Lawson Johnston, who also founded the business in 1884 in London. Before this he had worked as a butcher in Edinburgh and went to Canada where he canned tomatoes and a large consignment of beef for the French government. In 1889 the business became a limited liability company and in 1896 it was bought by the notorious company promoter, E.T. Hooley, and launched to the public at a capitalization over six times its previous value.[16] Hooley's involvement was shortlived: having drastically over-capitalized Bovril and removed most of the liquid funds comprising its working capital, he left the problems to Johnston and his son, George, to sort out. Hooley never sat on the board of Bovril and took no interest in its long-term prospects. Most of the work of securing the future of the company fell on George Lawson Johnston, as his father was in failing health and died in late 1900.

George showed great financial ingenuity and not merely kept the business going but expanded its activities by backwards vertical integration into land, cattle, transportation and processing plant in South America and diversified the product base by adding Virol, a malt extract tonic, Marmite, a vegetarian version of Bovril, and Ambrosia, a range of milk-based baby foods and later creamed rice, to the company's repertoire. The company prospered in the 1920s and despite being hit by the slump of 1929–32 recovered well in the later 1930s. By the Second World War, Bovril could boast several subsidiaries in Australia, Canada and Ireland, *inter alia*, and a balance sheet capitalization of over five million. George Lawson Johnston, who was elevated to the peerage as Lord Luke in 1929, remained chairman until his death in 1943 and added the role of managing director in 1932. In the former position it was his not wholly welcome duty to make the annual speech to the shareholders. He was not a natural or fluent speaker but, given the briefness of the printed statements, it was a necessary chore. The example is the last one which he made and reflects the problems and conditions of war-time business.[17]

On Luke's death in 1943, he was succeeded as chairman by his eldest son, Ian St John, who also inherited the title. The Lawson Johnson family retained effective control of the Bovril group until the early 1970s when it was taken over by Sir James Goldsmith's Cavenham Foods Group despite Rowntree Macintosh being invited to act as the 'white knight' by the board of Bovril. The Lawson Johnston family, although they wielded effective control of the company, had so diluted their shareholding in 1896 that from then on they had only a minority — though the largest single block — of the shares. Goldsmith's price was so high that the shareholders could not resist it and the founding family severed their managerial connections with the firm in the third generation. Bovril did not stay with Goldsmith long. He carved up the group, selling its bulk milk assets to Express Dairy and its Argentinian properties. In 1980 the rump of the Bovril business was sold to Beechams, the health drinks, pharmaceuticals and cosmetics firm. There it has stayed to the present day.[18]

Notes

1. 8 Edw. VII c. 69, first schedule, A 107.
2. 18 & 19 Geo. V c. 45, clause 39 (4).
3. 19 & 20 Geo. V c. 23, clause 123 (2).
4. K. Newman, 'Financial Advertising Past and Present', *Three Banks Review*, No. 140 (1983) p. 50.
5. Ibid., p. 48.
6. E. Green, 'Sir Edward Hopkinson Holden' in D.J. Jeremy (ed.), *Dictionary of Business Biography, Vol 3* (Butterworths, 1985) p. 295.
7. Newman, op. cit., p. 44.
8. Newman, op. cit., pp. 49–50; D. Porter, 'A Trusted Guide of the Investing Public: Harry Marks and the *Financial News* 1884–1916', *Business History*, Vol. 28, No. 1 (1986) p. 7.
9. 'During the period of the private company, Weir's Directors' Minute Books were also used to record Directors' Reports . . . From the formation of the public company onward . . . a complete series of published accounts accompanied each year by a Chairman's Review.' W.J. Reader, *The Weir Group: A Centenary History* (Weidenfeld & Nicolson, 1971) p. 208.
10. F.A. Wells, *Hollins & Viyella: A Business History* (David & Charles, 1968) pp. 259–60.
11. P. Richardson, 'Nobels and the Australian Mining Industry, 1907–25', *Business History*, Vol. 26, No. 2 (1984) pp. 162–3.
12. Ibid., p. 177.
13. S.G. Checkland, *The Mines of Tharsis* (George Allen & Unwin, 1967) p. 278.
14. F. Crouzet, 'When the Railways were Built: A French Engineering Firm during the "Great Depression" and after' in S. Marriner (ed.), *Business and Businessmen: Studies in Business, Economic, and Accounting History* (Liverpool UP, 1978).
15. Ibid., p. 125.
16. J. Armstrong, 'Hooley and the Bovril Company', *Business History*, Vol. 28, No. 1 (1986).
17. This section is based on the entries for John and George Lawson Johnston in Jeremy, op. cit., pp. 510–31.
18. G. Wansell, *Sir James Goldsmith* (Fontana, 1982) pp. 82–3, 89 & 188.

BOVRIL LIMITED

EVEN DISTRIBUTION OF SUPPLIES

LORD LUKE'S REVIEW

The FORTY-FIFTH ANNUAL GENERAL MEETING of Bovril Limited was held yesterday at the Chartered Insurance Institute, London.

The LORD LUKE, K.B.E. (chairman and managing director), presided.

The CHAIRMAN said: Gentlemen, Since the issue of our report we have suffered a sad loss in the death of our vice-chairman, the Duke of Atholl. He had a very distinguished career. He was a brave soldier, an active member when in the House of Commons, and a great chieftain in his own county. He joined this board 15 years ago, and was a helpful director, and was popular with the Bovril staff and employees both here and abroad. He made a great success of a visit to the Bovril estancias and factories in South America. We shall indeed miss his cheery enthusiasm at our board table. I would ask you to stand in his memory.

BALANCE-SHEET ITEMS

The meeting having stood in silence.

The CHAIRMAN continued: Turning to the balance-sheet, you will find the freehold and leasehold properties £9,544 down. This is due to depreciation. Plant, &c., on the other hand, owing to certain additions, is, after allowing for depreciation, up to the extent of £9,879. The interest in subsidiaries, including indebtedness, at £327,311, has been increased by some £28,000. Investments in associated companies, &c., at £793,399, is up £83,438. Three-fourths of this addition is due to the purchase of National War Bonds.

Stocks of cattle and raw material, at £900,907, shows an increase of £16,251. This is due to increases in raw material and finished stocks, the cattle interest being down. Sundry debtors is one of the few items showing a considerable change, at £472,542, against £232,982, an increase of £239,560. This is due to increases in the amounts owing by Estates Control Limited and Argentine Estates of Bovril Limited. Sundry creditors and provision for taxation is up by some £260,000, a large part of which is an increase in the reserve for taxation.

RESERVE REACHES £1,100,000

The reserve, at £1,070,000, shows the appropriation added last year, and the addition of another £30,000 this year will bring it up to £1,100,000.

You will see in the profit and loss account that the net profit shows £275,628, as against £263,860 in 1940. Of course these two figures are by no means representative of the actual trading profits of the two years, but they are as adjusted after making allowances for Excess Profits Tax.

The Excess Profits Tax standard is of course our ceiling and under the present Budget improvement in our final net profit can only show itself if additional capital is employed in the business and raises our standard, or Bovril receives larger dividends from its investments.

E.P.T. POSITION

A company's position as regards its Excess Profits Tax standard is simply a matter of luck. No doubt the standard years selected were in their wisdom wisely chosen by the Inland Revenue as years that on the whole would provide the largest possible revenue in the scheme of taxation. The years may suit some companies, but certainly on the whole they caught many at their very worst period. I do not think there ever was any suggestion that Excess Profits Tax was an equitable scheme as between various taxpayers, but it was a scheme of taxation that has produced a very large revenue, and no doubt in quite a few cases has prevented those in what might be called war industries making excessive profits.

At the beginning of the war I told you I intended to forego my chairmanship salary because, as you were paying income-tax and part of the surtax, it was costing you a considerable sum and I was only getting a shilling or two in the £ of it. I accordingly had it cut out, but now that owing to the Excess Profits Tax you have to pay 100 per cent. of your profits over a standard figure I have sometimes thought it was a pity I had done so, because it would not now be at your expense, even though I might only get 6d. in the £ of it. However, nowadays one is kept much too busy with more important things than bothering about remuneration.

You will have seen from the report that the profits were sufficient to provide our usual fixed dividends, £30,000 to reserve, and 9 per cent. on the Deferred.

There is no class more hardly hit than those who out of savings bought shares that to-day provide an income after deduction of tax of almost half what they received in 1938, and therefore we were very pleased to see our way to recommend a small increase on the Deferred dividend.

ELASTICITY OF ORGANIZATION

The Bovril organization, which has been built up during all these years, can show considerable elasticity at a period like this, not only in the production of Bovril but particularly of emergency rations and other food products, and by intensive work by day and night, &c., our output of all these is at least three times what it was in 1939. The factories are indeed to be complimented on their efforts.

During the period under review we have taken considerable trouble to distribute our supplies of Bovril as evenly as possible throughout the country. I believe our friends in the retail trade have been receiving at least as much Bovril as they did on the average of 1938-39-40—unless they live in an area where the population has been much reduced, as, of course, we take that into account in arranging the quotas.

NATION'S GENERAL NOURISHMENT NEVER BETTER

As chairman of the Ministry of Health's Committee on Nutrition, I listened during four years just before the war to some of the best informed dietitians, health experts, and statisticians discussing the question of the nation's diet and then come to their conclusions. They had little doubt about their findings, but were very sceptical as to whether, with party politics, &c., in the way, much would be done to tackle the matter and improve the nourishment of the people as a whole.

Many other sound dietitians had been thinking along the same lines, and there was, I should say, general agreement on the main facts, but I am sure progress would have been painfully slow if we had not come to a period of rationing. The last two years have given an opportunity that has so wisely been taken advantage of, and I should not be surprised if, in spite of all the difficulties of shipping and home farming, the people are on the average so well provided for that the nation is better nourished than ever before. This is especially noticeable as regards that considerable body who used to be somewhat under-nourished. I refer particularly to the large family with probably only one wage-earner to provide food for all.

MONOTONOUS MEALS

One, of course, hears talk of the monotony of our meals simply because we miss that infinite variety of tasty extras that used mostly to come from overseas in ships with great refrigerators. Obviously we must forget such dainties for the present, though after the war they should begin to come again. However, let us hope that the improvements in the main features of the nation's nutrition will not be discarded and cast aside lightly.

Team work has largely been a key to our success in spite of all the difficulties caused by the war, output had been increased. It has been a pleasure to me to work with this team, which I have referred to year after year, particularly Mr. Walker, the departmental heads, and the branch managers at home and overseas. To all these warm thanks are due.

NO INCREASE IN THE PRICE OF BOVRIL

We are rather proud of the fact that since Bovril was first marketed, over half a century ago, its price has never been raised during a period of war. There was no increase during the 1914-18 war, nor has the price been raised during this war, in spite of the general increase in prices all round. I hope we shall be able to maintain this record, as I am anxious that we should do so in order to avoid penalizing the many thousands of regular consumers of Bovril who rely on it especially during trying times.

The real difficulty in speaking to shareholders to-day is that there is so much of interest that one could say and yet so much of it has to be left unsaid, probably till this war is over, and I, therefore, make no apology for cutting the speech down this year, especially as shareholders have not got a great deal of time to listen to it, and the newspapers have very little space to spare.

After the formal business of the meeting to-day I shall again have pleasure in presenting long-service awards to members of the staff who have had 30 years' continuous service with us. This year eight of our staff qualify: Mr. H. W. Barnett, Mr. A. A. Gailey, and Mr. H. J. Taylor, of the head office staff; Mr. J. Britton and Mr. C. J. Spaughton, of the factory office staff; and Mr. E. J. Cummins and Mr. A. E. Frost, of the factory. In addition, Mr. J. P. Dutton, of Montreal, has served 30 years with the company and Bovril (Canada) Limited, and a suitable presentation is being made to him in Montreal.

The report and accounts were adopted.

---

5. Report of statement of Lord Luke, Chairman of Bovril Ltd, 26 March 1942. *Source: The Times*, 27 March 1942, p. 10.

6 Registers of directors

Original purpose

Since only joint stock companies have boards of directors, registers of directors exist solely for this type of firm; partnerships did not have any such document, the nearest being the partnership deed. One of the most potent reasons for keeping these registers was that the law required it. The 1844 Act, which made the formation of joint stock companies cheap and easy, stipulated as one of the conditions of being granted company status that the business make an initial return to the Registrar of Joint Stock Companies of the names of its directors, notify any changes, and make this list available gratis to the shareholders at the company's registered office.[1] These requirements were absent from the 1856 Act. Since that Act totally repealed the 1844 Act but contained no provisions about maintaining a register of directors or lodging any such list with the Registrar, the company was freed from this stipulation. At first sight the 1862 Act seems to rectify this omission, for clause 45 requires every company to keep a register at its offices, send a copy to the Registrar, and notify him from time to time of any changes.[2] However, the strange wording of the clause made it possible for most companies to avoid this responsibility as the phraseology 'Every Company under this Act, and not having a Capital divided into Shares, shall keep . . .' ruled out most companies because their capital *was* divided into shares.[3] This situation did not change until 1900 when the Companies Act of that year deleted the offending passage.[4] Thus from 1900 the company was again required to send an annual list of its directors to the Registrar. From then on, these stipulations have remained in force. Therefore, just as for the register of members, from 1844 to 1856 and 1900 onwards an overriding reason for keeping a register of directors was to comply with the law. The thinking behind this legal requirement was that the directors were the decision makers in a company, acting on behalf of the shareholders who had a right to know precisely who the current directors were and some basic information about them. They were entitled to judge whether they considered these individuals trustworthy and honest and thus good people to manage the affairs of the company. This entitlement extended beyond current shareholders to those who were contemplating buying a stake in the firm, for the returns of directors which were submitted to the Registrar were open to the inspection of the public subject to a maximum charge of one shilling.[5] Obviously shareholders or potential members might object to certain individuals being directors, for instance bankrupts, people with criminal records or a previous association with unsuccessful companies, those with a doubtful mental state (and indeed some of these were debarred by law from being directors).[6] In order to make their displeasure known, they had to be able to discover easily the names of the current directors. Similar considerations applied to creditors, either actual or potential, who had some right to know with whom they were conducting business and from whom they anticipated payment.

During the twentieth century the register of directors took on a wider role. Because of concern about the possibilities of corruption by directors, it was felt necessary to require them to declare their interests. It was feasible that a director of one company might grant a contract or order to another business of which he was a major or sole beneficiary. This would lead to a conflict of interest since as the director of the company putting out the contract he should strive for the lowest possible price while as a member of the contracting company he should wish to obtain the highest possible price. It was considered best that the directors of a company should know each other's interests. Accordingly the 1928 Act required all directors to make a statement to their fellow directors of the firms of which they were members.[7] This provision was also incorporated in the 1929 Consolidating Act.[8] These statements were often then bound into the board minute book. However, although this kept the directors informed of their peers' interests, the shareholders remained ignorant since they had no guaranteed access to these books. As a result, the 1948 Act considerably tightened up the provision of the 1929 Act by insisting that all companies keep a register showing each director's holding of shares and deventures in any corporate body, which was to be open for inspection at the company's registered office and available for perusal during annual general meetings.[9] Thus the shareholders were in a position to check on any conflicts of interest among their directors and bring this up at meetings if it was felt to be a threat. In this way the registers of directors became more than a mere listing of the individuals and took on the function of a check on them as well.

One final, rather minor, purpose was assumed by these registers during the

First World War. The registers were required to record the nationalities of the directors as well as any previous nationality they had held. The reason for this was that the government seized the property of many foreigners who were natives of enemy countries such as Germany, Turkey or Austro-Hungary, sold it to British nationals and used the proceeds to help pay for the cost of the war. The requirement embodied in the 1917 Act[10] was to allow the government to identify firms which were substantially or wholly managed by enemy aliens.

Sources

The survival rate of the contents of registers of directors is high when they were lodged with the Registrar of Companies who was charged with ensuring their preservation. From 1844 to 1856 and from 1900 the Registrar received annual returns or notification of any changes in all boards. Thus for live companies the returns of directors can still be accessed in Companies House, although the older versions will need a little notice, having to be brought from the Welsh out-station. For companies which have ceased to trade, these returns should be found, like other statutory documents, in the PRO at Kew among the Board of Trade papers. Unlike returns of shareholders, they are not usually weeded and so good runs can be found giving a comprehensive picture for the periods covered. Strictly, of course, these returns are not the actual registers, which would have remained in the company, but they do contain an abstract of the information in the register and as such are a good source.

The actual registers have often lived on within the company that created them. As the business was required by law or its articles of association to maintain them, they were well cherished and infrequently destroyed. Also, compared to registers of members which are usually very bulky volumes, one book will contain decades of returns of directors because the number of board members was normally kept down to a handful or two and frequent changes were not encouraged. The company secretary was often charged with maintaining these records and they were kept in his store. Where a company is defunct, these volumes may have been passed to a local repository and it is worth discovering the last-known address of a business and casting around a little. The NRA should have a listing if the records are in a public archive. There is therefore a very good chance that the researcher will find this type of source.

The information they contain

Originally the registers of directors contained only the barest facts: the full name of the director, his address, occupation or profession, the date he joined the board and the date he left. Although the register often contained a column headed 'reasons for ceasing to be a director and for appointment of new director', it was frequently left blank. In many early companies the large shareholders were also the directors and thus re-election was virtually automatic and changes in the composition of the board were infrequent. Where there was an alteration, the reason might be given, but it was not always the case, and when stated it could be brief and not very informative, such as 'resigned' or 'retired' or 'died'.

By the early twentieth century some additional information was being included, for instance the director's nationality, and nationality of origin if different had to be given after 1917, see page 87 above. However, they remained essentially a mere list of the directors' names, addresses and occupations and even the 1929 Act failed to alter this. Although it required directors to make a declaration of their interests, this statement was not for public consumption but only for the eyes of the other directors. Thus they were more likely to be bound in with the board minutes, which were usually only open to directors and senior management, rather than the register of directors which was open to all members.

It was the 1948 Act which changed these registers fundamentally. After that Act a director had to make a full and formal declaration of his interests in any other company whether by virtue of owning shares, stock or debentures or being on the board. The registers thenceforth contained a list of all the shareholdings of each director, the date he acquired them, the number obtained and the price paid or other consideration for which they were given. If there were any limitations or conditions upon that director's interest in these securities, that too had to be stated, for instance if he was one of a number of joint holders or the shares were in a trust of which he was the sole or part beneficiary. Similarly the register had to record when he disposed of this property with an equal level of detail as required at the acquisition stage. In addition to his shareholdings, the director was also required to list all his other directorships. If he added to this list, or indeed ceased to hold some positions, he was required to notify this for entry in the register. Thus since soon after the Second World War the registers of directors contain much detailed information on the interests of the board members in that particular company and all others.

Finally, one more piece of information became recorded after the 1948 Act: the date of birth of a director. This did not apply to directors of private companies, but all others had to comply. The reason for insisting on this was to make public the director's age, since the Act required that normally directors retire from the board after they had reached the age of 70, except in private companies.[11] Thus the registers become more informative as they become more modern, but the range of the information they contain is strictly limited.

Uses

Because the information contained in the registers is limited to pretty simple factual details of the directors, the uses to which they can be put are similarly restricted. For a biographer or genealogist who is collecting any information available about a specific individual, they will provide the dates of appointment and resignation to a particular board and the addresses at which the director lived while he held the position — for a change of address is normally recorded. After 1948 the registers provide more information for the biographer in terms of other shareholdings and directorships and this data paints a much broader picture of the individual's role in business. The biographer could construct a rough estimate of the individual's total shareholdings and thus the wealth he had in this form and the income he derived from it. Similarly, the ramifications of his directorships could be traced and thus the extent of his influence within the business community. However, a researcher interested in the life of a particular director will be frustrated by lack of information on, for example, why he abandoned his position. A formal statement such as 'resigned' may hide a conflict of interests between a director's many shareholdings in different companies, or failure to work amicably with other directors, or lack of attendance — the board minute books might reveal more. For recent history, judicial interviewing may reveal the answer.

In many respects these registers are not essential documents in trying to reconstruct the history of a company, as the limited information they contain, particularly in the early volumes, may be found in other sources, for instance minute books and financial returns. The list of directors' shareholdings after 1948 is, however, unique and adds to the picture of each director's overall business interests. A complete series of these documents gives a clear indication of the leadership of a company over time, in terms of the names, occupations and number of directors. Most early companies tried to limit the number of directors to the bare minimum, five was often regarded as sufficient. An increase in the board size usually reflects a change in the financial structure of the company, for example the Borneo Company admitted two more after its capital was increased, and the reduction of family interests was usually followed by an increase in outside directors. A private company when going public always appointed further directors. Thus major changes in the history of a company may be detected through these registers and compared with minute books and reports and accounts.

These registers can help in establishing relationships between different companies through the shareholdings of one person. Concealment of this before 1948, often with disastrous consequences for the shareholders, was a major defect in company law before that date. A factor influencing the promulgation of the 1948 Act was the Royal Mail Group scandal of 1931. Lord Kylsant had cleverly maintained control, although with a minority of the capital investment, of the many different companies in this Group by an elaborate system of cross-shareholdings strategically placed, which remained hidden from public view. The failure of this organization, which controlled about 15 per cent of British registered tonnage, threatened to shake the entire British economy.[12] The 1948 Act was designed to prevent a repetition by enforcing a statutory declaration of all directors' interests.

The registers are also useful indicators of the power of a certain group of people within the directorate of a company, such as those within the same family, or from the same town, or of the same occupation or religion. Studying a series of registers may give an idea of the power of particular groupings, such as Quakers, shipowners or bankers, within a company. The same is true for those with less obvious common interests. There were a number of syndicates of like-minded, and in some cases related, individuals who cooperated in floating family companies, or acting as underwriters of issues, or controlled a number of companies by interlocking directorships and shareholdings. These networks can be traced by a check of the shareholdings and directorships of a number of individuals in a range of different companies. The registers of directors are useful for this. If a large number of registers of directors from different companies and for a long period were used, it might be possible to address the questions who held the real power in Britain's companies, was it a stable elite, was there much movement in and out, and how large was this group?

If a register of directors is all that survives for a particular company, it could be used to sketch an outline of its history through the terms of office of various chairmen and directors. This is often a convenient way of dividing up company histories, as in many cases the change in leading personnel ushered in different policies and activities. The demise of an ageing but powerful chairman may result in a sudden and belated modernization programme.[13]

There are a number of drawbacks in using these registers. The major one is that they do not explain the changes at board level; they give the facts of who and when but do not say why the appointment was offered to or accepted by the individual or why it was terminated. Similarly, they contain nothing about the contribution of the individual at board meetings, whether he was a frequent attender and led discussions or vice versa, and no mention of whether he had a particular functional role within the company. A further caveat to be borne in mind is that the occupations and addresses given, especially in the early registers, are those the directors chose to give. In the case of the former they can be very general and uninformative, for instance 'merchant', 'gentleman' or 'company director', and in the case of the latter there is no guarantee that this is the director's main or only address; even more annoying, he may give only the address of the company rather than his residence. Thus these particular documents on their own are of very limited usefulness, especially before 1948. They contain only factual material with no explanation of causality and are best used as a supplement to other more revealing records.

Cross-references to other documents

Because of the limited nature of the information contained in registers of directors, it is particularly important to be able to supplement them with other documents from the same business. The board minute books (q.v.) are an obvious adjunct to the registers by revealing the regularity of attendance of an individual and perhaps why they were appointed or resigned. The better board minute books may also show the degree of influence an individual had on company policy through his contribution to the debates at board meetings. These documents also often contain the declarations of directors' interests between 1929 and 1948 as explained above on page 86.

The shareholders' registers (q.v.) are also a complementary source to the registers of directors for, before the 1948 Act made it compulsory to give details of a director's shareholdings, they can be used to gain an idea of the financial stake of each director in the company, whether in equity, debentures or loans. There are a couple of sources which will confirm the information given in the registers but will not add much to it. These are prospectuses (q.v.) and the annual reports for both of these usually listed the current directors. In addition, the chairman's statement (q.v.) often announced any changes in the composition of the board, thanking retiring members and welcoming new ones and in many cases giving some intimation of the reasons for a director stepping down. If a director deserved particular mention for any reason, an honour, or appointment, that too might appear in the chairman's statement. The latter may also allude to any alteration in the arrangements whereby the directors are remunerated. If their fees are to be increased or an additional fee is to be paid, this may appear in the statement. They may also be found in the profit and loss account, where it survives, though often only as an aggregate figure for the total board. Letter books (q.v.) may contain confidential references to the qualities of particular directors, especially where the director was making a tour of inspection of one of the branches, sites or factories away from the head office, and correspondence took place over arrangements for the trip and a report back followed it.

Works using this source

Many of the individual biographies in the *Dictionary of Business Biography* use the records of joint stock companies lodged with the Registrar.[14] Among the more useful documents in this archive are the returns of directors which give precise details of the board membership of the entries and show their spread of business interests across firms and industries and thus their overall importance in the business elite. Youssef Cassis used the registers of directors to show how many directors of joint stock banks were also partners or directors of merchant banks or financial firms in the City of London. In their capacity as merchant bank directors, they wanted the joint stock banks to channel surplus cash from the country into the City where it would be made available to finance the big international deals of the private financial firms. These deals, he argues, generated very large profits and accrued to the partners or few shareholders in the private companies rather than going to the anonymous shareholders of the joint stock banks, the shareholdings of which were more widely dispersed. This, Cassis concludes, explains why English joint stock banks, unlike their American or German counterparts, failed to play a large role in direct industrial investment or international trade.[15]

The example

The Bagdad Light and Power Company was formed as a private partnership of

British, Belgian, French and German businessmen with interests in the Gulf who wished to improve the operation of their trading activities by developing the local infrastructure. It was also a way of employing unconvertible local currency. The date of its formation is unknown but it appears to go back to the 1890s, when large amounts of capital earned overseas (supplemented by sums invested by entrepreneurs at home) were employed in such schemes as railways, mining and, like this, utilities. It was registered as a limited liability company in the UK in May 1930. The company by then was acting as an investment trust, dealing in various governments' bonds, but continued its initial interest in power production and municipal lighting using locally produced oil as well as dealing in property, advancing credit, and acting as agents or managers on behalf of other businesses.

By 1959, when it was acquired by Gilmans, a merchant house based in Hong Kong since the 1840s, its capital was £1.2 million. Gilmans appeared to be seeking a UK base and by special resolution the name was changed to Gilman (Holdings) Ltd. Thus the original title ceases to exist, but it is not a 'defunct company', because the unique company number was retained by the new Gilmans' business. This particular register of directors is included for two reasons: it includes individuals of foreign birth, required by the 1917 Act, and lists other shareholdings and interests of the particular directors to whom it refers.

Notes

1. 7 & 8 Vict. 110, clauses 7(10), 10 & 57.
2. 25 & 26 Vict. c. 89, clause 45.
3. Ibid.
4. 63 & 64 Vict. c. 48, clause 20.
5. For example: 7 & 8 Vict. c. 110, clause 18; 19 & 20 Vict. c. 47, clause 106(5); 8 Edw. VII c. 69, clause 243(6).
6. For example: 7 & 8 Vict. c. 110, clause 29; 8 Edw. VII c. 69, first schedule, table A, clause A77.
7. 18 & 19 Geo. V. c. 45, clause 81.
8. 19 & 20 Geo. V c. 23, clause 149(3).
9. 11 & 12 Geo. VI c. 38, clause 195.
10. 7 & 8 Geo. V c. 28.
11. 11 & 12 Geo. VI c. 38, clause 185.
12. E. Green & M. Moss, *A Business of National Importance: The Royal Mail Shipping Group, 1902–1937* (Methuen, 1984).
13. Such as when the first Earl of Inchcape took over the leadership of the amalgamation of P & O and the British India Steam Navigation Co in 1914.
14. D.J. Jeremy (ed.), *Dictionary of Business Biography*, Vols. 1–5 (Butterworths, 1984–6).
15. Y. Cassis, 'Management and Strategy in the English Joint Stock Banks 1890–1914', *Business History*, Vol. 27, No. 3 (1985).

Register of *Directors of *Bagdad Light and Power*

Gibson (Holdings) Limited formerly

When appointed	† The present Christian Name or Names and Surname	‡ Any former Christian Name or Names or Surname	Usual Residential Address
as at 1.7 1948	Sir *Kinahan Cornwallis* G.C.M.G. C.B.E. M.C.	None	Oak House Hartley Wintney Hants.
as at 1.7 1948	Georges Jules Francois Joseph Grandchamps	None	55 rue Mignot Delstanche Bruxelles, Belgium.
as at 1.7 1948	Samuel Henry Taylor	None	Thornfield Sandown Park Tunbridge Wells.
as at ...	Douglas Selby Warren	None	Old Bridge House Marlow Bucks.

6. Register of directors of the Bagdad Light and Power Co Ltd as at 1 July 1948. *Source*: Inchcape plc archives.

Company Limited

Nationality	§ Business Occupations and Particulars of other Directorships	¶ Date of Birth	Date of ceasing to be Director	Reason [...] Director and for Appointment [...] new Director

British — *Company Director / Director of The Imperial Bank of Iran Limited* — 19.2.1883 — 2[...].[...].[...] 907 — *Resigned*

Belgian — *Company Director / Other Directorships / None.* — 31.[...].90.25.2.59 — *Resigned*

British — *Retired Merchant / Director of Cawnpore Electric Supply Corporation Limited / Delhi Electric Supply and Traction Company Limited / Madras Electric Supply Corporation Limited / Madras Electric Tramways (1904) Limited* — 23.4.19[...] — [...]

British — *Stockbroker / Director of [...] / [...] African [...] Lighting Company Limited / Indian Copper Corporation Limited / [...] Electric [...] / [...] Electric Supply [...]* — 19.6.5[...] — 30.12.[...]

§ The names of all [...] corporate incorporated in Great Britain of which the Director is also a director should be given, except bodies corporate of which the Company making the return is the wholly owned subsidiary, or bodies corporate which are the wholly owned subsidiaries either of the Company or of another company of which the Company is the wholly owned subsidiary. A body corporate is deemed to be the wholly owned subsidiary of another if it has no members except that other and that other's wholly owned subsidiaries and its or their nominees.

¶ Dates of birth need only be given in the case of a company which is subject to Section 183 of the Companies Act 1948, namely, a company which is not a private company or which, being a private company, is the subsidiary of a body corporate incorporated in the United Kingdom which is neither a private company nor a company registered under the law relating to companies for the time being in force in Northern Ireland and having provisions in its constitution which would, if it had been registered in Great Britain, entitle it to rank as a private company.

6. Register of directors of the Bagdad Light and Power Co Ltd as at 1 July 1948.
Sources: Inchcape plc archives.

Register of *Directors of Bagdad Light and Power *Gilman (Holdings) Limited*

Companies Ltd.— The S.L.S.S., Ltd., London, Birmingham, Liverpool, Manchester & Glasgow. WD1650 7-46

When appointed	† The present Christian Name or Names and Surname	‡ Any former Christian Name or Names or Surname	Usual Residential Address
as as at 1.7.1948	Robert Philippe Albert Mathew Joseph Walthere Baron Hankar	None	D'Argentine, Sal Hulpe, Belgium.
as as at 1.7.1948	W... Nieuwenhuys	None	7. Avenue de la Clairière Brussels.
14.4.1954	Philippe de Selliers de Moranville	None	23 Rue Ducale, Brussels
as 17.9.1954	Cecil John Edmonds, C.M.G., C.B.E.	None	Horonden, Hawkhurst, Kent
30.12.1957	[illegible]	None	33 Leigh Gardens, Leigh-on-Sea
14.10.1955	Donald McKenzie McKechnie	None	Ingailla, Balmyle Road, West Ferry, Dundee
as 28.2.1957	William Halford Lawson	None	The Mound, Mimbridge, Chobham, Surrey
25.2.1959	Roger Dermot... Foote	None	33 Ennismore Gardens, London, W.8.

Company   Limited

Nationality	‡ Business Occupations and Particulars of other Directorships	¶ Date of Birth	Date of ceasing to be Director	Reason for ceasing to be Director and for Appointment of new Director

Belgian	Gerant de la Mutuelle Solvay Other Directorships None	15.2.1892	14.4.1934	Resigned
Belgian	Company Director Other Directorships None. Mutuelle Solvay	28.7.1889	28.2.59	Resigned
Belgian	Directorship none	11.11.1915	15.1.	
British	No Occupation No other Directorships	26.10.1879	25.2.59	Resigned
			28.2.59	Resigned in place of...
British	Stockbroker Director of Beaver ... Ltd	31.7.	25.2.59	Resigned additional
British	Engineer No other Directorships	25.5.1403		
British	Chartered accountant Directorships for ... & Armstrong Whitworth Ltd (Engineers) Ltd English General ... Ltd Company de Elektricidad de la Provincia de Buenos Aires Ltd	21.3.1899	25.2.59	in place of Sir K Cornwall Resigned
British	Business & Technical Consultant Other Directorships: Bowden Instruments Ltd. Jas. E. Pilgrim Limited (continued overleaf)	19.8.1916	30.9.1965	

‡ The names of all bodies corporate incorporated in Great Britain of which the Director is also a director should be given, except bodies corporate of which the Company making the return is the wholly owned subsidiary, or bodies corporate which are the wholly owned subsidiaries either of the Company or of another company of which the Company is the wholly owned subsidiary. A body corporate is deemed to be the wholly owned subsidiary of another if it has no members except that other and that other's wholly owned subsidiaries and its or their nominees.

¶ Dates of birth need only be given in the case of a company which is subject to Section 188 of the Companies Act 1948, namely, a company which is not a private company or which, being a private company, is the subsidiary of a body corporate incorporated in the United Kingdom which is neither a private company nor a company registered under the law relating to companies for the time being in force in Northern Ireland and having provisions in its constitution which would, if it had been registered in Great Britain, entitle it to rank as a private company.

6. Register of directors of the Bagdad Light and Power Co Ltd as at 1 July 1948.
Sources: Inchcape plc archives.

7 Registers of members

Original purpose

Every registered joint stock company was required to keep a record of the members or shareholders as part of the privilege of being granted incorporation by the Joint Stock Companies (Registration) Act of 1844.[1] The Acts of 1844 and 1856 used the word 'shareholders', subsequent legislation called such people 'members'. When applying for registration under this Act, an aspiring company had to submit a deed of settlement signed by 25 per cent of its subscribers by number and capital and after registration it was necessary to send annual returns of its shareholders and the transactions between them to the Registrar of Companies. Thus after 1844 registers of members were created in response to a legal requirement. This stipulation was contained in all subsequent company legislation as a condition of acquiring joint stock status.[2] However, before any general statutory requirement on companies to keep lists of shareholders, early chartered companies and those brought into being by private Acts of Parliament normally compiled registers. The Peninsular and Oriental Steam Navigation Company, for example, kept such information from its formation in 1837.[3] This was because it was one of the conditions of the charter or a clause within the Act bringing such companies into existence as well as for the practical reasons given below.

It was important that details of the shareholders were known by the directors and executives involved in the formation and running of a company for a number of reasons. Firstly, the names of the early subscribers, especially if well known and respected, could be advertised in any attempt to raise fresh capital and so attract further shareholders. Secondly, the officers of the company would be able easily to identify the most important shareholders, and thus most powerful voters, in general meetings. Thirdly, the registers provided an essential reference work for the company secretary in calculating and paying dividends and in noting unanswered calls on partly paid-up shares. The registers were essential when a company chose to make a scrip or rights issue. These entailed the company offering shares, either free or at a favourable price, to existing shareholders in proportion to their current holdings. Thus the company needed to have an accurate and up-to-date list of its members at the specific time of the issue. Similarly when the company chose, or was compelled by law, to send out communications to its members, such as copies of the balance sheet or profit and loss account, or later copies of the chairman's statement, it used the register of members as its mailing list. It was the responsibility of the shareholders to keep the company secretary informed of any changes of address, and any alteration in share ownership only became effective when it was recorded in the company's register of members. Thus the phrase used in announcements of dividends or rights issues, that the benefit would accrue 'to shareholders on the register at the closing of the company's books'; on such a day,[4] was a warning to shareholders to ensure their transactions were recorded by then and their addresses updated. Before the introduction of limited liability it was particularly important to maintain these records in case of bankruptcy or failure. For with unlimited liability, when a firm failed a shareholder could be called upon to meet a proportion (related to his shareholding) of the company's loss from his other sources of capital or income.[5] If he was unable to pay his share, then he was liable to be declared bankrupt. As a permanent record of the ownership of a company, the register of members, together with registers of debenture holders, preference shareholders and holders of convertible loan stock, were key working documents for all registered companies.

It could be argued that a harbinger of the registers of members were the books kept by HM Customs of the ships registered at each official port. These books contained, in addition to technical details of the ship, a list of the owners who held the sixty-four shares in each ship, their addresses and occupations. The privilege of joint stock ownership, to a maximum of sixty-four partners, was exclusive to shipping and conferred by Act of Parliament in 1786.[6] The reason for this registration of ownership was to ascertain that the ships were in fact owned by Britons for certain privileges accrued to British-owned and registered ships. All changes in ownership had to be recorded, so that from the late eighteenth century one branch of industry was effectively keeping 'registers of members'.[7]

Although registers of members contained details of the financial status of individuals, they were never totally confidential. All the returns kept by the Registrar of Joint Stock Companies were open to inspection by any member of the public on payment of the requisite fee and, indeed, they could require a copy of any return.[8] Thus although access was restricted by cost, it was available. Similarly, the Companies Act recommended that any shareholder of a company should be permitted to inspect the register 'at all convenient times. . . gratis. . . and require a copy thereof' at the company's registered office.[9] Again access was only restricted by economic ability to purchase one share, or if the company chose to write unusually restrictive clauses into its deed of settlement or articles of association.

Sources

The rate of survival of registers of members compared with other documents considered in this book is generally very good for two main reasons. First, because annual returns of shareholders had to be submitted to the Registrar of Joint Stock Companies from 1844 onwards, copies of these documents were preserved and are available for consultation. Secondly, the legal requirements to keep registers of members was continuous. From 1855 the submitting of some returns was optional but not shareholders' lists, which were specified as compulsory; for example, the 1900 Act laid down that within a month of their launch, registered companies had to file with the Registrar details of all shares so far allotted, for cash and other considerations.[10] Thus the researcher can usually hope to find a reasonably continuous series of these documents, for live companies at Companies House or at the registered office of individual companies. For defunct companies, the shareholders' lists are among those documents normally preserved in the files kept at the PRO at Kew in the BT31 or BT41 classification. Though some of these files have been weeded, there is usually enough left to give a good picture of the type of shareholders investing in the company.

As a document referring to the financial holdings of private individuals, each register was carefully stored, sometimes in a lockable bound volume. They are often to be found separately from the other archives in a company's store or basement, in the keeping of the company secretary. Interest in these documents can result in a profitable acquaintance with a company secretary, especially if any of the secretariat has served the firm for many years, which may bring insights into a company's history which cannot necessarily be gleaned from written or printed documents. Although many companies have transferred old documents to record offices and other repositories, most would not readily part with their register of members. Even in the case of the survival of relatively few items, the chances of finding these volumes at a company's head office are good. In the case of a group of companies, the registers of the subsidiaries are likely to be deposited in the group headquarters or the head office of the holding company.

In recent years the share transactions of one firm have sometimes been managed by another company, which keeps the documentation and submits the annual returns, for example Baring Brothers acts in this capacity for Inchcape plc.

This should be borne in mind, especially when seeking more up-to-date records. In the last decade or so it has become not uncommon for large firms with vast numbers of shareholders to maintain their lists of them on computer files, but they still need to produce 'hard copy' for the annual return.

The information they contain

Registers of members of companies were often large, leather-bound volumes, with gold embossed titles and printed headings; the text until recent times was kept in neat copperplate script, by a company secretary or clerk who took great pride in the work. The volumes were usually numbered in chronological sequence; as they became filled over the years, new books were opened. Each shareholder was normally listed in alphabetical order, with his or her address, and usually occupation or status. Aristocratic, military or naval rank was usually fully specified, if appropriate, as were any honours or decorations. As these details changed, the information in the registers was kept up to date, with various insertions and deletions, such as notifications of changes in address. The disposal of the shares on the death of an investor was recorded, either to a beneficiary of the will or to a purchaser from the estate.[11]

Precise details of the shares held by an individual were noted. In early cases this was the number of shares and their value, as in the example quoted for this entry: one of the early shareholders of the Australasian United Steam Navigation Company Limited was William Mackinnon, a merchant residing at Balinakill, Tarkert in Argyllshire, who held fifty £50 shares on 20 May 1887. Space was provided for details of 'additional shares held by existing members during the preceding year' including their number and the date of transfer. A further coloumn was allowed for 'shares held by persons no longer members' with a space at the end for remarks.

Later registers recorded more information about the shares: the amounts paid up on them at certain dates and the numbers allocated to the particular blocks held by each shareholder which corresponded to the numbers on the share certificates. Sometimes, of help to the researcher, a total figure of the number of shares and their value is stated after each investor's entry. Often a summary was given after a certain period of time, such as a year, detailing the shareholdings in a company at a glance. The registers also show where shares were held not by one individual, but jointly, as, for instance, by a partnership or group of investors. They also indicate where shares were owned by a corporate body such as a bank, investment trust or syndicate.[12] This can be of value when investigating the role of formal financial institutions in capital mobilization and formation. Finally, it should be noted that registers exist not merely for ordinary shareholders, the owners of the equity, but also separate volumes were kept for each class of capital: preference shares, deferred shares, debenture holders, any convertible or fixed-term loans.

Uses

These documents are essential to an understanding of the mobilization of capital in the formation and expansion of a company. To the business historian, registers of members give details of the identity of the original shareholders of a firm, with an indication of their backgrounds gleaned from their titles, places of residence and occupations. The earliest and largest shareholders are usually easy to spot. Details of shareholders' addresses can show, for example, British capital being invested overseas, the wealth of certain regions of Britain, and the width of the geographical spread of investment in a firm,[13] indicating its sphere of influence, that is the places with which it came into contact as a result of its activities. There were often family or business links between investors as many shareholders were attracted to a firm through acquaintance with existing investors.

Through considering the occupations of shareholders, it is possible to discern whether or not they were closely involved in a firm, such as being directors or employees, or hoping to supply the company with raw materials, fuel or machinery,[14] or indeed whether they were customers, as for instance grocers or provision merchants buying the shares of a large food manufacturing concern. Or were they purely passive investors, seeing the company as a means of employing their surplus capital, looking only for the opportunity of earning good dividends? Women shareholders were commonly placed in this category. They were often sisters, wives, mothers or friends of existing shareholders and early subscribers. These details give an idea of how capital was raised for the launching and operation of a company. There were three main ways that this could be done: by encouraging employees to take a pecuniary interest in a firm, hoping that this would have the spin-off of promoting company loyalty (though the opportunities for this were limited to managers and some white-collar workers in the nineteenth century;[15] it was rare for manual workers to have spare income for any form of investment and rarer still for them to buy shares in a company); through persuading wealthy relatives and friends to contribute to a company's success; and by convincing professional City businessmen and financial institutions to take an interest in the venture.[16] Many companies used all three methods either in the original launch or to keep going.

Through a combination of the registers of members and the articles of association, it is possible to discern the holders of voting shares, which may explain some decisions made by companies. Looking at the registers of a particular company over time can indicate changes in its ownership. Some shares were passed to sons and daughters and stayed in the same family for long periods, others passed from original shareholders to new investors, including other companies, such as investment trusts, banks and insurance companies, that is institutional investors. This source can also provide information on the behaviour of individual investors; did they hold their shares, and their interest in the company, for a few months or many years? Did the shareholders of a company become increasingly concentrated in the hands of a particular family, such as in the case of the AUSN, the example quoted here, which became dominated by the Inchcape family, or was family shareholding diluted and its influence waned? Thus the registers provide details of the sources of capital in a firm, and whether or not the investors were predominantly from one group, such as a family, banks or other business organisations whose activities were possibly linked to the company in question.

This source can also be of considerable use to the genealogist. For a researcher seeking information on a particular person, a detailed and well-kept register can give a series of changes in address, status and occupation, and give an indication of the individual's wealth. Did they make subsequent investments in a firm? Did they pay up the calls on shares? By finding out the rate of dividend paid on shares at a particular time, from the annual reports and accounts, it is possible to calculate the income from a particular block of shares over time, and thus the money remitted to a shareholder. Many investors had holdings in other companies, so a range of firms might need to be approached by a researcher, or a number of separate volumes consulted in Companies House. In this way it would be possible to reconstruct an individual's portfolio of shares and hence his wealth and annual income from these investments. Another interesting line of research using registers of members is to investigate the degree of overlapping and interlocking shareholdings and directorships in a number of apparently separate companies. In this way, various informal familial or business networks could be revealed. A similar exercise would be to try to reconstruct the shareholdings of various semi-secret trusts, syndicates or investment companies. One aim of these bodies was to keep the real shareholders hidden. However, sometimes addresses can be matched or the directors and shareholders of the nominee body can be discovered and so the real pattern of shareholding exposed. The registers of members could also be used to see if a reduction in the denomination of shares had any effect in widening share ownership. It has been postulated that the trend in the nineteenth century was towards lower-priced shares and that this increased the market available for them.[17] The registers of members can throw light on this.

One of the major drawbacks in using the register of members has already been mentioned, namely that many prominent shareholders used nominees or nominee companies. Another great inhibitor is the volume and size of the books. Because even a medium-sized company in the late nineteenth century could have thousands of shareholders, one return occupied many pages. If it is appreciated that a company might also have four different categories of capital, each with its own separate return, this multiplies the bulk. Finally, the alphabetical niceties of the compiling clerk could be eccentric, so that finding an individual in the list can be time-consuming. This said, the registers of members are vital documents for capital formation and deserve greater attention than they have received to date.

Cross-references to other documents

Documents giving similar information include share certificates, which show the individual number, value and details of ownership of a share, with the company's name, nominal capital and date of founding. A collection of different share certificates held by an individual can be used to track down further details of their holdings through the appropriate registers. Prospectuses (q.v.) advertising the launch of a company, in order to attract investors, often listed the original large shareholders. Certainly a list of worthy, wealthy businessmen or aristocrats and details of their stake in a firm played a large part in persuading others to invest. Agenda books and minute books (q.v.) listed the directors present at each meeting — these were usually prominent shareholders. Some minute books recorded transactions in shares — as part of their records of the business of the firm — or noted an issue of new shares or the rights of loan holders to convert to equity.

The raising of capital by an established company was often by preference shares or debentures — these normally paid a fixed rate of interest, and the latter could be redeemed by the company at a later date. Registers of the holders of these shares were kept and can add to the picture of the equity shareholders in a firm already seen in the registers. It is usually necessary also to consult the articles of association (q.v.) of a company if the voting rights of shareholders are under investigation. For not all classes of capital carried votes: some classes carried proportionally more than others, and the votes might not be directly proportional to the number of shares held. All these details should be stated in the articles of association. In the case of registers of members, the need to reconstruct information is less likely than for many other documents because of the generally good survival rate of this source.

Works using this source

Most modern business histories have consulted registers of members in analysing the nature of ownership of companies. For example, Edwin Green and Michael Moss, in their work on the Royal Mail crash, looked at several. These included the lists of shareholders of the King Line Limited held at Companies House in Edinburgh and the papers of the Royal Mail voting trustees kept by the National Maritime Museum, which include lists and proceedings of meetings of shareholders and debenture holders.[18] Philip Cottrell also makes use of details of share ownership in his work on the finance of industry before the First World War.[19] Another example of a study using this source is T.C. Barker's histories of Pilkington in which the family control of the firm's equity looms large.[20] The holding of a specified number of shares in the firm, essential in qualifying as a director, shows that in the case of this firm, the registers of members are of particular importance.

On the more macro-scale, some historians have tried to make generalizations about capital formation in particular industries from an examination of the shareholders' lists. For example, Ward has tried to determine who financed canal construction in the late eighteenth century and Broadbridge has attempted the same exercise for the early railway companies.[21]

The example

Formed by an amalgamation between the Queensland Steamship Co and the Australian Steam Navigation Co, the Australasian United Steam Navigation Co Ltd was launched in 1887 with a capital of £600,000 made up of 12,000 £50 shares. The nominal capital remained the same for the rest of its life until 1961.[22] A sample was taken of 185 persons and four companies investing £378,690 in the AUSN from 1887 to 1892, in order to show how this source can be used in analysis.

A total 10,000 shares were offered for sale in Britain and 2000 in Australia. Only £12,970, representing 259 £50 shares, was invested by Australians, showing a lack of interest locally in the company (which was solely concerned with the Australian coasting trade) and that the capital required was predominantly raised in Britain. The largest single investor was Sir William Mackinnon, who attracted further investment from his family and colleagues in Scotland, and from the Dumbarton shipbuilders, Denny, who built many ships for the AUSN. Merchants associated with Mackinnon who resided abroad, such as James Lyle Mackay, who became the first Lord Inchcape, also invested in this undertaking, probably encouraged by Sir William, who employed him in his first job in the East.

In studying occupations, the majority of AUSN shareholders were passive investors, looking for employment for their surplus capital, and probably did not play an active part in the running of company. Very few people linked to the industry, except the shipbuilders, were attracted to invest. The day-to-day running of the company was undertaken in Australia — the London AGMs mainly confirmed the level of dividend paid. The occupational structure may be summarized thus:

	%
Merchants	31.8
Private*	24.5
Other companies	11.7
Military, naval	10.1
Shipbuilders	6.9
Civil servants	5.2
Bankers, law etc.	4.9
Manufacturing	3.5
Ship agents etc.	0.7
Others	0.7

* This included persons giving their occupations as gentleman, lady, widow, spinster etc.

The geographical spread of shareholding may also be summarized:

	%
England	62.7
Scotland	32.8
Australia	3.4
Others	1.1

Notes

1. 7 & 8 Vict. c. 110, clause 49.
2. For example, 19 & 20 Vict. c. 47, clause 16; 25 & 26 Vict. c. 89, clause 25.
3. B. Cable, *A Hundred Year History of the P & O* (Nicholson & Watson, 1937).
4. Usually the date of the publication of the interim or annual report and accounts.
5. As examples, see the case of Gilman & Co in S.K. Jones, *Two Centuries of Overseas Trading: The Origins and Growth of the Inchcape Group* (Macmillan, 1986) and the City of Glasgow Bank in R.N. Forbes, 'Some Contemporary Reactions to a Banking Failure', *Three Banks Review*, No. 121 (1979).
6. 26 Geo. III c. 60.
7. R.S. Craig, 'Shipping Records of the Nineteenth and Twentieth Century', *Archives*, Vol. 7, No. 36 (1966) pp. 191–2.
8. For example, 7 & 8 Vict. c. 110, clause 18; 19 & 20 Vict. c. 47, clause 106(5); 25 & 26 Vict. c. 89, clause 174(5).
9. Clauses 50, 22 and 32 respectively of the Acts cited in note 8 above.
10. 63 & 64 Vict. c. 48.
11. Sometimes separate registers of probate were kept, recording the estates of shareholders on their death; this is true of the example used in this chapter.
12. Green & Moss, drawing on the Price Waterhouse papers which were compiled from the registers of members, show that of the eleven principal companies comprising the Royal Mail Group in 1930, only about 10 per cent of the shares were held by the public, the vast majority being owned by other shipping companies, financial trusts or nominees: E. Green & M. Moss, *A Business of National Importance: The Royal Mail Shipping Group 1902–1937* (Methuen, 1982) pp. 223–6.
13. See, for example, Forbes Munro's work on the group of companies founded by Sir William Mackinnon which demonstrated the importance of Scottish investment overseas: J. Forbes Munro, 'Scottish Business Imperialism', ESRC Report B00/23/0049.
14. For instance, the shipbuilding firm of Denny was a large shareholder in the AUSN, the example used in this chapter.
15. A good example is Dodwell & Co Ltd, founded in 1899, in which 80 per cent of the initial capital was put up by its senior partners, branch managers, mercantile assistants, clerks, book-keepers and compradores: S.K. Jones, 'George Benjamin Dodwell, a shipping agent in the Far East, 1872–1908', *Journal of Transport History*, 3rd ser. Vol. 6, No. 7 (1985).
16. For example, Napier was able to persuade the Law Guarantee and Trust Society to take all £20,000 of its first mortgage debentures in 1906: C.H. Wilson & W.J. Reader, *Men and Machines: A History of D. Napier & Son Engineers Ltd 1808–1958* (Weidenfeld & Nicolson, 1958) pp. 83–4.
17. P.L. Cottrell, *Industrial Finance 1830–1914: The Finance and Organization of English Manufacturing Industry* (Methuen, 1980) pp. 81–4.
18. Green & Moss, op. cit., p. 265.
19. Cottrell, op. cit., pp. 81–4.
20. T.C. Barker, *Pilkington Brothers and the Glass Industry* (Weidenfeld & Nicolson, 1960) and *The Glassmakers: Pilkington 1826–1976* (Weidenfeld & Nicolson, 1977).
21. J.R. Ward, *The Finance of Canal Building in Eighteenth Century England* (Oxford UP, 1974); S.A. Broadbridge, 'The Sources of Railway Share Capital' in M.C. Reed

(ed.), *Railways in the Victorian Economy: Studies in Finance and Economic Growth* (David & Charles, 1969) pp. 184–211.

22. S.K. Jones, 'The Decline of British Maritime Enterprise in Australia: The Example of the Australian United Steam Navigation Company, 1887–1961', *Business History*, Vol. 27, No. 1 (1985) pp. 59–74; and N.L. McKellar, *From Derby Round to Burketown: the AUSN Story* (St Lucia, Queensland, 1977).

N⁵ Form F

REGISTER OF

ANNUAL LIST

SUMMARY of CAPITAL and SHARES of the *Australasian United Steam Navigation*

Nominal Capital £ 600,000	divided into
Number of Shares taken up to the 20th	day of
There has been called up on each Share ...... £ 50 ... 600	20 ... 200
Total Amount of Calls received ... £ 14000	
Total Amount of Calls unpaid ...... £	
Total Amount of Shares forfeited ...... £	

LIST OF PERSONS holding Shares in the *Australasian United Steam Navigation Company* at any time during the year immediately preceding the said *twentieth* day of *May*

NAMES, ADDRESSES, AND OCCUPATIONS

Surname	Christian Name	Address	Occupation
Mackinnon	William	Balmaghie, Patel	Merchant
Sutherland	Thomas	122 Leadenhall St	Shipowner
Seary	Peter	Launston	Shipbuilder
Mackask	Alexander M	Bradlands, Weybridge	Civil Servant
Laurie	George Saudy	49, India Place 86	Merchant
James	Anthony	67 Cannon Road St	Gentleman
Leo	Charles E	Munich Park, William	Manufacturer
Mackinnon	Lawrence	5 Kensington Palace Park	Merchant

7. Register of members of the Australian United Steam Navigation Co Ltd, 20 May 1887. (Left hand page of Register on p. 107).
Source: Inchcape plc archives.

8   Diaries

Original purpose

Most great men kept and still keep diaries if only to provide a basis for writing memoirs when their days of action or high-level decision making are over. Judges, politicians, generals, top policemen and literary figures can all expect to achieve a degree of immortality and significant earthly reward from such activities. Here interest is rather more narrowly focused on diaries which were kept by businessmen in the course of their commercial career. They may have kept them originally for exactly the same reason as other notables as there was much interchange between the world of business, politics, the military and finance,[1] that is to act as an *aide-mémoire* when the diarist came to write his reminiscences.

More significantly, many businessmen kept diaries at work, either as an appointment book to remind them of future meetings and subsequently record who had been seen and when, or as a confidential record of conversations held and decisions made in order to ensure that appropriate courses of action were pursued. The former are the more common but less informative. In the latter case, the diary might constitute a private record, outside the company's records and not processed by the staff, of personal views on policy, the performance of fellow directors, or links with other businessmen outside the company. Sometimes a diary was kept for a specific purpose or period, such as a business trip abroad, a visit to a conference or an exhibition. Depending on the purpose, business diaries might be kept by the great man himself; more often a clerk or secretary took shorthand notes of meetings and wrote up the entries subsequently, or took dictation from his employer. Those diaries which were personal records dealt with high-level strategic decisions or staff matters and were highly confidential documents. They were often fitted with their own integral lock and kept secure in a personal safe.

Where a leading figure in business believed in keeping a diary, he might well institute the practice on his subordinates as a means of ensuring a proper record was kept of their activities, decisions and expenditures which he could inspect. In these cases, business diaries acted as a means of control on the actions of managers by their superiors. In some cases, as well as entering meetings, discussions and decisions, the diarist might also copy important outward letters to act as a reminder and record of his decisions.

Sources

Real business diaries are likely to have been preserved in the firm with any other business archives, when the firm survives or has been absorbed into a group which is concerned to preserve the heritage of its past. However, from the relatively few specimens that survive, it seems that the majority of businessmen did not keep the confidential record type of diary and the appointment book type did not long outlive the year it was current. The example is drawn from one of the diaries kept by Edward Holden, managing director of the Midland Bank from 1898 to 1919.[2] He maintained a series of diaries for most of this twenty-year period; they survive in the Midland Bank archives and amount to nine volumes. In addition, partly at Holden's insistence, his lieutenants also kept regular diaries and the bank's archives have examples from the 1890s to the 1960s of several joint general managers' diaries. They also have 'reference books' which were the diaries kept by branch managers, and a good proportion of these survive for a range of geographical areas and periods of time. In cases where the businessman achieved fame in some other field, his diaries may lodge with his main body of papers, so Lord Beaverbrook's diaries which do not distinguish between his business and political activities are now housed in the Beaverbrook Collection at the House of Lords Record Office.

There are some printed guides to diaries such as those of William Matthews and John Stuart Batts.[3] Both list the diaries by year of origin and within that alphabetically by name of the diarist. Both also have an index to the diarists and Batts has a subject index. Apart from any limitations indicated in their titles, their main drawback is that very few of the diaries listed are of businessmen or relate to business or industry. Most of the diaries are of clerics, travellers, military or literary persons. A few exceptions stand out: for instance, Henry Pease, Quaker industrialist of Darlington, and Lord Alfred Baldwin the iron master appear as diarists in Batts; and David Stevenson, civil engineer of Edinburgh, is listed in Matthews. Although there are few such gems for the student of business history, they should be consulted initially.

The best single source to find the location of diaries of named individuals is undoubtedly the National Register of Archives at the Historical Manuscripts Commission where the alphabetical computer-based personal names index can be accessed. If the name is unknown and it is more a case of seeking diaries relevant to a company or industry, then again the NRA is a good source. It has a 'companies index' arranged by industry and within that alphabetically by company name, and a 'businesses and trades' index listing alphabetically by industry. The latter index contains firms which are small, or not household names. These two sets of indexes run to over 40 volumes, so are well worth consulting. The NRA also has five volumes of 'diaries and papers' indexes, which although of some use suffer from the defects of containing only the diaries of people not in the public eye and very few entries relating to business. The Business Archives Council is another useful source as it maintains a card index system, and copies of lists of records arranged by company name and trade. Where the diaries were kept by the individual as a personal record, they may remain with family papers rather than the company's archives and thus it is necessary to determine if a family archive exists and where it is located.

The information they contain

Because business diaries were kept for personal use only or to be seen by only a few select people, they are both full and frank. They can contain information on a vast range of topics related to the business and some personal matters and can be very honest in the comments: 'I am at the end of my tether' being one straight-forward entry in Holden's diary. When these diaries are of the chairman, managing director or somesuch luminary they tend to be mostly concerned with high-level decisions but, given the very tight rein on which some directors kept their managers, they can contain surprisingly detailed information on relatively minor topics.

Staff affairs often took up a large amount of space: holiday arrangements, the level of salaries, contributions to a provident fund, appointments, promotions and dismissals are all regular matters requiring a decision. On occasions there is an enormous amount of detail on relatively junior staff. For example, one branch of the Midland found a bag of silver had been cut and much of the contents was missing. This required a thorough investigation by the branch manager of the cashiers who were responsible for the bag, all duly recorded in the managing director's diary. It included the cashiers' names and ages, where they lived and the rent they paid, the salaries they received and their length of service, their friends, how they spent their evenings, any debts outstanding, and even whether they were engaged or 'associated with' any young ladies and if so their occupation and address.[4] Such massive detail is not common and required an exceptional circumstance, but is fascinating reading when it appears. There are entries containing warnings to managers who were not up to scratch; another is a note of a clerk who had been dismissed on being sent to prison for knocking down a man in a public house and then giving a false name to a policeman; another indication of the very real problems posed by drink before the First World War is the manager of the St Anne's branch who was encountered by a superior coming out of a public house 'the worse for drink. . . as this is the third time he has transgressed he must be transferred to a subordinate post at another branch'. On a happier note, there is the suggestion by the chairman to the wife of an ill branch manager that the bank would be willing to allow him a generous pension if he chose to retire early; on another occasion, notice of salary rises to some branch managers is entered, as their branch profits had risen, and at the time of the South African War the bank agreed to hold open the posts of any clerk who joined the volunteer force and continued to pay their salary. Staff affairs took significant space and are full of delightful detail.

Premises is another area which features largely in diary entries when the firm is a multi-site activity, such as banking or multiple retailers. Leases, the need for and cost of renovations, decisions on tenders, expenses incurred, problems of obtaining suitable premises for new branches, concern by the architect of damaging nearby leaseholders' ancient lights, all took up much time and space. Since premises represented expensive, long-lasting fixed capital, senior men were concerned to ensure expenditure was really necessary and that value for money was obtained.

High-level corporate decisions figure fairly frequently in business diaries and in the example, at the turn of the century, Sir Edward Holden of the Midland Bank was trying to enlarge his company by absorbing other banking companies. Holden was impressed by size and had an affinity for things American because they tended to be on a grand scale, and so he was keen to negotiate with independent firms who might be eligible. In 1901 he was having talks with at least two separate prospects, the Yorkshire Banking Company, and the Lincoln and Lindsey Bank. Because of the need to maintain secrecy, these meetings rarely occurred in the office, rather Holden and his clerk travelled the country meeting the other negotiators in various hotels — the Chine at Boscombe, the Midland at Derby and the St Pancras Hotel. All three sets of negotiations were recorded in his diary.

Another important area covered by business diaries is relations with customers. In the case of the particular example, since the business was a bank this meant dealing with the clients who deposited with it or more normally who wished to borrow from it on overdraft or via a loan. The managing director was kept informed by his branch managers of any customers who looked as though they might fail. When overdraft limits were exceeded, Sir Edward wanted to know why, and often insisted on additional securities being lodged, overdraft limits were set for specific customers, and interest to be levied was set — always calculated at bank rate plus a given per cent — or business was refused because the borrower was not a good risk or the business was 'so far away from our base'. When necessary, the level and type of guarantees required were determined, balance sheets were requested before any advance was made and, if all went wrong, receivers were appointed or discussions took place on capital restructuring. Midland Bank boasted many important customers — Elswick, the cycle firm; Maxim Sons and Vickers in armaments; W.G. Armstrong, shipbuilder and steel master; as well as a whole host of lesser lights. They appear in the pages of business diaries.

Scattered throughout the business diaries are comments on the general state of trade in a particular town or area. The managing director wished to know where bad debts might be anticipated, how his local branch was doing in comparison to rivals, the names and abilities of local solicitors, the social standing of various groups of local residents, and thus the most noteworthy customers and their prospects. In Holden's diary there are entries of discussions with his local managers on the state of the wool trade in Halifax, land values and social standing in Guernsey poursuivant to opening a new branch there, and the state of the iron trade and local iron masters in Ulverston.

There are a multitude of further matters on which diary keepers had discussions with their colleagues. Negotiations with suppliers is an important area for any business; in the case of the Midland Bank, not being a manufacturer, this is less important; however, they were keen to buy Burroughs' office equipment and some of the entries deal with quantities, prices and discounts required and offered. The Bank was also concerned with external agencies whose services it used and so, when a bundle of cheques took inordinately long to arrive at a branch and then turned up apparently having been opened, a strong protest was ordered to be despatched to the Post Office authorities.

Finally, matters of policy such as the desirability of being involved in issuing, underwriting or taking up a portion of foreign loans; or of rediscounting bills for various foreign banks wishing to place some of their paper in London; or the amount of discretion which should be given to branch managers by head office and the concern that head office 'must know its commitments' to explain the limited discretion actually granted; all are regular subjects. In some cases much more personal affairs are noted, as when Holden is seen to be canvassing support for a particular candidate to become the treasurer at a specific Freemason's Lodge, or in April when it is noted he is absent on holiday in Blackpool. Personal diaries may also highlight the link between a family and a business firm, showing informal decision making or chains of command. They are particularly important for businesses owned, managed or controlled by a founding family. In private firms and partnerships they may give useful information about the distribution of profits, or other financial data, particularly valuable if a firm's accounts have not survived. Their other significant role is in showing informal links between businessmen, or between captains of industry and other professions such as politicians, clerics and the military. The range of topics covered by business diaries can be enormous in the best examples, into which category Holden's undoubtedly falls, although in some specimens the entries can be tantalizingly cryptic, whetting the appetite but providing no substance.

Uses

Just as the range of topics covered in the fuller diaries is vast, so are the uses to which they can be put. Family historians and genealogists who know, or believe, an ancestor worked for a particular firm may strike lucky in finding mention of that antecedent. It is a very long shot as only a small proportion of employees were mentioned and, perversely, if the employee was in trouble or suspected of misbehaviour — because of drink, misconduct or poor work — he is more likely to appear among the staff entries. Labour historians will also find some good examples of the conditions in which employees worked, the levels of remuneration, likelihood and frequency of promotion, perks such as company houses or other allowances, the causes of dismissal and the attitudes of senior managers and directors to their juniors.

Architectural historians will profit from a perusal of diaries, particularly when the firm was known to employ a subsequently famous architect; for example, the Midland Bank employed among others T.B. Whinney and Woolfall & Eccles[5] and thus details of layout or design and the related expenditure, source of fixtures and fittings, and discussions between architect and client recorded in the diaries would shed light on how they worked and the relationship between client and architect. Although more awkward to access, since it is difficult to foresee what areas might appear in any specific set of diaries, the general social or economic historian would find nuggets of pure metal in the discussions of the trade of a particular town or the state of an individual industry, or the social status and wealth-owning classes of a region or town. Such insights add a new perspective which augments more usual sources. Again the discussions of customers and suppliers gives information on the micro-scale for particular firms which may be typical of a region or industry and if sufficient entries accumulate may indicate a trend which can be confirmed from other external sources.

Obviously for anyone brave enough to contemplate writing a business or company history, business diaries could be invaluable where a given firm's suppliers, customers or bankers are known or, indeed, where it is suspected that a business relationship may have existed. They are also a boon where the historian is investigating links between business and politics or business and the military. Diaries may show the social status of the diarist and his role within the establishment, or the informal influences brought to bear to further or constrain his business. For example, the diaries kept by Mrs Edith Lawson Johnston for 1904 show that both she and her husband were keen supporters of the Tariff Reform League, which might have benefited her husband's business, and that they were not infrequent visitors to Buckingham Palace and the court and thus mixed in the highest circles in the land.[6] At its best the business diary can be used for a wide range of research interests but it must be stressed that many are much less informative than the best and thus, even when they survive and have been located, they may turn out to be disappointingly thin. Additionally, the entries in some diaries are tantalizingly cryptic, using initials, titles or surnames only, and the researcher may have to do a significant amount of background research on people, their positions and status to make much sense of the entries. It must also be borne in mind that diaries are often an unofficial source, recording the personal opinions of the individual diarist, not necessarily the consensual view of the board. Few businessmen appear to have kept the confidential record sort of diary and and even fewer survived. The appointment book sort was often destroyed soon after the period it covered had terminated. That said, at their best diaries are an invaluable source: they are among the three 'most important documents of all' because they 'give evidence about policy decisions' according to Professor Mathias, one of the doyens of British business history, and 'provide primary evidence for the explanation of change'.[7]

Works using this source

Quite obviously any biography or autobiography will be much enhanced if the subject has kept diaries. All great men who have written memoirs or volumes of reminiscences have drawn upon their formal diaries, as well as their less reliable memories. Such works are numerous and outside the scope of our consideration here, except where the great man is notable for his business acumen as well as political or other activities. Thus A.J.P. Taylor's massive biography of Lord Beaverbrook, though mostly concerned with his political career, also deals with his company flotations in Canada before the First World War and his proprietorship of a number of national newspapers such as the *Daily Express* and *The Evening Standard*.[8] This work drew on the whole range of the Beaverbrook archives, including his diaries and appointments book. Similarly a number of biographies have been written on Montagu Norman the eccentric governor of the Bank of England from 1920 to 1944; again, although using a range of his surviving papers, his diaries were invaluable in showing the proportion of interviews he had in the depression of the 1930s with financiers and City men, compared to manufacturers and industrial magnates more normally resident in the provinces.[9]

Some of the entries in the *Dictionary of Business Biography*[10] lean heavily on diaries kept by entrepreneurs. The award-winning work on the business career of Dudley Docker[11] also utilized a range of business, political and social diaries to show Docker's relationships with the top layers of society, his attempts to further the idea of a businessmen's government, and his close links with some members of the Conservative Party. Among the diaries Dr Davenport-Hines used were those of Christopher Addison, H.A. Astbury, Sir Maurice Hankey, Sir Edward Holden and J.M. Madders. A more straightforward biography of a business leader which made use of the subject's diaries is that of William Lever, the soap magnate, later Lord Leverhulme, especially for his periods abroad in the Congo or Solomon Islands.[12] For a much earlier period, a much smaller scale business and a much less sophisticated activity, the diary of Thomas Turner was the basis of a full-scale book, an article in an archaelogical journal and was widely quoted by among others Charles Dickens.[13] For a village shopkeeper this is unanticipated fame and although the diary ranges over a whole spectrum of personal and social affairs, it also casts light on his business dealings. Business diaries were among the 'chief manuscript sources' used by Professor Hyde in his pathbreaking work on the Ocean Steam Ship Company.[14] In particular, the diaries of Alfred Holt, who founded the company and was its main entrepreneur for over a quarter of a century, which he kept continuously from 1866 to 1898 were invaluable in building up a picture of his motivation and beliefs.[15] Equally valuable were the diaries of his father, George, in providing insights into Alfred's schooling, his boyhood delight in things mechanical, and how he gained his early training in business.[16] For a later period, Sir Richard Durning Holt's diaries were used to show how the second generation of the family fared in donning the mantle of leadership. Sir Richard's 'Diary of a voyage to the East' of 1892–3 was especially important for it was during this inspection tour that he perceived that the Blue Funnel Line was no longer the leader in steamship technology and was losing out to more dynamic competitors. As a result, in collaboration with the shipping firm's agents, Swires, he put pressure on the older generation, Alfred and Phillip, to modernize the fleet using some of the reserve fund that had been built up out of retained profits.[17] Diaries were essential in this book to understand the motivation of the founder and later why a new policy had to be formulated and actioned.

On a smaller scale the diary of Thomas Cook, one of the partners in Hagues and Cook, a woollen spinning and weaving partnership founded in 1811 in Dewsbury, Yorkshire, was an important source, among others, used to show their role as government contractors.[18] In 1815 the firm began making blankets and heavy woollen cloth and in 1818 began trying to secure government contracts for heavy woollen blankets and uniform cloth. Cook's diary shows the considerable difficulties the firm faced in breaking into this lucrative market, having its goods accepted as of proper quality and specification, and then persuading the authorities to pay for the goods delivered. It is unnecessary to labour the point that when they survive business diaries are a highly useful source for both the biography of individuals and the history of companies.

Cross-references to other documents

Where confidential diaries exist, they are an invaluable source to complement board minute books (q.v.) for they will provide an insight into the thinking of one of the board members. Where the board minutes record the decision made and the official line, the diary may well provide the counter arguments and show the position taken by the diarist and his appraisal of the attitudes of the other members. If the series of board minute books is incomplete or none have survived, the confidential business diary may provide an alternative source for uncovering the discussions on business policy.

Given the paucity of information which a prospectus contains about the individuals involved and the events which preceded the formal registration, diaries would help put flesh on the bare bones of such documents. As prospectuses gave the names, addresses and occupations of the promoters/ proposed directors, it should be easy to establish identity. If a diary is extant of any of the individuals named in the document, it should show the negotiations leading up to the issuing of the prospectus, may indicate who were the main advocates, why the company was to be formed and what its prospects were considered to be. It is a pretty slim chance that any particular individual kept a diary and that it survived, unless he were a figure of national importance, but if he did it would be an invaluable aid. Similar remarks apply to a patent. It too is low on biographical explanation and causality and thus if the inventor kept a diary it will complement the patent. There is a little higher probability that an inventor entered up a diary as, being of a scientific bent, he would wish to record his experiments systematically; also, in the event of someone else patenting 'his' idea prior to the inventor doing so, a properly maintained diary or log of experiments would be valuable evidence of prior invention which would be grounds for challenging the validity of the competing patent. If it exists, a diary may be invaluable in showing how long an inventor has been working on a project, how many dead ends were pursued before the successful process was discovered, what he thought were its commercial possibilities and then post hoc how successful it really was in business, the problems in mass production, the keeness of others to licence his invention.

Diaries would similarly enchance bare documents like shareholders' lists or registers of directors. These records are little more than litanies of names with addresses and occupations and so say nothing direct about motivation or causality. If diaries were written up by any of the individuals, they would provide a great deal of explanation. At their best, diaries can be one of the most fruitful sources in revealing the thinking and motivation of individuals and the causality of events which are known to have occurred from other papers. These other records are, however, unlikely to point to the contemporary existence of such diaries as this would not be widely known and certainly have no place on official documents. It is, therefore, up to the researcher to search for the diary of any individual in which he is interested.

Diaries can serve as a similar complementary source for other documents such as the chairman's speech, licences or agency agreements. Because the latter two are fairly dry legal material, they contain little explanation of why and how they came into being. If the diaries of any of the parties to such agreements can be located, they will provide background and context to these contracts and perhaps motivation too. If the diary of a particular chairman is found, it may indicate how and why he came to make the speech, the discussions leading up to its drafting, whether he wrote it himself or employed a speech writer, the degree to which he then imposed his own ideas, language and emphasis, how he thought the speech was received and any reflections or follow ups to it. Again diaries when they survive provide contextual material and possibly explanation. It must be emphasized that when they can be traced, diaries are worth their weight in gold as they are usually a frank source, full of human interest and likely to provide explanation and motivation to other documents, and this causality is unlikely to be found elsewhere.

The example

The example used to illustrate this chapter is drawn from the business diaries kept by Edward Holden when he was managing director of the Midland Bank.[19] Holden's rise within the Midland was paralleled by the Midland's rise to world pre-eminence. In 1881, when Holden joined the Midland Bank as an accountant, it was still based in Birmingham where it had been founded in 1836 with a handful of branches. He was one of the architects of its growth by taking over dozens of its competitors so that by 1898, when he became managing director, it comprised about 250 branches and had deposits over £30 million. By 1908, when he was made chairman as well as managing director, it had over 400 branches and about £70 million in deposits. By his death in 1919 the Midland boasted over 1300 branches, around £350 million in deposits and was the largest bank in the world. The Midland moved its head office to London through acquisition of the Central Bank of London in 1891, in which negotiations Holden was instrumental, and so acquired a seat on the prestigious London Clearing House. This London presence Holden reinforced in 1898 when he added the City Bank, one of the largest London independent banks, to his bag.

Holden, as well as being personally involved in acquisitions, took a keen interest in staff development and training, encouraging employees to attend evening classes to learn languages, stay abreast of company law or appreciate accounting. He also took major decisions on office procedure and the standardization of accounting and record-keeping methods throughout the many acquired companies. As part of these two interests he introduced the idea of managers at many levels keeping diaries as a record of decisions made, appointments kept and conversations. They obviously aided the work of the manager's superior in keeping a check on him as well as his own. The result of Holden's enthusiasm was that the Midland Bank Archives now contain a plethora of business diaries.

Notes

1. For example, see W.J. Reader, 'Imperial Chemical Industries and the State, 1926–45' in B.E. Supple (ed.), *Essays in British Business History* (Oxford UP, 1977) pp. 227–43; R.P.T. Davenport-Hines, *Dudley Docker: The Life and Times of a Trade Warrior* (Cambridge UP, 1984).
2. Midland Bank Archive (MBA), Diaries of Sir Edward Holden.
3. W. Matthews, *British Diaries: An Annotated Bibliography of British Diaries written between 1442 and 1942* (Univ. of California Press, 1950); J.S. Batts, *British Manuscript Diaries of the Nineteenth Century: An Annotated Listing* (Centaur Press, 1976).

4. MBA, Sir Edward Holden's Diary, 8 March 1900.
5. I am most grateful to Edwin Green, archivist of Midland Bank, for this point.
6. Bedford Record Office, Ms LJ 1/1, Diary of Mrs E. Lawson Johnston for 1904.
7. P. Mathias, 'Historical Records of the Brewing Industry', *Archives*, Vol. 7, No. 33 (1965) p. 10.
8. A.J.P. Taylor, *Beaverbrook: A Biography* (1972) chapters 2, 8 & 9.
9. A. Boyle, *Montagu Norman* (Cassell, 1967); H. Clay, *Lord Norman* (Macmillan, 1957).
10. D.J. Jeremy (ed.), *Dictionary of Business Biography, Vols 1–5* (Butterworths, 1984–6).
11. Davenport-Hines, op. cit., was joint winner of the Wolfson Prize for 1985.
12. W.P. Jolly, *Lord Leverhulme* (Constable, 1976).
13. T. Turner, The Diary of a Georgian Shopkeeper (Oxford UP, 1979); *Sussex Archaeological Collections*, Vol. 11 (1859).
14. F.E. Hyde, *Blue Funnel: A History of Alfred Holt & Company of Liverpool 1865–1914* (Liverpool UP, 1956).
15. Ibid., p. 186.
16. Ibid., pp. 10–12.
17. Ibid., pp. 90–3.
18. F.J. Glover, 'Government Contracting, Competition and Growth in the Heavy Woollen Industry', *Economic History Review*, 2nd ser. Vol. 16, No. 3 (1964); reprinted in K.A. Tucker, *Business History: Selected Readings* (Cass, 1977).
19. This chapter draws heavily on Edwin Green's fine vignette of Sir Edward Holden in Jeremy, op. cit., pp. 290–7. The reader is heartily recommended to it.

18

25 January

Tredegar Iron & Coal C?? — 9?? — Limit £30,000.

Interview with Mr. W. S. B. McLaren and Mr. Arthur Keen.

The works were formerly laid out for manufacturing steel and the collieries were made subordinate to that. The steel production is now abandoned and the Co are confining themselves to working coal. The quality is the best in the district for making Coke. The Co have recently booked an order for Coke 28/, though last year they were selling at 12/. When the trade falls back to its old level, the Tredegar Co. will be in as good as any Co. in the district.

Mr. Holden. — Our Board is very prejudiced against Collieries. They refused an a/c of that kind the other day with a Cr. Balance of £20/30,000. If your a/c works debit and credit, that will make a difference

Mr. McLaren. — The a/c will not be constantly in debit. The overdrafts of the Co with Williams Deacon, and the London & Provincial were not secured — terms:

Bank Rate (Lond. & Prov? — Min: 3%)
Comm? — 1/6 ? — now negotiating to reduce

Deposits — London Deposit Rate
The a/c would be kept in London & Cardiff. He doesn't think that the London & Prov? will make any objection to his opening another banking a/c. The London a/c is kept now kept at Williams Deacon. The a/c with the L. C. & M. would be kept at Ca...

8. Pages of diary of Sir Edward Holden, managing director of Midland Bank, 25 January and 21 February 1900.
Source: Midland Bank plc archives.

Mr Holden will bring the question before the Board and then write to Mr McLaren.

D. Armitage & Sons Ld, Mirfield

Interview with Messrs J.P. Armitage Spedding and W.H. Armitage (Accountant) See Mr Murray's diary

23 January 1900

Elswick Cycle Co, Newcastle on Tyne

Interview with Mr Dixon Davies who reported that arrangements have been made with all the creditors of the Co except one in Sheffield. The Co propose to reduce the Capital to £100,000. Mr Holden stated that the Bank as Debenture Holders would support the scheme. They will keep their hands in till the meeting is over. They stipulate, however, that Buckingham is to be removed from the management if the Bank's money is to remain.

The Co have orders for 1000 machines on hand.

25 January 1900

Ealing Corporation — Loan of £10000 beyond present O/D of £35,000 at the London & County.

Interview with Old Bond St. Mgr who stated that the ratable value is £230,000 producing £50,000 a year. The Corporation have been attempting too much in acquiring works & property for the ratepayers eg. for electric supply and

21 February 1900.

L. B. Cº

Interview with Mr. G. at the St. Pancras Hotel. He stated that he had received a letter from John Dun, and that one of his directors had re ewed a message from Bemrose of Derby which led him to believe that negotiations were coming on. He didn't see how he could agree to less than a divd of 13½% as our shares were at a low figure and his shareholders would be put at a disadvantage if he agreed to a lower dividend.

I agreed to submit the matter to my board on Friday and write to Mr. G. on Friday night. If it goes through then, I am to arrange for Lawford to come to my house on Saturday, and the investigation is to begin next.

22 February 1900.

Y. B. Cº

Interview with Mr. W. at Midland Hotel, Derby.

He enquired whether I seriously considered that an amalgamation would be for the benefit of both institutions.

I replied that it was the policy of the day to form large institutions; our bank combined with his would command the best business and destroy active competition.

Mr. W. spoke about his health; he is nearly 65 and he should like to see his institution in good hands. He asked about price. I replied that I had not got so far as that, but whatever was

8. Pages of diary of Sir Edward Holden, managing director of Midland Bank, 25 January and 21 February 1900.
Source: Midland Bank plc archives.

22 February 1900

done the equality between Reserve & Capital would have to be maintained.

He thought that their scheme of issuing new Capital would assist in doing that. The reduction of his shares had been a complete success (in 1898. the £50 shares with £12.10.0 paid were subdivided into 5 £10 shares with £2.10.0 paid). The dormant a/cs amount to about £60,000.

We did not discuss the price as I did not want to press matters further until the next half year. I told him we should increase our dividend in June.

He was evidently making up his mind to go thro' with the transaction. He had come to the interview with the consent of Sir James Kitson, and we agreed that the answer to be given to him if he asked the result of the discussion was, that he had not yet decided whether it would be for the benefit of both institutions.

It was arranged that the next interview should be held about the time of the Bankers' Dinner.

26 February 1900
to
7 March 1900

L. B. Co. ✓ Investigation of a/cs with Mr. Lawford at the Chine Hotel, Boscombe.

Mr. Holden came up to town to attend the Board Meeting on Friday, March 2nd.

9 Book-keeping records: journals and ledgers

Original purpose

Virtually all businessmen at all times have had to keep some sort of financial record, even if the process was too scrappy to justify the title of 'book-keeping'. At the simplest level, a businessman might have kept a list of payments due to him from workmen who had been advanced money, or customers whose accounts had not yet been settled, or money owed to suppliers of raw material whose invoices remained unpaid. The purpose of the books in these cases was little more than to act as an aide memoire to ensure the businessman did not fail to collect a debt or pay a bill. The books might have served the additional purpose of providing a method of recording how and when he paid each bill or collected each payment. Over time, this *ad hoc* method of keeping financial records became formalized.

For those firms organized as joint stock companies after 1844, there was a legal imperative to keep proper books of account. The 1844 Act charged the directors of every company with the responsibility for keeping such books and gave shareholders the right of inspection.[1] These requirements became diluted in subsequent company legislation. Although the 1856 Act laid down fuller requirements, specifying that books should be kept on the double-entry principle, mentioning different types of books such as cash book, journals and ledgers, and indicating the items to be included, as these were not embodied in the actual Act but rather in the model regulations in Table B,[2] this meant that companies could choose to ignore these provisions. They only had full legal force by default — if a company failed to register any articles of association, they were deemed to apply. However, if a company registered articles which did not contain these provisions, then the model regulations were overruled. It was only from the 1928 Companies Act that the requirement to maintain books of account was re-enshrined in the body of the law.[3] This is not to say that few companies kept such books before 1928, quite the contrary. All companies kept some book-keeping records for the reasons previously discussed, though their quality can be very variable. This is not the place to go into when double-entry methods of accounting were introduced into this country and became the normal practice. This discussion will be confined to two of the commoner types of financial record.

The *journal* was kept originally as a daily record of all transactions as they occurred.[4] The entries were in chronological order and no distinction was made between different types of payment or the reason for the payment. The book was sometimes kept in single entry using two columns for the figures on the same page, one for receipts, one for disbursements. The journal was also an integral part of the double-entry system when receipts appeared on one page and payments out on the other. In some cases the journal was accompanied by a waste book which functioned as the rough working document in which the clerks initially noted the transactions. Subsequently each entry was transferred to the journal by the book-keepers in a standard form, in copperplate, when there was less immediate pressure, so ensuring a neat, clean comprehensible entry. Once the entry had been recorded in the journal, the entry in the waste book was crossed through or ticked off. Because they were rough working records, waste books were perceived as ephemeral and their survival rate is correspondingly low. In later periods the waste book ceased to exist as the business kept files of invoices or goods inward receipt notes instead. The waste book was often the genuine 'book of original entry', though the journal is technically also placed in that category.

Thus the original purpose of the journal, up to the early nineteenth century, was to record all transactions in chronological order in one book. This allowed the businessman to check whether a particular payment had been made or when a specific transaction occurred. As businesses grew in size and complexity, the single journal became a clumsy device and to facilitate finding particular items it was often broken down into a number of separate journals, each covering one specific class of transaction, such as cash book, sales journal, purchases journal, wages book. The words journal and book were used virtually interchangeably in the title or on the spine. This arrangement considerably eased reference to the journal to find a specified entry since fewer irrelevant items had to be processed. Once the unified journal had been broken down in this way, the original journal, with no specific type of transaction indicated in the title, became relegated to a rag-bag containing any items which did not fit into the neat categories, unusual or non-standard transactions, or those which were very infrequent.

The *ledger* was a second plank in the financial platform of a business. It recorded the transactions of a firm but in specific categories. With a unified journal, the ledger was the first attempt to break the heterogeneous daily entries into specific groupings, such as individual customers or suppliers, types of income or expense, variety of good or venture, each on a separate page. These entries were brought from the journal ('posted' from the journal is the normal jargon) and the two books were cross-referenced by some sort of numbering system. The ledger was a more useful management tool than the unitary journal as it allowed the businessman to see the state of any individual customer's account, or his outstanding debt to a specified supplier, much more quickly and simply. Over time the single ledger with separate pages for different categories of transactions gave way to separate books for each type of transaction: sales or debtors' ledger, creditors' or purchase ledger, capital goods ledger, each merited their own book. The general ledger was then relegated to the role of containing summaries of the various specific ones. When the business had moved to both multiple journals and multiple ledgers, the two are readily distinguished, quite apart from the title on the cover, since the ledger will devote one double page to each customer if a sales ledger, or each suplier if a purchase ledger. Thus the ledger has its entries broken down and categorized to a greater extent than the corresponding journal.

The two types of financial record were closely interrelated and served very similar original purposes. At the simplest, they provided the businessman with a record of all transactions, therefore acting as an aid to his memory. He could check if and when a payment had been made and follow up any omissions on his or his customers' part. They were also crucial documents providing the basic material for drawing up a balance sheet or a profit and loss account. This presupposes that the businessman balanced the accounts, however irregularly, and drew up such documents. Although there is much debate about the regularity of this activity, and indeed, if it was done at all in the firms of the eighteenth or early nineteenth centuries, the majority of firms from the mid-nineteenth century imposed regular balancing of the books on themselves by writing such a requirement into their articles of association. A further original purpose of the journal and ledger was to act as a check on the probity of various individuals in the firm. Partners could check on their fellow partners' honesty and their clerks' and book-keepers' trustworthiness. In a period when fraud, misappropriation of funds and felony were frequent, accurate book-keeping was likely to show up any such malpractices. When the firm was constituted as a partnership and the partners drew out differing amounts of cash or bills, the ledger and journal allowed the individuals to ensure that one partner was not making excessive drawings, or if he was that his capital share was accordingly reduced. Since the books were occasionally used in courts of law to prove a point in a dispute between partners or a firm and its customer, they were generally entered up meticulously and preserved carefully.

Sources

As previously mentioned, because they were intended as only ephemeral documents, waste books rarely survive. Journals and ledgers, on the other hand, as they were meant to be permanent records, were assigned much greater value and were likely to be preserved most assiduously while the firm survived. However, as there was no legal necessity to lodge copies of journals or ledgers with any external body, such as the Stock Exchange or Registrar of Companies and, indeed, their bulk and weight effectively precluded there being more than one set of a firm's accounting records, there is no single repository with a comprehensive collection of ledgers or journals. Where the firm survives, either independently or as a subsidiary of a larger group, the journals or ledgers for some previous period may well survive in their archive or library, or with the company secretary. However, their sheer volume over a long time period meant that the firms that generated them were often impelled to dispose of them once the transactions therein inscribed seemed ancient enough not to impinge on current activities. The most thoughtful firms deposited their past journals and ledgers with a local record office or library, or donated them to a national archive such as the Adam Smith in Glasgow. It has to be said, however, that many fell victim to salvage drives, fire, bombing and neglect.

When ascertaining whether any journals or ledgers survive for a particular business, the best place to start is the firm itself or, if it has been absorbed, the current parent company. The business should know whether it still holds any accounting records or if it has made deposits to a particular archive. For a company no longer in existence or one which is unable to provide the researcher with any information, the NRA is probably the next port of call. In their trade books they have deposits classified by type of industry and by firm, with details of the type of records and where they are located. The other useful source is the Business Archives Council which maintains an index of business archives in public and company depositories arranged alphabetically by company name and lists of specific deposits. This source contains some documents which have not yet found their way on to the NRA files. In addition, there are a number of printed guides to specific types of business documents, mostly inspired by the Business Archives Council. They are listed in the Bibliography (q.v.) under the heading 'Guide to collections of business records'. These books indicate what records now survive for various firms and where any accounting records are included such as journals or ledgers. Other than these national sources, it may be worth approaching record offices or libraries local to where the firm was situated when it was in business.

The information they contain

Essentially journals and ledgers contain the same information arranged in different ways, obviously mainly of a financial nature. The book may contain details of all payments received for goods sold and the value of all goods despatched; similarly, the value of raw materials received may be recorded and the corresponding payments for them. There may be wages books, showing how much was paid and to whom, capital expenditure accounts showing how the firm bought plant, equipment or land. There may be accounts for particular ventures, such as individual voyages of a particular ship or separate accounts for various mines sunk. In the service industries there may be details of expenditure for a hotel chain arranged both by type of expenditure — linen, laundry, cutlery, tobacco, meat etc. — and also by each hotel. The Spiers and Pond ledgers in Kensington Library are a massive example on these lines.[5] 'Private ledgers' often give details of the partners' drawings from the firm and may even show how these sums were spent or invested. The private ledgers of Birley Brothers, nineteenth-century Manchester cotton manufacturers, are excellent examples of these, though now sadly resting in the University of Florida Archives in the USA, making them expensive to use for British researchers.[6]

In addition to the particular transaction and the monetary value, some journals and ledgers also contain details of the volume of goods involved or some comment on their quality. This is unusual and becomes less common in the more modern period. This also indicates one of the weaknesses of this class of records: they do not contain any qualitative information, only quantitative. Although invaluable to ascertain the financial and statistical history of a firm, they can be frustrating if other records have not survived alongside them.

Uses

The best use of a series of journals and ledgers is to reconstruct the financial history of a company. Since they contain a wealth of financial material often already partly categorized, it is possible to carry out significant analyses of the financial affairs of the firm. Using sales ledgers, the researcher could work out monthly and yearly sales figures to show seasonal trends and how the business grew or declined over time. When these aggregates are broken down in the ledger by customer, it is also possible to determine the nature of the customer base and how that changed through the company's life. Was the company dependent on a few major customers who each took a large proportion of output, or were there numerous customers taking only a small proportion of output each? How did this pattern change? Since the customers are usually named in the ledger it might be possible, using old directories, to trace their location and so work out the geographical distribution of a firm's sales. Was it selling essentially to a local market or did it sell nationwide? Did it export any goods and, if so, to which countries? How did this pattern change over time?

Obviously similar exercises could be carried out for suppliers if the purchase ledger survives. The wages book might shed light on wage rates and earnings, the sex ratio of the workers, how their number altered seasonally and in the longer term; if both sales' and workers' books survive it may be possible to compute a crude measure of labour productivity by comparing sales value and number of workers employed. Again, where the ledger contains details of particular ships' voyages or ventures such as mining it is possible to calculate the total expenditure for a particular enterprise and perhaps also the profit on that activity. When the ledger contains entries of capital expenditure, a reconstruction of the firm's fixed capital can be made, and the record examined to see if there were any replacement cycles, long waves or other such patterns. When the private ledgers survive, an analysis can be made of the partners' drawings and some idea made of their personal wealth and life-style. They may show the withdrawal of capital from the business to invest in a country estate which may indicate the entrepreneur adopting a more gentlemanly life-style and concomitant neglect of the business. They may alternatively show the entrepreneur spreading his risk by investing some of his profits into other industrial areas or assuring supplies of raw materials. There are an almost infinite variety of time series, tables and graphs that might be constructed from a set of simple accounting records such as the ledger or journal.

There are, however, one or two drawbacks to using accounting records. First, because of their specialist nature, the researcher either needs to have a good working knowledge of accounting conventions and techniques or to be able to call upon the services of an interested accountant, which can be off-putting. Secondly, if the journal alone now exists, it can be a very tedious and time-consuming process to try and assign each entry to a proper category and so reconstruct the ledger and build up a classified financial history. Where solely the journal survives, probably the most practical course is to reconstruct only some of the more significant ledger accounts. Thirdly, it must be recalled that not all firms either tried to keep or succeeded in keeping their books in a clear revealing manner. Some companies deliberately obfuscated matters in order to cover up errors, dubious ploys or straight shenanagans. Others tried to keep a full and fair set of books but were sadly lacking in the quality of their clerks or book-keepers. Some modern accountants examining past books have been quite unable to make any sense of them. It should also be borne in mind that some firms, especially before they became joint stock companies and were still partnerhips, kept 'private' or 'partners' ledgers which were maintained by the partners themselves or a long-serving, trusted clerk. These recorded what was considered sensitive information, such as the partners' drawings, their capital in the business or figures of profitability. If these ledgers have not survived, then some of the most interesting aspects of the firm will remain permanent lacunae and the normal ledgers will have otherwise inexplicable omissions. An important weakness in all accounting records is that they do not contain any qualitative material and do not explain why certain courses of action were taken. It might be inferred from a sales ledger that a certain customer was refused further supplies because he had not paid outstanding invoices but there is likely to be nothing in the ledger itself to support or deny this. A final complication which has as yet had little effect on historians is that from the 1950s there has been a trend towards computer-based accounting records, and this has become *de rigeur* even for quite small firms with the advent of the micro-computer. The sales ledger may now only exist as a rearrangement of the magnetic field on a floppy disc. At the least, future researchers will need to be *au fait* with reams of print-out and electronic data-processing techniques, at the worst they will find no records, because electronic files have been wiped and re-used. On a more optimistic note, many ledgers are indexed and this aids the researcher significantly.

Professor Mathias has neatly summarized the pitfalls and value of accounting records:

> the books of original entry, made in chronological order as transactions occur, may be tedious to handle, because they are not divided into separate sections by types of account. Working out sales or purchases of a particular raw material, or isolating the accounts of any other single theme of a business will therefore involve laborious reconstruction. But the general day book [or journal] enables the historian to see in great detail the total flows of transactions over time and . . . to see the cash position of the business in detail — for example, to analyze the seasonal variations in outgoings and receipts — . . . far more conveniently from the comprehensive chronological account book than from a collection of more specialized ledgers.[7]

Cross-references to other documents

The nearest neighbours to the journal and ledger among business documents are the balance sheet (q.v.) and profit and loss account (q.v.). These documents are more public and are drawn up using the information in the journals and ledgers. Thus where both a reasonably full set of accounting records and the balance sheet or profit and loss account survive, the former can be used to show how the aggregate figures in either of the latter were derived. In this way the ledger may elucidate the balance sheet or profit and loss account. It will certainly make explicit some of the financial thinking behind the more public — and sanitized — balance sheet figures. However, one of the great weaknesses of accounting records on their own is that they do not explain the motives for a given course of action. It may be obvious that sales figures have risen but whether this is a result of a price rise or increased volume will probably not be indicated. Similarly it may be clear that expenditure on capital equipment has risen, but the rationale for this, whether in order to increase volume of output, or decrease costs at the same level of output, or to commence in a brand new line, will not be spelt out by anything in the journal or ledger. Thus to understand these actions, the researcher needs to have access to a source which provides qualitative information. The best complement to accounting records which provides explanations, if it survives, is the board minute book (q.v.). This should record resolutions and decisions of the directors such as price increases or investment plans. In the best examples, as well as the bare decision there may be some outline of the anticipated outcome or the debate which took place in the board meeting. Where the minute books have not survived, the letter books (q.v.) may throw some light on the thinking, for explanatory letters may have gone out from head office to subordinate outposts, or to customers, trying to justify the course of action. Where neither of these documents have survived the various ravages that beset old records, the business diary (q.v.) of a director may throw some light on events, or possibly the chairman's statement (q.v.) made at the annual meeting. In the latter case, because the speech is for public relations purposes, inspiring confidence in 'the City' and among present and potential investors, it may be a very tame and insipid document which will reveal only a fraction compared to the less public and therefore more frank and full documents already mentioned.

Works using this source

Very few works have been written drawing solely on the ledgers or journals of a firm. As has been said for other documents, these are not likely to be the sole source for a book or even an article. This is partly because they do not explain a trend or event. A journal may show that sales are falling but not why, or that a particular customer is buying more but again no causality is offered. Because of this, accounting records need to be supplemented by letter books or diaries which will provide some explanation of the figures in the account books. Journals and ledgers are purely quantitative sources, they contain no qualitative material and this militates against them being used as a major source for any work. They may be invaluable for drawing up tables, charts or graphs but will not provide much material for narrative or analysis on their own. An even more important reason for journals and ledgers being little used is that the information they contain is conveniently summarized in the annual balance sheets and profit and loss accounts of the company. Thus where a full run of these documents survive, it is much easier to use the published accounts rather than the disaggregated sources from which they have been compiled. By using balance sheets or profit and loss accounts, the historian is using semi-processed material rather than the raw ore and so saving time and effort which would have been needed for refining and amalgamating. Finally, because of their bulk, the technical problems of interpreting them, and the fact that they were unique documents never reproduced, neither circulated to shareholders, nor publicly deposited, they have not survived in large numbers. Too often an author has a comment like: 'Unfortunately, no business ledgers or account books are included in either the business or the family collection and, consequently, very few accounts have survived'[8] or 'Although the directors have taken great pains for many years to amass these records, it was realised that many items, particularly ledgers, cash books, and journals, were missing.'[9] In the latter case the story did have a happy ending as 'During the writing of the book some of these items were discovered. They had been deposited for safe-keeping in a bank, and despite careful enquiries, no member of the present generation knew of their existence.'[10]

Where an author wishes to get behind the published figures, an examination of the journals or ledgers is a must. In some cases this is because the published accounts were misleading and the object of the research was to discover what really went on. Green and Moss's work on the Royal Mail Group is a good example of this type of work. In untangling the knotty affairs of this major shipping enterprise, which effectively went bankrupt between the two world wars and was dismembered into numerous component parts, the authors used, *inter alia*, the private ledgers of D. & W. Henderson in the Harland and Wolff Archives.[11] The pioneering business history of the shipping agency, Swires, also drew upon a variety of accounting records such as 'ledgers, journals, and cash books . . . to supplement the private ledger' to give more detail about 'the range of produce trades and how these trades were financed . . . the sources of commission earnings during the 1870s . . [and] the accounts of the members of the Butterfield family' and so 'sharpen many of the blurred lines of the picture and fill in the detail in some of the blank spaces'[12] which would otherwise have remained.

Anderson used the investment ledger of the Union Marine Insurance Co to show the investment policy of this firm, particularly its overseas holdings, and so show changes in the size and composition of its foreign portfolio to see if it cast light on British overseas investment generally just before the First World War.[13] He was using business documents to see if they could illuminate a wider issue, namely why and how Britain invested abroad, what sort of securities were attractive and how long they were retained, all important issues in the debate about British investment abroad and the degree to which this caused under-investment in 'new' industries at home in the period 1870–1914. To support the contention that accounting records do not often survive, Professor Payne's words may be quoted: 'Among the records of the Govan Colliery has survived a single account book . . . This volume covers the operation of the undertaking for the two years 1804–1805.'[14] However, from this apparently unpromising single source, Payne was able to draw numerous conclusions. The output levels of the miners could be calculated as the account book contained the quantities of coal raised from each pit each day; the existence of 'St Monday' was dramatically demonstrated as output on Mondays averaged only 55 per cent of the daily output of the rest of the working week.[15] Methods of payment for different types of job were revealed, which men were on piece rates and which on time rates. The practice of binding labour was introduced in this period because skilled men were so scarce and bounties were paid of a guinea or two as binding money. Payne was also able to show that capital expenditure was a relatively small proportion of total expenditure, lending support to the thesis that fixed capital formation was not a pressing problem for England in the industrial revolution,[16] and most of it was met from current revenue. He also showed that the colliery was highly profitable with possibly a 50 per cent return on sales for these two years.[17] All in all, this is a gem of an article showing how a single document cleverly used can be made to throw light on a whole range of important topics in business and economic history. It is a paradigm, if not a representative example, of what can be gleaned from an account book.

An American example using a fuller set of accounting records to good effect is Johnson's articles on the Lyman Mills.[18] Using a variety of books of account —

general ledger, factory ledger and sub-ledgers such as inventory, payroll and production — he showed that the Lyman Mills operating water-powered cotton mills along the Connecticut River in Holyoake, Massachusetts, developed a sophisticated, integrated, double-entry cost accounting system as early as the late 1850s. Although it is impossible to determine how representative this firm is of the total population of firms in the US at the time, Johnson feels that this may well demonstrate that cost accounting systems were introduced at an earlier date than normally claimed and for reasons of internal management control rather than because of increased external competition. Although open to criticism, this is an interesting example of the use of ledgers to trace the development of accounting techniques and management control systems.

The example

The example is drawn from the archives of the Charles Barker Group, a leading international advertising agency. It was one of the earliest such agencies, founded in 1812 as Lawson and Barker at Birchin Lane, London. It had a very close relationship with *The Times*: Lawson printed it, Baker distributed newsletters for it to provincial papers, and some *Times* correspondents regarded the agency's offices as their workroom. From this beginning the agency moved into placing newspaper advertisements for clients, often in *The Times*.[19] Barkers really took off in the 1830s and 1840s when it inserted advertisements for applications to subscribe for foreign loans on behalf of clients such as Rothschilds and for the shares of a whole range of railway companies.[20]

The document is reproduced from their 'Shipping Advertising Ledger' of 1837–42. It records the details of advertisements placed by Barkers on behalf of a number of shipowning firms. The pages for the Norfolk Steam Packet Company are typical, giving the cost and dates of the advertisements, the papers used and a monthly total expenditure. The delays between presentation of an account and receiving payment are noteworthy — in one case nearly eight months — as are the promotion of special events such as the Yarmouth races. Once the account was settled, the receipt was noted and the account crossed through in red ink. Among Barker's clients were the P & O Steam Navigation Company, Anglo Brazilian Mail, the General Steam Navigation Company and the Antwerp Steam Packet Company. The P & O had one of the largest accounts; in July and August 1840 for advertising its prospectus alone, it used fourteen newspapers and over 100 insertions costing nearly £100.[21]

Notes

1. 7 & 8 Vict. c. 110.
2. 19 & 20 Vict. c. 47, clause 69 of Table B.
3. 18 & 19 Geo. V c. 45, clause 39(1) & (2).
4. A useful introduction to accounting records is to be found in T.C. Barker, R.H.

Campbell & P. Mathias, *Business History* (Historical Association, 1971) pp. 33–9; and T.S. Ashton, W.T. Baxter *et al.*, 'The Publication of Business Records', *Archives*, Vol. 1, No. 6 (1951) pp. 17–30.

5. Kensington & Chelsea Central Library, Spiers & Pond, impersonal ledgers, 1890–1911.
6. W.E: Stone, 'An early English Cotton Mill Cost Accounting System: Charlton Mills 1810–1889', *Accounting & Business Research*, Vol. 4, No. 1 (1973) p. 72.
7. P. Mathias, 'Historical Records of the Brewing Industry', *Archives*, Vol. 7, No. 33 (1965) p. 9.
8. S. Marriner, *Rathbones of Liverpool, 1845–73* (Liverpool UP, 1961) p. xii.
9. S. Marriner & F.E. Hyde, *The Senior: John Samuel Swire 1825–98* (Liverpool UP, 1967) p. 207.
10. Ibid.
11. E. Green & M. Moss, *A Business of National Importance: The Royal Mail Shipping Group, 1902–1937* (Methuen, 1982) p. 264.
12. Marriner & Hyde, op. cit., pp. 209–10.
13. B.L. Anderson, 'Institutional Investment before the First World Ward: The Union Marine Insurance Co 1897–1915' in S. Marriner (ed.), *Business and Businessmen: Studies in Business, Economic and Accounting History* (Liverpool UP, 1978).
14. P.L. Payne, 'Govan Collieries, 1804–5', *Business History*, Vol. 3, No. 1 (1960); reprinted in K.A. Tucker, *Business History: Selected Readings* (Cass, 1977) p. 66.
15. Ibid., pp. 68–9.
16. See F. Crouzet (ed.), *Capital Formation in the Industrial Revolution* (Methuen, 1972) for a general introduction to this subject.
17. Payne, op. cit., p. 78.
18. H.T. Johnson, 'Early Cost Accounting for Internal Management Control: Lyman Mills in the 1850s', *Business History Review*, Vol. 46, No. 4 (1972); reprinted in K.A. Tucker, op. cit.
19. T.R. Nevett, *Advertising in Britain: A History* (Heinemann, 1982) pp. 64–5.
20. Ibid., pp. 30–1.
21. Guildhall Library, London, Ms 19,994.

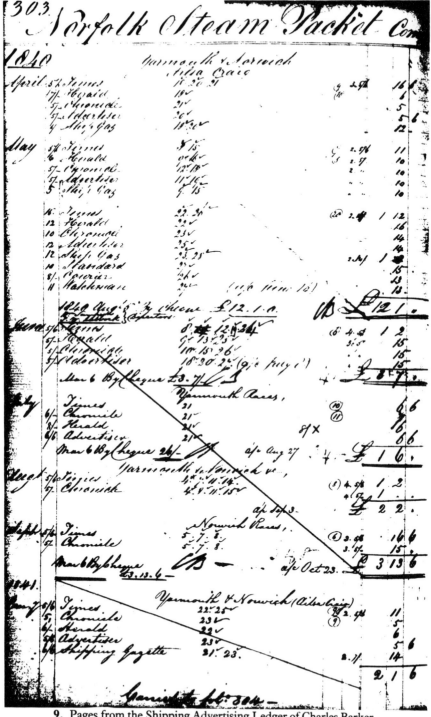

9. Pages from the Shipping Advertising Ledger of Charles Barker,
April 1840–August 1842.
Source: Guildhall Library, London Ms 19,994, pp. 303–4.

9. Pages from the Shipping Advertising Ledger of Charles Barker,
April 1840–August 1842.
Source: Guildhall Library, London Ms 19,994, pp. 303–4.

10 Balance sheets and profit and loss accounts

Original purpose

The purpose of these documents was to provide the shareholders of a company — or the partners if joint stock form had not been adopted — with a summary of the financial affairs of the business made up to a specific date and thus reassure them that their capital was safe. Both documents drew much of their information from the journals and ledgers which were the day-to-day financial records of the organization. The balance sheet showed the assets and liabilities of the firm at a particular point in time and thus, by deduction, its net worth or value. The profit and loss account showed the flow of funds into the firm and from it to suppliers, workers and other creditors. The two should complement each other and equipped with the pair the capitalist should have a pretty good idea of the firm's past financial activities and present position.

In the early family firms of the eighteenth century, balances were not necessarily struck regularly or even frequently and, when they were drawn up, the *balance sheets* were often handwritten and circulated to the few partners who were entitled to them. Joint stock companies set up by royal charter or Act of Parliament often had clauses written into their constitution requiring them to produce an annual balance sheet, or 'an abstract from their books showing the state of their funds and debts'.[1]

Thus it became not unusual to have a periodic balance sheet. The reason for such stipulations was that publicity was perceived as providing protection for shareholders and creditors alike. This became a legal requirement for all joint stock companies set up under the 1844 Act which insisted that the books were balanced and a 'full and fair' balance sheet was compiled to be presented to the shareholders at each ordinary general meeting.[2] In addition, this Act stipulated that the balance sheet should be printed and a copy sent to every shareholder at his registered address ten days before the meeting. However, the clause also contained a phrase which allowed companies to duck out of this obligation if they chose, by making the requirement 'subject to the provisions of any deed of settlement or bye law in that behalf'.[3] The 1844 Act also demanded that a copy of the balance sheet was sent to the Registrar of Joint Stock Companies within fourteen days of the general meeting.[4] Therefore, after 1844 one very compelling reason for joint stock companies to draw up a balance sheet was because the law required that they do so, at the minimum in order to file a copy with the Registrar and in most cases also to inform their shareholders.

However, from 1856, when limited liability status became freely available to joint stock companies, as explained in the Introduction, company law took a backward step as far as disclosure was concerned, for the clauses on balance sheets ceased to be in the body of the Act and instead were relegated to the model regulations in Table B.[5] These only had the force of law if the company failed to register separate by-laws or failed to state that Table B did not apply. In this way a company could avoid circulating its shareholders with a balance sheet. The 1856 Act did not stipulate that a copy of the balance sheet be lodged with the Registrar. Thus both the legal sanctions were removed in one fell swoop. This state of affairs was perpetuated in subsequent company legislation until 1907 when the requirement to file the balance sheet at Companies House was reinstated.[6] However, it was not until 1929 that the full rigour of the 1844 Act was regained and the balance sheet had again to be made up and presented at annual general meetings and a copy had to be sent to every shareholder at least seven days beforehand.[7] Since that date this requirement has never been rescinded from company legislation. The rationale for this pre-circulation is to give shareholders sufficient time to examine the balance sheet and prepare questions about it before the general meeting.

Because the law was lax between 1856 and 1928 does not mean companies ceased making up and keeping balance sheets. Any well-run business, whether joint stock company or family partnership, saw the value of an annual or even half-yearly balance sheet. It was likely to reassure partners or shareholders that their capital was safe since total assets exceeded liabilities. By comparing the figures shown on one balance sheet with those of the previous, it gave directors and shareholders some indication of how the business had fared in the period between. It was a useful internal discipline for the firm as it compelled it to check balances in each of the ledger entries and so ensure the book-keeping records were up-to-date and accurate. However, it should also be borne in mind that the balance sheet was for external consumption in the case of a joint stock company and so the directors had a strong motive for putting the best figures possible to the shareholders. If the business seemed to be faltering, then the directors might face a hostile general meeting and indeed might lose their seats on the board. Thus the tendency was to manipulate the figures in an optimistic direction. Given the newness of accounting as either an art or science, that there was no national professional accounting body until after 1880,[8] and that the law did not enforce rules on how a balance sheet was to be prepared, it was not too difficult for the directors to indulge in 'creative accounting'.

Profit and loss accounts were rather slower in finding their way into legislative enactment. The 1844 Act made no mention of them or any similar document. The 1856 Act did suggest that 'a statement of income and expenditure' should be made up annually and laid before the general meeting[9] but this was not part of the Act itself but instead was one of the clauses in the model rules and, as already explained, these could easily be ignored by any company choosing not to adopt them. This remained the *status quo* until 1928 then for the first time legislation stipulated, in an unavoidable way, that companies must present a profit and loss account or, if a non-profit-making institution, a statement of income and expenditure to each annual general meeting.[10] Thus from 1928 onwards all joint stock companies had to draft and present such a document. However, there was no requirement on companies either to lodge these profit and loss statements with the Registrar or to circulate the members of the company before the general meeting. This only came with the 1948 Act, which therefore provided a double incentive for drawing up such an account.[11]

If before 1928 there was no legal necessity to present a profit and loss account to the shareholders this, as in the case of balance sheets, did not mean that all companies avoided such paperwork as though fever infected. Some saw the advantage of providing their members with such data, especially when it came to the question of the dividend to be declared. The courts ruled that dividends could only be paid from profits, not out of capital, and therefore to justify a particular dividend the company needed to declare an equal level of profits. In a joint stock limited liability company, many of the shareholders' main interest was in the payment of a regular, and preferably rising, dividend. They therefore wished to see steadily increasing profit figures from which the dividend payment could be made. It was in its own interest for the company to publish some rudimentary form of profit and loss account.

Throughout the nineteenth century there was no tax on profits. It was only in the First World War that such a tax was levied and then it was on 'excess' profits, that is the increased level of profit attributable to the extra economic activity that a fully-employed economy generated.[12] The reason for the tax was to still accusations of profiteering rather than any belief that profits were legitimate sources of tax revenue. At this time a new imperative arose for drawing up profit and loss accounts, namely as a method of showing the level of profits for tax assessment purposes. It ceased to be a concern after 1921, when the duty ended. It was not again an issue until the threat of war reappeared in 1937 when a 'national defence contribution' tax was introduced as a percentage of profits. This was supplemented in 1939 by a re-introduced version of the excess profits tax of the First World War.[13] So again the business firm had to produce profit and loss statements from which the tax men could calculate its liability. From that date, a tax of some sort on business profits has remained. Although the name and rate has changed fairly frequently, all businesses have had to draw up profit and loss accounts to allow a calculation of their liability for profits or, since 1965, corporation tax.

A further purpose of the balance sheet and profit and loss account which has only developed in the last few decades is to act as a form of public relations and advertising. Once the balance sheet, profit and loss account, chairman's report, auditors' report and other documents began to be incorporated in one glossy booklet, with charts and graphs, colour photographs of products and operations, they could serve as a measure of the firm's prestige — the thicker, glossier and more colourful, the sounder the firm was the anticipated analogy — and act as publicity in attracting new investors, both individuals and, more importantly, institutions such as pension funds, unit trusts and insurance companies.[14]

Sources

All joint stock companies formed under the 1844 Act had to send annual copies of their balance sheets, *inter alia*, to the Registrar of Joint Stock Companies. For live companies these have been preserved among the papers kept at Companies House. For those companies which have ceased trading, that is the vast majority of businesses started under the 1844 legislation, the balance sheets will be found among the 'dead company' files in the PRO at Kew, among the BT31 and BT41 classes. For partnerships, there was no similar requirement to lodge a balance sheet. These firms preserved their current balance sheets carefully, often under lock and key, for they were regarded as highly confidential documents, giving much information of value to a rival. Sometimes, when the partnership converted to corporate form or was taken over by a joint stock company, the balance sheets were passed on intact and survive in the archive of the acquiring company. However, their frequency of survival is very spasmodic, as the usual destructive influences have taken their toll, and partnerships normally produced only a very small number of copies of these documents to reduce the risk of revealing financial secrets.

Under the 1856 company legislation the situation changed dramatically. There was no longer any requirement for companies to lodge the balance sheet with the Registrar and therefore this safe haven ceased to accumulate the documents. As a result, neither the PRO nor Companies House contain any balance sheets from 1956 until 1907 when the stipulation was re-introduced by that year's Companies Act.[15] There is therefore a grievous gap in the publicly deposited records covering the last half of the nineteenth century, a period when business was growing fast, amalgamating and taking on a new shape. This cannot be studied from the balance sheets in public repositories. Some of this caesura can be made good from the Stock Exchange records held at the Guildhall Library in the City of London. The London Stock Exchange required every company whose shares were traded on its floor to submit copies of all circulars which were sent to the shareholders and which might have a bearing on the value of its shares;[16] thus the balance sheet and the profit and loss account, which were key documents in any evaluation of a company's worth, had to be sent in. These were bound up by year in alphabetical order of company name and have now been handed over to the Guildhall Library for safekeeping. Thus for companies quoted on the Stock Exchange these financial documents for the period 1856–1907 can still be accessed. It should be borne in mind, however, that a minority of businesses, only the largest, used the formal financial market in this period, and most stayed as partnerships or private companies. Fortunately for the researcher, from 1907 to date without break, the law has insisted on public companies lodging annual balance sheets with the Registrar, where they may still be found. However, one lacuna still remained: the 1907 Act established the notion of a 'private' company, that is one with a limited number of shareholders, which does not go outside this circle of members to raise capital and thus does not directly approach the public to buy shares or take up debentures.[17] Such companies did not need to file balance sheets with the Registrar and a number of family-run firms chose to become private companies rather than disclose their asset structure.[18] So again there is a gap in the publicly deposited records. This only became filled when either the private company went public or was absorbed by a public company, thus needing to file balance sheets, or after the 1967 Companies Act when all companies had to file them irrespective of their status or number of shareholders.[19]

Unfortunately the statutory requirement for a profit and loss account to be lodged with the Registrar did not come until 1948[20] and so before that date none are to be found in either Companies House or the PRO. For publicly quoted companies they can be found in the Stock Exchange papers at the Guildhall Library in the same volumes as the balance sheets. The most difficult type to trace, where they ever existed, are those for non-public companies. They may survive in the firm but even this is dubious for the usual reasons.

In modern times the balance sheet and profit and loss account have been part of the annual report published by all public companies. These are widely distributed not merely to all directors and shareholders, but also to city experts such as share brokers, unit trust managers and insurance fund managers irrespective of whether they are shareholders. The individual company normally holds an unbroken set of its reports since the last war and the City Business Library in London Wall keeps a five-year run for all public limited companies (see 'Useful addresses'). Thus for recent years and the large public companies there is no problem in getting hold of the balance sheets and profit and loss accounts.

The information they contain

It is very difficult to generalize as to the information which is given in the average balance sheet or profit and loss statement before very recent times. These documents vary enormously from firm to firm and over time. Given that the profession of accountancy was not born on a national scale until 1880 and then had a prolonged infancy,[21] there was no general consensus rigorously imposed of what should be included. This was compounded by company law failing to enforce strict guidelines as to the contents of a balance sheet. The 1844 Act confined itself to requiring the balance to be 'full and fair' but no more.[22] The 1856 Act laid down firmer guidelines on what was to be included and attached a model example to Table B.[23] For the period this model set a high standard, separating items such as the number of shares, amount paid per share, any arrears of calls, and if there were forfeited shares under capital. Debts and liabilities were similarly differentiated; headings were specified for loans, debentures, mortgages, trade debts, law expenses, unclaimed dividends and interest due on loans. The asset side was also broken down into detailed headings, the company being encouraged to show its property under freehold land, freehold buildings, leasehold buildings; property was divided into stock in trade and plant; debts were classified as secured, good but unsecured, and bad.[24] By contemporary standards this was a useful set of categories and would have provided shareholders with some idea of the firm's position. However, there was no compulsion upon companies to adopt this layout since the balance sheet only appeared in the model regulations and, as explained above, companies could choose not to adopt these. Additionally, the clause in Table B which recommended the use of the model balance sheet contained the qualifying phrase 'or as near thereto as Circumstances admit'.[25] This again provided a loophole for any business which chose to present its balance sheet in a different, less informative format.

This remained the position until 1907 when the prescribed format for the balance sheet was dropped completely. The body of both the Acts of 1907 and 1908 contained clauses about the balance sheet, but the wording was so vague as to provide little guidance to companies, or information to shareholders. The balance sheet was to contain 'such particulars as will disclose the nature of such liabilities and assets and how the values of the fixed assets have been arrived at'.[26] Effectively companies had complete freedom in the construction of their balance sheets. The 1928 Act was much more specific in its requirements, specifying separate disclosure of: authorized and issued share capital; fixed and floating assets; intangible and tangible assets; and assets consisting of shares in or loans to subsidiaries.[27] However, these clauses were shown to be deficient in dealing with hidden reserve funds and movements of cash into or out of them and, because they only specified aggregate amounts to be given for assets in subsidiaries, this remained a meaningless figure. In addition, private companies remained exempt from the requirements on balance sheets.

The 1948 Act was the first piece of legislation both to lay down full guidelines on how a balance sheet should be presented and to compel all companies to follow this model.[28] It devoted several pages to overcoming the defects of the 1928 Act in disclosure of reserves and the question of group accounts.[29] Its main defect from the historian's viewpoint is that it continued the exemption given to private companies as there was no need for them to register their accounts.[30] The reluctance on the part of the legislature before the 1940s to introduce any hard and fast rules about format is understandable. If the experts — businessmen, book-keepers and auditors — disagreed, it would have been perverse and perhaps counter productive for government to impose one set of conventions over competing ideas. The upshot was that each business was largely free to pursue its own path in the method of presenting its balance sheet, although gradually by the late nineteenth and early twentieth centuries a measure of agreement was to be found among the larger public companies.

A similar caveat has to be lodged about the contents of the profit and loss statement. For over one hundred years the law eschewed any edicts on what it ought to contain. The 1844 Act, for instance, did not even mention a profit and loss account, let alone what should be in it. The 1856 Companies Act specified the contents of any 'statement of income and expenditure':

> statements so made shall show arranged under the most convenient Heads the Amount of gross Income, distinguishing the several sources from which it has been derived, and the Amount of gross Expenditure distinguishing the Expense of the Establishment, Salaries, and the other like Matters: Every Item of Expenditure fairly changeable against the Year's Income shall be brought into Account.[31]

However, the breakdown specified was sufficiently vague and general as to leave plenty of room for interpretation. Also this clause appeared only in the model regulations, not in the body of the Act itself, and thus a company could avoid adhering to it simply by stating in its articles of association that specified clauses of Table B did not apply. The logic of leaving the definitions loose was on the same lines as for the balance sheet. As was the case for balance sheets, the 1856 definition of what an income statement might include was perpetuated in the 1862 Act,[32] but disappeared completely in the 1907 legislation where no hint of such a document appeared, except to say that the balance sheet did not need to include one.[33] Although the 1928 Act required the directors to draw up a profit and loss account, it ignored totally any specification of the content.[34] It was not until 1948 that the format of an income statement was again prescribed.[35] The only exceptions, until 1967, were private companies.[36] The result of this lack of specificity was even more marked in those profit and loss accounts which do survive than is the case for balance sheets. Many are paragons of brevity, giving only two or three headings and lumping together a range of incomes or expenditures to make them totally unamenable to any analysis.

This said, most balance sheets did contain a common fund of information. They were drawn up on the double-page basis, liabilities on the left and assets on the right. On the liabilities side, the first entry was invariably the capital of the company: the number of shares issued, the amount paid up per share and thus the total nominal equity value; if there were preference shares or debentures, or any other class of share or loan, these would be similarly specified to show the total capital raised from the public and which in theory was owed by the company to the individual investors. Although the precise level of detail varied from company to company, it was quite normal for there to be a note of shares on which calls had not been paid and any which were forefeited or not taken up. The balance sheet also indicated the level of creditors, sometimes distinguishing between types — 'trade' and 'others' or 'pre-payments' made to the company — though this distinction was not always very helpful. There was often a provision for bad and doubtful debts which were anticipated but not yet proved, and if a reserve fund had been built up by transfers from the profit and loss accounts of previous years it too would feature on the liabilities side as in theory it belonged to the shareholders and was therefore owed by the company to them. The balance from the profit and loss account was brought forward to the balance sheet, but often this was minus certain payments such as an interim dividend on the ordinary shares, or payments of interest on loans or debentures. Sometimes there was a provision for bills drawn (meaning bills of exchange) but not yet presented; this was another form of liability as it represented a creditor who would have to be paid eventually.

The assets side of the balance sheet could contain some interesting figures but it often concealed as much as it revealed. The basis of the valuation of some of the assets was open to much crticism, as for instance in 'The example' of the Assam Company where there was no attempt to arrive at an independent current value of the company's plantations, factories and other property in Assam nor yet was a historical cost figure used; rather they were put into the books at the same figure as the company's capital and the shareholders were left to make their own estimate![37] This smacks of circular accounting and was an abrogation of the duties of the directors. In other cases it was not unusual to lump together both the tangible assets of the company, such as the freehold and leasehold property, with the intangible assets, such as trademarks, goodwill and patent rights. This single consolidated figure was meaningless and, since it appeared unchanged year after year, was purely arbitrary. In modern accounts, firms do not list intangibles as assets because it is impossible to arrive at any objective judgement of their value. Before the 1930s it was also unusual for firms to separate out their investments in wholly or partly-owned subsidiaries. There was no requirement even after the 1929 Act to disclose precise holdings or even the names of the subsidiaries and many companies had one category on the lines of 'holdings in subsidiary companies' and whether this was a shareholding, loan or other investment was not specified nor were the sums differentiated.

There were some entries on the asset side which were likely to be rather more firmly based in reality. The value of plant, office furniture, vehicles and other items of fixed capital was usually indicated, though again the precise basis of valuation was not always given, so that it is difficult to work out if this was a historic cost or historic cost less depreciation. The stocks of both raw materials and finished goods were another item on the assets side, normally stated separately, but again the basis of valuation was frequently not made explicit; it is fairly safe to assume historical cost was used for both raw materials and the finished goods. The assets side of any balance sheet also generally contained a note of the debtors of the company, those who had received goods but not yet paid for them although payment was anticipated in the near future. Even more liquid, there was a note of the cash assets of the company often broken down into that in the bank and that on hand, that is in notes and coin within the company, and if the company was involved in foreign activities there might well be two or more entries, for cash in London and that held abroad at the sites where operations were taking place. This was the stock of working capital which the business needed for its day-to-day activities.

The profit and loss accounts are subject to similar qualifications to the balance sheets. The quality and quantity of information that they contain varies enormously between firms and over time. At their best they are a detailed breakdown of the expenses of running the company for a year. The example quoted, the Assam Company, is particularly good because of its wealth of detail with five pages devoted to expenditure, at what was a relatively early stage in financial accounting. There are plenty of opposite examples where, as late as the 1930s, public companies were publishing profit and loss accounts which had less than six headings on each side. The best profit and loss accounts contain vast amounts of information on the costs of running a business and its sources of income. On the expenditure side, that is on the left-hand page, each of the items of expense are listed: the costs of obtaining raw materials and fuel; the costs of wages, salaries and the fees of directors and any other officials; commission paid to agents; the allowance made for depreciation of the firm's fixed capital, plant or equipment that has had to be written off; costs of tools; costs of running the office such as rent, rates, heating and stationery; legal charges such as stamp duty plus the amounts that have been allocated for future claims such as a reserve fund, contributions to the staff pension scheme or for bad debts. It must be stressed that the precise headings will depend very much upon the nature of the business being conducted. Obviously because the Assam Company was growing tea in the Indian sub-continent and then shipping it home to the UK, many of its expenses were incurred in India and were related to the hiring, support and transport of its coolie labour force. Its expenses in the UK were relatively slight as were those of most UK companies which had their main base of operations abroad, for example Ashanti Goldfields Corporation, Rio Tinto Company or Bovril Australian Estates.

On the right-hand page of the profit and loss account appear the flows of income into the firm. The most important component of these is likely to be the sales of the main product the company is manufacturing or merchanting, in the example tea, for other firms items such as soap, glass or bicycles. There may be some deductions to offset against this income and in lucky cases there may be a volume figure as well as a value figure, such as pounds of tea or head of cattle. In addition to this inflow, the business may have other subsidiary sources of income. This was true in the early stages of industrialization when organizations often chose to spread their risks over a number of products rather than specialize, and again in the twentieth century when companies relearned this lesson but implemented it on a much greater scale by indulging in multi-product mergers. When businesses had wholly-owned subsidiaries, or indeed investments of any sort in other firms, there was likely to be an income from this in the form of interest, dividends or a share of the profits. Although not always broken down, it was usually listed separately as a group. Thus in the good examples a profit and loss account can give an accurate picture of the nature and size of the various flows of income going into a firm. Modern examples in the glossy booklets normally issued by public companies will not merely conform to modern accounting conventions but will have several pages of notes to the accounts making these conventions explicit and clear even to the lay reader. In addition, they give notice of the date and place of the annual general meeting and include proxy forms to enable those who cannot attend to vote.

It needs to be stressed, however, that many profit and loss accounts, especially before the Second World War, can be singularly frustrating documents, lumping together a range of expenditures or incomes, in some cases not giving the total figures for sales but only the gross profit on trading and then deducting one aggregate sum for cost of sales and establishment. In such cases the figures are virtually meaningless and conceal so much that they are of no real use.

Uses

Sheila Marriner has already written a definitive piece on the problems inherent in using balance sheets or profit and loss accounts as a source for business historians.[38] This summary draws heavily on that article, and the reader is warmly recommended to it. This section will point out the more important pitfalls and then the uses for which these records are particularly valuable. The main problem with using these records is the complete lack of uniformity in their construction. Not merely did different firms compile their accounts in different ways, but a given business changed the methods and practices it used in drawing up its statements from year to year. The law was very lax on the contents of both a balance sheet and a profit and loss account until 1948 as explained in the section on 'The information they contain', above. The 1948 Act was the first to stipulate, in the body of the legislation, a full breakdown to which companies had to conform when drawing up their balance sheets. As we have had occasion to observe previously, the law did not set stringent standards for firms to follow, rather it lagged behind best practice and acted to round up those laggard companies who were significantly behind average practice. Thus the improvement in the quality of these statements stemmed more from the growing professionalism of accountancy and the desire of well-run companies to keep their members informed than any stipulations of company law. For instance, it was not until 1928 that the law required the balance sheet and profit and loss account be drawn up to the same date.[39] Prior to this an unscrupulous company could choose two different dates so that the two documents could not be compared and some analyses could not be made, for instance of returns on sales. Similarly, because the standards of disclosure were sufficiently vague before the 1930s, it was quite possible for firms to shift large amounts of cash out of the profit and loss account into secret reserve funds, as was shown most dramatically by the Royal Mail Group crash and Lord Kylsant's subsequent prosecution.[40] This was carried out via provisions for future taxation, or over-rapid depreciation, or over-provision for bad debts. There was no requirement to state explicitly that such a reserve fund existed and these monies could then be used to make good any trading losses by bringing sums from the reserve back on to the profit and loss statement with again no explicit indication that this was what had been done. Although the Royal Mail Group is the most famous example, there were plenty of other respected names using similar practices, including Napier, the car and aero engine manufacturer, and the Ocean Steam Ship Company which owned the Blue Funnel Line.[41] Thus any researcher using balance sheets or profit and loss accounts before the Second World War must be aware that they often conceal as much as they reveal. This stems largely from their main function, as far as the company was concerned, which was to reassure investors and maintain the share price. These public financial statements had a public relations role and as such are biased towards optimistic results. Another drawback from which the balance sheet suffers is that it is only a snapshot at one particular date. This is chosen quite arbitrarily and with no necessary consideration of the natural cycles of the business.[42] The balance sheet will not show the fluctuations in the business between the dates of its compilation and may give a false impression because of this. Finally, of course, a major drawback to using these types of document is that there is no explanation given to them. They are only the crude figures. Although relationships can be established, ratios calculated and time series constructed, however diffidently, the financial statements never contain any reasons as to why these relationships occur or which way causality lies, or why certain ratios or trends exist. For causes, the researcher will have to look to other documents.

Bearing these major reservations in mind, let us consider the uses to which the more informative and consistent balance sheets and profit and loss accounts can be put. The most common use is for the historian of an individual company to construct long-run time series of a firm's financial results — its sales, profit, dividends and capital employed — and from this draw some conclusions about the growth of the company over time and its profitability. If the figures will bear it, the key ratios such as the return on sales, return on capital employed, liquidity or gearing may be calculated. This is the sort of analysis which is carried out by the research department of a modern stockbroker to give some indication of the financial health of a company. Where the balance sheets and profit and loss accounts are sufficiently detailed, the calculation of these figures will show how the firm controlled its cash flow, whether it was making large returns on small volumes or vice versa, and so help explain the policies pursued by the firm to foster growth or the reasons for its decline or demise. In addition, some of the more detailed statements can be used to determine how a firm's activities broke down in terms of geographical area, or by type of product, whether some lines were particularly profitable while others were loss makers, whether operations in some countries subsidized those in others.

The historian of accounting finds balance sheets and profit and loss figures particularly fascinating. They throw light on a whole range of issues in the development of accounting practices, such as depreciation policies or their total absence, the acceptable relationships between risk capital and loan capital, the methods of presenting figures in the documents and how this practice changed over time. From this it is possible to see how far company law affected current best practice and to what degree the law lagged behind best practice. The extent to which reserve funds were used, whether provision was made for bad debts, and the proportion of profits retained for plough back compared to that distributed as dividends to the shareholders, can all be investigated from these documents. The valuation of assets and the treatment of intangibles can also be deduced from balance sheets, and an examination made of how these practices changed over time. To the accountant interested in the development of his art, the balance sheet and profit and loss account are indispensible sources like ledgers or journals, though they can also be, as explained above, frustrating and enigmatic.

Cross-references to other documents

The chairman's statement (q.v.) is the document most closely associated with balance sheets and profit and loss accounts. The chairman's statement normally commented on the salient financial results of the year. At the minimum, there would be a mention of the progress of sales and profits, even if the former was expressed in general terms — 'a substantial rise' or 'continued growth'. In the better speeches there was some explanation of the more important factors underlying the bare financial results: rises in prices of raw materials, a strike or industrial relations problems. The balance sheet and profit and loss account contain only the bare financial figures, the chairman's statement often helped to explain the underlying causes. This practice was formalized when it became normal to issue a written report, usually called the directors' report. This was recommended in the 1907 Companies Act but not made compulsory until 1928 when such a statement had to be laid before the general meeting. The 1948 Act required that in addition the report be circulated to all members previous to the meeting. Nowadays it is best practice to present the balance sheet, profit and loss account and directors' report in one glossy colour brochure.

To discover more detail on how the balance sheet and profit and loss statement were constructed, the internal financial records of the firm, such as the ledgers and journals (q.v.), are essential. The balance sheet and profit and loss account summarize one year's entries in these books and from them, in theory, it is possible to see how and why certain figures were put in the annual statements. In fact, of course, as explained in previous sections, it is often extremely difficult, verging on the impossible, to reconstruct the precise process as the underlying assumptions, conventions and policies are not known. Similarly, where a company is presenting group or consolidated accounts, access to the ledgers, journals and other internal financial records are necessary if these aggregate figures are to be broken down into individual operating companies. Again the caveat mentioned above needs to be re-iterated. It is often a frustrating task and historians with a sound knowledge of modern accounting practices and indeed practising accountants benevolent enough to try and help a struggling business historian have often retired from the field defeated.

The balance sheet and profit and loss statement may augment the premises records (q.v.) in that the former may give separate values for the company's freehold or leasehold property, though equally frequently they may be lumped together with other of the company's assets, and the latter may show the costs of maintaining and improving such property, or the level of depreciation considered necessary. The latter should also contain details of any rents paid out and on the other hand any rents received from leasing out surplus property. Finally, these public financial statements may contain some figures to augment the often sparse staff records (q.v.). In the more detailed profit and loss statements, some breakdown of total wage costs may be given which will allow greater analysis of the make-up and wage levels of the workforce. There may also be reference to other costs incurred on behalf of the labour force such as, in twentieth century examples, transfers to a pension fund or, as in the example, the costs of bonuses, raw materials found for the coolies and the cost of recruiting and transporting them. Such detail is rare in a profit and loss statement but where it is given it can amplify the staff records.

Works using this source

Collins in a recent article[43] draws on the balance sheets of nearly forty English banks in the nineteenth century to try to come to some general conclusions about their cash ratios and liquidity, the relationship between current and deposit accounts and between the banks' assets and liabilities. He shows that even in the 1840s note issue was a tiny proportion of the banks' total liabilities compared to deposits which made up the vast majority. Current accounts were considerably more important than deposit accounts and this meant bank directors had to keep an eye on their liquidity. As others have suggested, bills of exchange declined in importance after the late 1860s when bank advances expanded. Cash ratios fell in the period from about 7 per cent to about 13 per cent in the 1870s. This pioneering study was based almost entirely on the appropriate balance sheets in the various banks' archives. A good example of how the published accounts of a public company can be used, what they reveal and the pitfalls to be avoided in using them is the paper written by Lee.[44] He uses the balance sheets of the Distillers Company from 1881 to 1944 to show how accounting conventions changed over time. For instance, he shows that before 1945 the published accounts refer only to the holding company not the group as a whole. He believes the 'shareholders received, if at all, inadequate explanations of movements in reported data' and 'at no time were the financial statements supported by explanatory notes'. He blames this squarely on the 'inadequate legal provisions for company financial reporting . ˙. . prior to the Companies Act of 1948'.[45] Lee also points out that there was no formal depreciation policy until 1930 and that balance sheets were 'no more than a reported trial balance and the profit and loss account no more than a reconciliation and justification for the proposed dividend'.[46] This said, Lee implies these accounts were fairly representative of the time for they were 'entirely within the bounds of generally accepted accounting practice of the periods covered'.[47] This is an interesting example of the use that can be made of balance sheets and profit and loss accounts to explore the development and conventions of company accounting.

Julian Mason was sufficiently provoked by an article explaining the drawbacks of using published accounts that he put pen to paper to extol their value, as well as indicate some of the problems he had encountered.[48] His study was of those firms in the brewing industry which had Stock Exchange quotations in the period 1870 to 1914. By 1900 there were over 250 firms in this category, although his sample is much smaller. He accepts that published accounts were the most processed and so the most misleading form of accounting record, that they say nothing about personalities or why decisions were taken and are a dubious measure of profitability because of the great latitude given to directors when constructing them.[49] However, Mason feels they show how contemporary businessmen saw things, especially where the figures show a trend over a number of firms. He also argues that there was significant use of accounting data for management information, that is for the internal control of the firm, because much of the material was broken down by department to allow comparisons and reach decisions on relative performance and profiitability.[50] Other examples of articles written using published accounts abound. The brewing industry was the subject of another investigation, this time by Gourvish and Wilson, for the period 1885 to 1914.[51] They drew on the published accounts of a number of large brewers to explore how profitable the business was in a period conventionally famed for an upsurge in temperance activity and a decline in per capita consumption. They suggest that although a number of London and Burton brewers did experience hard times with a fall in profits, dividends being passed and eventually a capital reconstruction, a number of provincial brewers continued to enjoy solid profitability. This they explain by 'financial conservatism . . . the purchase of houses principally out of profits, the creation of a healthy reserve against which losses and revaluations after 1902 could be written off'.[52] Lewchuk conducts a similar investigation into the motor car industry during its first forty years of life.[53] Using published accounts lodged in the Guildhall Library, London, he shows that profits before 1914 tended to be above the average for the economy as a whole, thus casting doubt on ideas of 'entrepreneurial failure', although after the First World War profits in his sample tended to be more in line with average returns. In this they demonstrated the normal pattern of profitability to be expected once an industry had become mature.

The example

The Assam Company, formed in 1839, is the oldest tea company in India and although registered initially in London is now an Indian company managed in both India and London. C.A. Bruce, who has strong claims to be the first Briton to discover that tea was growing in India, popularized its use in Britain against the established China tea and was the company's superintendent of tea forests. At its formation, the company had a nominal capital of £500,000 with which it bought the experimental tea nurseries established by the government in Assam as well as the indigenous tea-growing areas. The company soon tried running river steamers to get their tea out and supplies in.[54] The Assam Company held two annual general meetings yearly, one in London in May, the other in Calcutta in August, for the first twenty years of its existence. Different financial statements were issued at these meetings, made up to different dates. The London board decided the dividend which was paid in sterling to the members on the London register and its equivalent in rupees to those on the Calcutta register. After initial teething troubles, these were paid from 1843 at 3 per cent to instill confidence and allow the directors to make calls on the shareholders for further capital. The company experienced hard times in the late 1840s but by 1855 was paying 6 per cent rising to 12 per cent by 1860. By the late 1860s Kilburn & Co, a British-based merchant partnership, had become the managing agents of the Assam Company, at a time when the tea industry was suffering from its previous over-rapid expansion, and the resultant decline in profits is shown in the balance sheets.

The 1920s included seven years of the greatest prosperity the tea industry has ever known, followed by several years of deep recession in the world slump. Production costs increased enormously in the Second World War and Indian independence brought more changes, including a new managing partnership Macneill & Barry who acquired Kilburn & Co in the 1950s. The Assam Company (India) still flourishes and plays a dominant role among the present-day tea companies; it is based in Calcutta with gardens in Assam, Cachar and Darjeeling.

Notes

1. 24 Geo. III c. 57.
2. 7 & 8 Vict. c. 110, clauses 35 and 36.
3. Ibid., clause 42.
4. Ibid., clause 43.
5. For example, 19 & 20 Vict. c. 47, Table B, clauses 72 and 73.

6. 7 Edw. VII c. 50, clause 21.
7. 19 & 20 Geo. V c. 23, clauses 123(2) and 130.
8. H. Howitt, *The History of The Institute of Chartered Accountants in England & Wales & Its Founder Bodies 1870–1965* (Heinemann, 1966).
9. 19 & 20 Vict. c. 47, Table B, clause 70.
10. 18 & 19 Geo. V c. 45, clause 39(3).
11. 11 & 12 Geo. VI c. 38, clauses 127 and 158.
12. S. Pollard, *The Development of the British Economy 1914–1967* (Arnold, 1969) p. 64.
13. Ibid., pp. 214 & 325.
14. The latest development in this field is the preparation of reports and accounts in the form of a video to supplement a written statement.
15. See note 6 above.
16. See 'Introduction'.
17. 7 Edw. VII c. 50, clause 37(1).
18. Ibid., clause 21.
19. 16 Eliz. II c. 81.
20. See note 11 above.
21. See note 8 above.
22. 7 & 8 Vict. c. 110, clause 35.
23. 19 & 20 Vict. c. 47, clause 72.
24. A copy of this model balance sheet is reproduced in S. Marriner, 'Company Financial Statements as Source Material for Business Historians', *Business History*, Vol. 22, No. 2 (1980) pp. 228–9.
25. As note 23 above.
26. 7 Edw. VIII c. 50, clause 21.
27. 18 & 19 Geo. V c. 45, clause 40(1).
28. 11 & 12 Geo. VI c. 38, clause 149.
29. Ibid., schedule 8, clauses 2 to 11.
30. Ibid., clause 129.
31. 19 & 20 Vict. c. 47, Table B, clause 71.
32. 25 & 26 Vict. c. 89, Table A, clause 80.
33. As note 6 above.
34. 18 & 19 Geo. V c. 45, clause 39(4).
35. 11 & 12 Geo. VI c. 38, schedule 8, clauses 12 to 14.
36. Ibid., clause 129.
37. Inchcape archives, ACL 1/2 (305).
38. Marriner, op. cit.
39. 18 & 19 Geo. V c. 45, clause 39(4).
40. E. Green & M.S. Moss, *A Business of National Importance: The Royal Mail Shipping Group, 1902–1937* (Methuen, 1982) is the latest and most comprehensive account.
41. C.H. Wilson & W.J. Reader, *Men and Machines: D. Napier & Son 1808–1958* (Weidenfeld & Nicolson, 1958) pp. 112–3; F.E. Hyde, *Blue Funnel: A History of Alfred Holt & Company of Liverpool 1865–1914* (Liverpool UP, 1957) pp. 145–6 & 147–9.
42. The date of commencement of the firm's financial year was often changed in the course of its history for tax or other reasons. Occasionally a company facing particularly hard times lumped two years' figures together to produce a reasonable set of results.

43. M. Collins, 'The Business of Banking: English Bank Balance Sheets, 1840–80', *Business History*, Vol. 26, No. 1 (1984).
44. T.A. Lee, 'Company Financial Statements: An Essay in Business History 1830–1950' in S. Marriner (ed.), *Business and Businessmen: Studies in Business, Economics and Accounting History* (Liverpool UP, 1978).
45. Ibid., p. 259.
46. Ibid.
47. Ibid., p. 261.
48. J. Mason, 'Accounting Records and Business History', *Business History*, Vol. 24, No. 3 (1982).
49. Ibid., pp. 293–4.
50. Ibid., pp 295–7.
51. T.R. Gourvish & R.G. Wilson, 'Profitability in the Brewing Industry, 1885–1914', *Business History*, Vol. 27, No. 2 (1985).
52. Ibid., p. 157.
53. W. Lewchuk, 'The Return to Capital in the British Motor Vehicle Industry 1896–1939', *Business History*, Vol. 27, No. 1 (1985).
54. A detailed study of this company is H.A. Antrobus, *A History of the Assam Company 1839–1953* (Constable, 1957); see also P.J. Griffiths, *A History of the Indian Tea Industry* (1967).

THE ASSAM COMPANY.

Dr. Profit and Loss Account,

	£ s. d.	£ s. d.	£ s. d.
By weight received ...	3,107 6 9		
	10 4 5		
Cost of Sundries ...		3,117 11 2	
Amount standing against Mr. Kimmond in suspense, now written off ...		160 7 10	
CALCUTTA AGENCY—			
Agents' charges for 12 months, from Dec. 1st, 1869, to Nov. 30th, 1870 ...	1,200 0 0		
Do. commission of 6 annas per chest on 10,788 chest ...	404 11 9		
		1,604 11 9	
Freight of Tea from Assam to Calcutta ...		1,424 12 9	
Brokerage on bills negociated on London ...		147 10 11	
Premium on Treasury drafts remitted to Assam ...		419 6 0	
		£73,082 17 2	
PAYMENTS IN ENGLAND—			
Rent of Office, Salaries, Directors' and Auditors' Fees, and other charges of London Establishment ...	2,836 12 0		
Miscellaneous charges ...	269 4 10		
Office Furniture written off ...	222 3 9		
Interest on advances ...	384 2 10		
		3,712 3 5	
Balance ...		*43,342 6 1	
		£120,137 6 8	

*(Out of this an interim dividend of 5 per cent. was paid in January last.)

JOHN BENNETT, *Accountant.*

COMPANY.

Cr. CROP 1870.

	£ s. d.	£ s. d.	£ s. d.
By proceeds of Tea of this crop, sold to June 16th, 1871, as per account sales—			
Invoice weight ... 1,182,522 lbs.			
Loss by taring ... 17,583 "			
Account sales weight ... 1,164,939 lbs.		121,092 11 2	
Less—Insurance ...	3,726 9 4		
Freight, dock charges, and brokerage ...	8,260 13 8		
Discount allowed to buyers on teas sold ...	1,570 15 2		
	13,557 18 2		
		107,534 13 0	
Remaining to be sold—			
114,405 lbs., estimated at ...		9,300 0 0	
By Sale of Tea in India ...		8 12 0	
" Sale of Tea Seed ...		1,043 2 0	
" Rent of Rookang Gardens ...		100 0 0	
" Difference between irrecoverable advances, and fines and penalties recovered from sundry contractors and others ...		302 3 6	
" Exchange (in favor of the Company) ...		1,848 16 2	
		£120,137 6 8	

THE ASSAM COMPANY.

Dr. BALANCE SHEET OF THE ASSAM COMPANY, TO 31ST DECEMBER, 1870. Cr.

CAPITAL AND LIABILITIES.

	£ s. d.	£ s. d.
To Capital—10,000 Shares at £50 each.		
Amount paid on 9,358 Shares	187,160 0 0	
Forfeited 419 "		
Not issued 223 "	6,177 10 0	
10,000 Shares.		193,337 10 0
To Liabilities—		
Balance of Bills drawn in India previous to 31st December, 1870, not yet due	39,000 0 0	
Open accounts in England and India	4,466 15 8	
		43,466 15 8
To Profit and Loss, 1868 crop		528 18 3
" 1869 crop, as per last statement	18,663 4 4	
Less difference in finally adjusting with Brokers	51 13 9	
	18,611 10 7	
Deduct 2nd Dividend of 3½ per cent. declared and paid on this crop	6,550 12 0	
		12,060 18 7
Profit and Loss, 1870 crop, estimated at		*43,342 6 1
		£292,736 8 7

*(Out of this has already been paid a dividend of 5 per cent.)

PROPERTY AND ASSETS.

	£ s. d.	£ s. d.	£ s. d.
By probable value of the several Gardens and Factories the property of the Company in Assam			193,337 10 0*
" Value of Live Stock, Tools, Boats, &c.			6,484 19 2
" Cash in hand—			
ENGLAND—At Bankers	1,271 16 2		
Petty Cash	17 7 3		
		1,289 3 5	
INDIA—In Calcutta	1,548 5 5		
In Nazerah	1,789 19 8		
		3,338 5 1	
" Advances in Assam		5,717 8 8	
" Debts due to the Company—			
Messrs. Thompson	6,753 1 10		
East and West India Docks	2 8 11		
Sundries	562 3 8		
		7,317 14 5	
" Stock of Tea of 1870 crop remaining to be sold on 31st December, 1870		76,251 7 10	
			£292,736 8 7

*Having no reliable data on which to estimate the value of our gardens, we put their value at the amount of the paid-up capital, say £193,337..10. The Shareholders will of course estimate them at more or less, according to their own views and knowledge.

H. M. KENNEDAY, *Chairman.*
WM. TITE, *Deputy Chairman.*
H. W. WINSHURST, *Secretary.*

We, the undersigned Auditors of the Assam Company do hereby certify that we have carefully examined the above Accounts of the Company, by comparing them with the Books and the English Vouchers, and find the same to be correct.

London, 2, East India Avenue,
June 16th, 1871.

JAMES CARSON,
SAML. S. BANKART, } *Auditors.*
JOHN BENNETT, *Accountant.*

10. Pages from the profit and loss account and balance sheet of the Assam Co for year ending 31 December 1870.
Source: Inchcape plc archives.

11   Staff records

Original purpose

Records of the employees of a firm are scanty for the nineteenth century and appear in quanity only as a result of legislation affecting pay, conditions, pensions and national insurance in the later twentieth century. Although some record of staff who held shares in a company was kept in the register of members, it was only by virtue of them being shareholders and the information is meagre. In the eighteenth or early nineteenth centuries, employers kept some records relating to their staff but by modern standards they were unsystematic and casual. In the domestic system it was quite normal for the capitalist to keep workmen's books in which to set down his transactions with his labour force.[1] Given the irregular contacts between master and men, the shortage of coins and notes, the regular indebtedness of some families and that the workmen usually used materials supplied, and paid for, by the merchant, it behove him accurately to record all these scattered transactions in order to keep a track of debts owed him, and materials outstanding.[2]

Even with the growth of factory employment, personnel records remained primitive. Wages books were the most likely form of documents to be kept, combining a list of employees and their wage rates.[3] Where workers were on piece rates, their earnings were often based on a card or ticket which recorded their output for each day. These, however, were seen as ephemeral and rarely survive. Where records were kept of a more durable nature, they might note the production of each employee or the aggregate output of a team or shop for the day or week and the employer used this as much for recording output as checking on employees. The Govan Collieries certainly kept such records as did Kenricks the Midlands hardware firm in the early nineteenth century.[4]

The reasons for this paucity of documents about employees lies partly in firm size. Although large-scale factories caught the attention of contemporaries, they were in fact not typical: the average size of work unit was only 20 or 30 in the mid-nineteenth century.[5] With such small-scale firms the employer knew all his workers personally, and thus had less need to keep detailed records. He could remember names and skills, personal details of background and address, and roughly how long the individual had been with the firm. There was little necessity to commit these details to paper; without the pressure of employment legislation or strong trade unions, the employer often kept many of his personnel files in his head.

There were, of course, the exceptional firms which took an above-average interest in their employees. The Crowley dynasty commenced as manufacturers of iron goods in the north-east in the late seventeenth century. Later they integrated backwards into iron rolling and slitting and also opened a large warehouse at Greenwich. This firm drew up a very full set of instructions for its workforce, not merely on how they should carry out their duties but also their conditions of employment. This was necessary because the family chose to live in London near their market and where they could exert influence on government, for many of their sales went to fulfil navy contracts, while most of the work was carried out in Northumberland and Durham. This entailed delegation from the family to managers, and to minimize the managers' discretion the family drew up detailed instructions covering all aspects of the operation of the business.[6] In general those firms started by Quakers were concerned to be fair to their workforce and so kept rather more detailed records. The Reading biscuit makers, Huntley and Palmers, were considered good employers in the mid-nineteenth century and certainly showed a desire to improve the lot of their workforce, but even so very little evidence survives of their workers' pay, conditions or even names and dates of service.[7]

By the late nineteenth and early twentieth centuries a number of factors combined to encourage employers to keep fuller records of their labour force. The growth of large-scale firms, partly through internal growth and partly through the merger manias which came in waves commencing in the late 1880s, meant that it was increasingly difficult for employers to remember details of workforces that were measured in hundreds and might be on several sites.[8] The slow growth of trade-union membership following the legal changes of the 1870s, which permitted the formation of unions and granted the right to strike and picket peacefully,[9] caused employers to give more thought to their labour relations and to feel the need to write down more, for example writing rule books or drawing up contracts of employment. The other influence was the beginnings of professionalism in the field of employee relations. In the late nineteenth century some firms began engaging lady welfare workers whose specific task was to look after the female staff. Firms like Cadbury, Rowntree and Hudson Scott, which were all run by Quaker families, and Boots, were among the first to adopt this practice.[10] Their appointment came about because some firms were employing large numbers of women in their factories and the lady factory inspectors, who were first appointed in 1893, began to show up the poor conditions among female employees. This was reinforced by the social investigations of the late nineteenth century into the causes of poverty and aided by employers beginning to see their labour force as a resource to be used efficiently.

These lady welfare workers began to systematize the information kept on employees, instituting staff record cards, becoming involved with recruitment and so introducing application forms. This brought into being a comprehensive set of personnel documents for the first time in many firms. The welfare workers were also important in that they marked the first steps on the path to professionalism of the personnel function. In 1913 an Association of Industrial Welfare Workers was established with sixty members and this was to lead in 1946, via a number of other like-minded associations, to the formation of the Institute of Personnel Management[11] which is now the premier society concerned with employee relations. Just like other professional bodies, these organizations encouraged the introduction of standard systems of keeping records in a wide range of areas: application forms, references, absences caused by sickness, disciplinary actions, wages or salaries earned, from the 1930s the administration of aptitude tests, holiday entitlement, training courses and pension rights.

Today certain staff records have to be kept by law, for example the Employment Protection Act of 1978 and the Employment Act of 1980. Staff records are also maintained so that data is available in case of any dispute with a trade union or staff association, or in the event of needing evidence before an industrial tribunal. Generally, however, until very recent times employees were not perceived as requiring extensive documentation and thus the bulk of such records were created only in the modern period.

Sources

Staff records are found mainly in the archives of the company itself. As confidential documents, access to them is usually restricted. The files on employees, even after their resignation or retirement, are usually closed for many years: 50 or 100 is not unusual. As a result this is one of the most difficult sets of documents to track down and explore fully. Modern staff records are often maintained for many years by the departments and officers who created them: by recruitment personnel, pension staff, payment offices and office administration generally. This type of document is among the last to be sent to archives or record repositories — especially in the case of pension details. They must be kept until the person and his/her dependents are dead and the firm no longer has any obligations or responsibilities to the individual, which can be decades after the employee originally joined the firm.

Records of staff are not found among the statutory documents kept by most firms in the nineteenth century. The Public Record Office files of defunct companies, for example, relate principally to the capital structure of firms and their activities, rather than the details of the workforce. There are some exceptions, however. In so far as crews of merchant ships may be regarded as employees of shipping lines and master-owners, albeit temporarily, the certifications of their employment, known as crew lists, are available. Current lists are kept by the Registrar-General of Shipping and Seamen at Cardiff, non-current crew lists are to be found at individual county record offices, at the PRO, National Maritime Museum, and in the archives of the Maritime History Group, Memorial University of Newfoundland.[12] They give details of place of birth, place of joining ship, age, wages and rations issued to seamen. The census returns kept by the PRO in Portugal Street, London W2, also indicate details of employment. However, they describe occupation in general terms rather than specific employment in a particular firm. They nevertheless give an indication of staff numbers in the case of a town or locality dominated by a particular company. The census could be used to complement scanty staff records elsewhere.

Much information on staff can be gleaned from company magazines, but these are generally confined to large companies and to the modern period. Old albums can occasionally be found of works outings and celebration dinners, with photographs of employees. Photographs taken in the works may also be found, giving some idea of manning levels, the total number of workers and the sexual breakdown in a firm or department. Often such mementoes of working for a company, which dominated the lives of many people for whom social, geographical and employment mobility was rare, are to be found in the personal possession of ex-employees, rather than in the archives of the company itself. The employees were likely to be interested in this material and keep copies as souvenirs. Thus, in seeking staff records, it can be a good idea for a researcher to contact a firm's personnel director, or senior employees, to try and gain information on previous workers. Here oral history techniques are especially useful.[13] The reminiscences of employees of their conditions of work, their attitudes to the firm and their relationships with other people at work can help fill gaps in written documentation. Some employees note down memoirs of their companies, which are especially useful in understanding employment conditions as well as the history of the company as a whole. For example, many expatriate workers write reminiscences on their return to Britain, and some have been known to compile these whilst interned by the enemy during the Second World War.[14]

Retired staff members are often willing to assist researchers considering the human relations side of a company's history. They are surprised that anyone should be interested and usually have time to help, pride in their working achievements and strong opinions on the company. They may turn up useful press cuttings, photographs, items presented on retirement and anecdotes of fellow employees. The main problem in finding personnel records is that the vast majority of firms in the nineteenth century did not keep systematic information on their workers. Those businesses that did create any such documentation often perceived it as of no lasting interest and disposed of it fairly rapidly after its immediate functional use was past. This, of course, is not to deny the survival of wage books, or workmen's books in public and corporate archives, but they are the exceptions rather than the general rule. Although more firms began maintaining staff records in the twentieth century, it was not until after the Second World War that these became anything like comprehensive, and then they are most likely to be closed to a researcher outside the firm because of their personal nature.[15] Thus where they would be open to the researcher they rarely exist; where they exist they are rarely open.

The information they contain

From twentieth-century personnel files it is possible to build up considerable insight into individual employees from such records as application forms, appraisals of individual performance, disciplinary notes, details of negotiations with trade unions, overtime slips, holidays and sick leave, pension and redundancy details, information on temporary staff and notes on staffing generally, such as their mobility through departments and their relationships with new technology. However, it must be emphasized that the amount and depth of material available to the researcher usually decreases as one goes further back into a company's history.

Some staff records give the date of joining a company, age, wages and responsibilities. The India General Steam Navigation Company Ltd, for example, kept this data together with notes on performance and ability, relationships with colleagues, social background and marital status, attitude to work and prospects for promotion. The survival of documents as old as this, dating from the 1930s is rare. Most such material was destroyed when the personnel they referred to died or left. This volume, which describes nearly a hundred individuals, was constantly updated to include reports on their progress, with a view to pay rises or cuts, promotions or demotions, and transfers to other departments or branches. The comments are generally candid and the personnel officer or manager is obviously stating exactly how he feels. It is very unlikely that the people discussed in this volume would have been allowed access to it. It is less common to find such full information on operatives, as distinct from salaried staff who were 'white-collar' workers. The distinction between the two types of employee was sharper before the Second World War and as staff enjoyed higher status, less fluctuating incomes and might aspire to junior management they were of more interest to their employers and fuller particulars were kept about them.

Other staff records which may be discovered by a business historian include overtime books, giving the reasons for requiring overtime to be worked, such as in the case of a firm's dividend payment needing extra administrative work, the hours worked and rates. Informal notebooks, kept as aides memoire by branch managers for example, can provide details of names, ages and wages. For the nineteenth century and earlier, the information available is much more patchy and less systematic: survival is a matter of accident rather than intent. That said, those documents which do still exist can contain much interesting material. Workmen's books are found occasionally and these give the names of workmen, their trade or skill, their earnings or payments and whether these were in cash or kind. They usually also show whether an individual was in debt to his employer as was not uncommon for workers in the 'domestic system', whether the earnings were subject to seasonal or weekly variation, the frequency of payment and whether it was based on time or piece rates.

In some cases there are rule books still extant. The iron-working dynasty of Crowley drew up extensive 'laws' for the conduct of their workmen and fortunately these have survived to portray working conditions and practices.[16] Similarly, some of the early factory masters maintained books recording conditions of employment such as any bonuses or holidays granted; the works outings as a special occasion was often recorded[17] as were any meals, feasts or other social event organized and paid for by the employers. These also provide some idea of the negative side of motivation, the fines levied for misconduct, wasting materials, or arriving late, and occasionally a note of a workman being sacked. How representative those records are which do survive may be open to question but, since it is mainly a matter of chance as to which survived and which have been lost, there is no systematic bias to them. Although sporadic and patchy, they contain some fascinating insights into employment conditions.

Uses

Staff records are of particular use and interest to genealogists and biographers, and are also vital to the company historian for no narrative of the life of a firm would be complete without discussion of the role of the workforce. A measure of a company's size and importance may be gained from the number it employed. Details of labour force can show whether a business was capital- or labour-intensive and if it specialized in a particular activity, or carried on a range of operations. Staff records can show the proportion of employees that were 'white collar', the range of their ages and the breakdown between the sexes. Staffing levels can give an indication of a firm's growth and decline for usually when it was expanding and its profits rising it could afford more workers; when it fell on hard times, sackings and redundancies often followed.

A company's attitude to its staff, as seen in its records about them, reveals much about its overall nature — was it an old-fashioned firm, or modern and progressive? In the nineteenth century, was it caring and paternalistic? Did it provide housing or schools for its workers, did it try to influence the attitudes and values of its operatives by careful control of the social infrastructure? Did it provide savings banks, libraries and churches but not pubs as Cadbury at Bournville or Lever at Port Sunlight.[18] In the twentieth century, does it provide many 'perks' such as scholarships for employees' children, company cars, Christmas presents, discounts on its products or services, interest-free loans for season tickets, help with mortgages, bonuses related to the profits of the business, medical and dental facilities, social clubs and various outings? What is the management's attitude to misdemeanours by its workers? Were they encouraged to hold shares in the company? Does it try to inspire loyalty among its employees by creating an image of care and community? These questions can be answered from a systematic examination of staff records. The impact on the labour force of new technology may also be assessed from these documents.

Another area of concern to both the economic and social historian is the role of labour organizations such as trade unions and friendly societies. Most labour history has been written from the point of view of the inevitable growth of trade unions with more than a little of the Whig view of history creeping in. Equally important, but little explored, are the attitudes of management to labour, how managers tried to train and motivate their workforce, whether they hindered or encouraged operatives to organize and whether they recognized trade unions. These managerial facets of labour could be explored from a study of staff records in combination with other business documents. Thus staff records are useful to the general historian as well as the genealogist. Their main drawback is their paucity in the early period. However, with time and patience a reasonably full picture of an employee may be built up. Personnel documentation of some companies, such as the India General Steam Navigation Co, are very full and detail the personality and attitudes of the employees so that they begin to emerge as real people. Altogether these records can provide great insight but they vary enormously from company to company in quality and quantity and can pose great problems for researchers in terms of access because of confidentiality.

Cross-references to other documents

Registers of members (q.v.) can also include information on employees. When family firms were launched as public companies, it was usual for some of the richer staff to take shares in the company. If the share denomination was small enough, quite junior employees might buy a few. The names, addresses, occupations and details of the investment may be found in this source. It was in the interest of the firm for its employees to hold shares in order to promote loyalty to the company and concern for its best interest. Some firms aided their employees to purchase shares. Details of staff numbers and wages are occasionally shown in annual reports and accounts (q.v.) as an expense of the company. A total wage bill alone is not of much use unless the number of employees is known and can be used as a divisor to calculate average wage per employee. If only the aggregate wage bill is known, the approximate average wage for that industry and that period derived from other sources can be used to give a rough idea of employee numbers.

Sometimes details of staff appointments were given in board minute books (q.v.), especially if they were senior or key people or recruited for special duties. Another reason for the board to discuss employees was when there were problems of indiscipline or misdemeanour of any sort. Such matters were usually reported to the directors for their information and approval of the course of action proposed. Similar causes might lead to individuals being mentioned in diaries (q.v.) or, if they were working at some distance from the head office, in letter books (q.v.). This was particularly true for mining companies based in Britain whose centre of operations was in a foreign country where the metalliferous ore was to be found. Often a chairman's statement (q.v.) would include references to particular achievements, such as help in securing contracts, exceptionally long and distinguished service, exemplary behaviour in times of stress, such as in wartime, and in their contribution to the success of a firm generally. Few chairmen finished an annual summary of their company's performance without thanking the people who made it possible.

Works using this source

A good example of the use of memoirs and oral history to describe the living and working conditions of staff is Charles Allen's trilogy on expatriate workers in the early twentith century, which was serialized on BBC Radio 4.[19] More formal business histories have employed this source too. Besides the copious quantity of material published on the trade union movement, some of which in passing uses staff records of firms, most accounts of the development of a business pay attention to the attitude of the firm to its employees. Extensive use of workmen's books was made in studies of the domestic system such as that of Sigsworth on Black Dyke Mills and Ashton on the file-making activities of Peter Stubs of Warrington.[20] Those industries which were labour-intensive were often the pioneers of new methods of dealing with labour and Corley's study of Huntley and Palmers, the Reading biscuit makers, show how a paternalistic Quaker firm treated its labour force,[21] while Chapman's work on Boots the Chemist and Reader's on Metal Box show the beginnings of the emergence of a professional personnel approach via the lady welfare workers.[22] Many histories draw on material falling under the general category of staff records, including Coleman on Courtaulds, Floud on the British machine tool industry in the late nineteenth century, Hume and Moss on Beardmore, and Trebilcock on Vickers.[23] The article referred to as an example of the use of board minute books, by Church and Miller on the British motor industry, makes interesting use of oral history records provided by members of staff, especially from the oral history section of the Ford archives.[24]

The example

The India General Steam Navigation Company was formed in the 1850s to run river steamers which carried the tea crop from Assam in India to the country's principal ports. It was registered in London, which assisted in the survival of its documentation, but was operated only in India, where it employed engineers, pilots, masters of its vessels, clerks, cleaners, cooks and shipyard workers to maintain its vessels and railway interests. European staff generally filled the management posts but a great number of native staff were employed across the board. It is clear from reading these reports that living in India was far from easy — reports of ill-health, broken marriages and general feelings of dissatisfaction are common. This volume provides considerable insight into expatriate working life — the importance of home leave, relatively early retirements, social events and facilities planned by the firm, and the relationships between European and native staff.[25]

Notes

1. For example, T.S. Ashton, *An Eighteenth Century Industrialist, Peter Stubs of Warrington 1756–1806* (Manchester UP, 1939) pp. 9–11.
2. D.C. Coleman, *The Domestic System in Industry* (Historical Association, 1960) remains a good introduction to the subject.
3. For example, John Foster kept a 'spinners' wage book' from 1828–41 for his female mill workers: E.M. Sigsworth, *Black Dyke Mills: A History* (Liverpool UP, 1958) pp. 154–8.
4. P.L. Payne, 'The Govan Collieries 1804–05' *Business History*, Vol. 3, No. 1 (1960); R.A. Church, *Kenricks in Hardware: A Family Business 1791–1966* (David & Charles, 1969). The latter firm kept a 'Hiring Book' for the period 1827–40: p. 55.
5. P. Mathias, *The First Industrial Nation* (Methuen, 1969) p. 207; E. Jones, *Industrial Architecture in Britain 1750–1939* (Batsford, 1985) p. 47.
6. M.W. Flinn, *Men of Iron: The Crowleys in the Early Iron Industry* (Edinburgh UP, 1962) chap. 13; *The Law Book of the Crowley Ironworks* (Surtees Soc, 1957).
7. T.A.B. Corley, *Quaker Enterprise in Biscuits: Huntley and Palmers of Reading 1822–1972* (Hutchinson, 1972) p. 96.
8. L. Hannah, *The Rise of the Corporate Economy* (Methuen, 1983) pp. 21–4; P.L. Cottrell, *Industrial Finance 1830–1914: The Finance and Organization of English Manufacturing Industry* (Methuen, 1980) p. 189.
9. J. Lovell, *British Trade Unions, 1875–1933* (Macmillan, 1977).
10. S.D. Chapman, *Jesse Boot of Boots the Chemist* (Hodder & Stoughton, 1974) pp. 168–70; W.J. Reader, *Metal Box: A History* (Heinemann, 1976) pp. 28–30.
11. M.M. Niven, *Personnel Management 1913–63* (IPM, 1967) pp. 31–7.
12. Approximately 10 per cent of this archive is preserved at the PRO and a further 10 per cent at the National Maritime Museum with a few scattered holdings at local record offices. The remainder is preserved in Newfoundland.
13. For an interesting example, see G. Lanning, C. Peaker *et al.*, *Making Cars* (RKP, 1985).
14. Memoirs of expatriates living in Bahrain and Basra, and others working in the Siamese teak trade in the early years of this century were useful in writing S.K. Jones, *Two Centuries of Trading* (Macmillan, 1986) as were notes of life on the East African coast in the 1920s.

15. P. Buckland, 'The Public Responsibilities of Record Keepers' in Y. Buckland, *Approaches to Problems in Records Management: 1. Personnel Records* (Records Management Group, 1985).
16. See note 6 above.
17. A. Delgado, *The Annual Outing and Other Excursions* (Allen & Unwin, 1977) chap. 3.
18. I.A. Williams, *The Firm of Cadbury, 1831–1931* (Constable, 1931) chaps. 3 & 4; C. Wilson, *The History of Unilever: A Study in Economic Growth and Social Change* (Cassell, 1954) Vol.1, chap. 10.
19. C. Allen, *Plain Tales from the Raj* (Futura, 1977); *Tales From the Dark Continent* (Futura, 1980); *Tales from the South China Sea* (Futura, 1984).
20. Sigsworth, op. cit.; Ashton, op. cit.
21. Corley, op. cit.
22. See note 10 above.
23. D.C. Coleman, *Courtaulds* (Clarendon, 1969); R. Floud, *The British Machine Tool Industry* (Cambridge UP, 1976); J.R. Hume & M.S. Moss, *Beardmore. The History of a Scottish Industrial Giant* (Heinemann, 1979); C. Trebilcock, *The Vickers Brothers; Armaments and Enterprise, 1854–1914* (Europa, 1977).
24. R. Church & M. Miller, 'The Big Three: Competition, Management and Marketing in the British Motor Industry, 1922–1939' in B.E. Supple (ed.), *Essays in British Business History* (Oxford UP, 1977).
25. More details will be found in A. Brame, *The India General Steam Navigation Company Limited* (London, 1900) and P.J. Griffiths, *A History of the Joint Steamer Companies* (priv pub., 1979).

Date of appointment ... 1931 ... ...

T... ... ...

Mr. _____ - Panchugunj. Joined 1931 - age 39.
At the time of serious shoal trouble - necessitating transhipment between Markuli and Panchugunj - Mr. _____ showed a remarkable lack of initiative and interest and we had to send up special traffic officers to deal with the situation. We also had considerable difficulty in forcing him to retire his Head Clerk who was inclined to run the Agency's affairs, rather than Mr. _____ Two or three Senior Planters, whose opinion we respect, suggested that it would be in the interests of the Joint Companies' Tea Traffic from Cachar if we were to transfer Mr. _____ elsewhere.

We then warned Mr. _____ that, unless his work showed a considerable improvement, he had better look out for other employment when the time came for him to go on furlough. This suggestion succeeded in shaking him out of his complacency and, during the Silchar floods in July 1946, he displayed some welcome activity and interest. His relationship with planters, however, apparently continues to be unimpressive and we feel compelled to take their advice to transfer Mr. _____ elsewhere, without waiting for the R.S. to insist on this course.

Mr. _____ is very difficult to place as there are so

many posts which, under present conditions, are definitely beyond his ability and activity; we shall have to find a quiet spot like Monghyr for him and we would, in fact, gladly exchange this nomination with the R.S. for Kokilamukh. Married - no children.

... May ... ... 1st ... 1931 ... ...

Furlough

(commenced) ... of R.S. ... of ...

Managing Agent Report.

... letter ... 7.9.31 ... ... an appointment ... ... of ... ... as to ... promise & prospects.

D/o ... ...

_____ (1st Assistant Goalundo). Was appointed 1st Assistant Naraingunge in November/32 and transferred to Goalundo in October/33. Has generally done good work, and can be considered a fairly promising officer.

Is being transferred at the beginning of this month to the Head Office Accounts Department in place of Mr. Jackson on leave.

L/O letter of 7.1.37.

Goalundo. Mr. _____ has given satisfaction on the whole and it is obvious that such ability as he has is of more value at Mofussil Stations than in Head Office. We fear he will never be a brilliant officer, but he is at any rate fairly reliable and most industrious. Lack of initiative seems to be his chief failing and this may, of course, be eradicated in time.

11. Pages from a staff record book of the India General Steam Navigation Co of the 1930s and 1940s.
   Source: Inchcape plc archives.

———— Was transferred to Narayanganj this month
to act as 1st Assistant during Mr Berry's absence on leave. This
appointment is usually reserved for an R.S.nominee but, since we
have agreed to Mr Macaulay acting for Mr Berry, we have, temporarily
the nomination for the post of 1st Assistant.

This is likely to be a critical period in Mr ———— career
with the I.G. He has never been very severely tested and has
managed to worry along so far without getting into trouble, but
we fear that he is rather slow and lacking in initiative.

D/O letter of 30.12.37.

"Chhatak. Owing to the unfortunate death of Mr Aidya,
"it has been found necessary to transfer Mr ———— from
"J'ganj to carry on until the return of Mr Phelan, who is
"expected back at the end of March, 1938. Mr ———— has made
"a satisfactory start at this Agency."

Mr.———— commenced the year as 1st assistant, but was
very shortly thereafter transferred to Narsingnj to act as 1st
assistant at that Agency. Later, on the return of Mr. Berry
from furlough, Mr. ———— was transferred to J'ganj to relieve Mr.
Johns who, in his turn, went on Home leave ———— Mr. ———— place
at Goalundo was taken by Mr. Howard who, we are pleased to state,
has been quite a success. Both Messrs. ———— and Howard have
come on a lot during 1937.

D/O dated Calcutta 17/7/40.

Mr.———————— - joined 1931. Aged 32. Narayanganj.
Considering his youth and limited experience, he has made a good
start at Narayanganj. His ability is still developing and he is
acquiring more confidence in himself. Somewhat apt to leave too
much to his assistants and, in other cases, to leave the responsibility for a decision to Head Office without having made definite
recommendations himself - a fault which should be eradicated with
more experience. A tendency to "take things for granted" - he
needs to take more pains in some of his case work and to acquire
the knack of spotting "snags".

Relations with superior authority quite satisfactory,
and these would be improved considerably were he not so frightened
of "Calcutta authority". Relations with fellow employees good,
except that he sometimes finds difficulty with the Senior men in
other Departments, which is somewhat aggravated by an air of pomp-
osity which he has. Relations with the R.S. quite satisfactory.
He is popular in the District with Europeans and Indians alike,
but he would carry considerably more weight if and when he is able
to develop a "civic sense of responsibility" and undertake more
public duties. Married.

D/O dated Calcutta 1/5/41:

Mr.———————— Narayanganj - joined 1931 - aged 33.
Mr ———— still continues as our Agent at Narayanganj, but we have
not felt able to confirm him in this post. He has been very
fortunate in having the able assistance of two very good
Assistants in Mr Matthews and Captain Bell (R.S. nominee for the
post of Transport Officer). The Agency runs very smoothly, but
in its working we discern the hands of Messrs. Matthews and Bell
rather than the directing control and inspiration of Mr

Mr   ability continues to develop, but not as
rapidly as we had hoped for in view of the valuable experience
which he has been enjoying at Narayanganj. Mr   is undoubtedly
trying his very best, but he has his definite limitations. He
has, of course, the advantage of now knowing this rather
complicated district very thoroughly.

The good results shown by Messrs. Matthews and Cell are,
we feel, due more to their own loyalty, keenness, initiative, and
ability rather than to the direction and control of Mr   and
he somewhat lacks personal authority in his dealings with the
European staff, although he is quite good with Indians. A little
wooden and stubborn, Mr   is not receptive of other people's
hints or ideas, and he prefers to plod along his own line - he
should be more adaptable.

The time has come for us to decide whether or not we
should press the R.S. to agree to his confirmation as Joint Agent
at Narayanganj, and in view of the claims of Assistants like
Messrs. Allaker and Jackson who are three and four years senior
to Mr   we would not be justified in trying to keep Mr
at Narayanganj. We have therefore decided to transfer him to
Kokilamukh to relieve Mr Priggs who will in turn relieve
Mr Allaker at Penchuganj to go to Narayanganj.

D/O dated Calcutta 10.5.41

Mr   removal from Narayanganj does not involve
him in any discredit. In being given the chance in what was
expected to be Mr Berry's temporary absence, he was stepped
over the heads of several seniors, and only an exceptional
performance would have justified his confirmation. To this
extent only has he proved a failure, in that he has not proved
to be better than others who have prior claims to such a senior
post, and we have no reason to doubt that he will give every
satisfaction in some less exacting post.

Relations with superior authority quite satisfactory,
but he seems unable to benefit from advice given to him.
Relations with the R.S. quite satisfactory, but they do not
feel that he is the right man in the right place at Narayanganj.
Popular in the district with those Europeans and Indians with
whom he comes into contact, but he does not carry much weight.
Married.

D/O dated Calcutta 22/4/43

Mr   Kokilamukh. Aged 35½. Service 12 years.
Married. No child. Mr   of whom considerable hopes were held
at one time, failed to acquit himself sufficiently well when given
the opportunity of succeeding Mr Berry at Narayanganj, and has
reverted to the status justified by his length of service. He does
not like Kokilamukh residential arrangements and has made several
totally unacceptable proposals with a view to ameliorating his lot.
We doubt if these attempts have endeared him to the R.S., but we
understand that they held quite a good opinion of his capabilities,
and so far as we are aware, he has given average satisfaction and
need cause us no immediate anxiety.

D/O dated Calcutta 3/5/46.

Mr   Penchuganj. Joined 1931 - age 37. Was
transferred from Kokilamukh to Penchuganj
in November 1943 to take the place of Mr Priggens who was transferred
to Tezpur to take over from Mr. E.A. Smith.

During his last six months at Kokilamukh, Mr.   work
deteriorated and subsequent incumbents at Kokilamukh have shown up Mr.
unfavourably by comparison.

11. Pages from a staff record book of the India General Steam Navigation Co
    of the 1930s and 1940s.
    Source: Inchcape plc archives.

When he was moved to Fenchuganj we warned Mr. _____ that his
tenure of Kokilamukh and done nothing to erase the not too happy
feelings resulting from his charge of Maraingang Agency and we
emphasised that Fenchuganj would be his last chance of convincing us
that he was capable of charge of senior Agencies, and that he should
not be relegated to minor Agencies. We regret to report that Mr.
Morby's record at Fenchuganj has been most unsatisfactory. He has
been slack, weak and incompetent and quite incapable of dealing with
normal emergencies which have arisen in the form of labour difficulties
and blocks on account of shoal troubles. The Head Clerk is a strong,
though not in other respects desirable, character and Mr. _____ has
been content to let him run the Agency and he has failed to appreciate
the fact that the responsibility is the Agent's and not the Head
Clerk's.

We quite realise that Mr. _____ is long overdue furlough and
we had in fact placed him No.1 on our list - Mr. Morby however refused
to consider furlough until well after the War in Europe has ended - we
endeavoured to persuade him that it was in his own interests to take
furlough as soon as possible but he was adamant though very inconsistent
in giving five different and contradictory reasons for wishing to defer
his furlough. He assured us that he felt in the best of health and we
therefore agreed to allow him to postpone his furlough which we think
will have to be his last. When he does eventually take his furlough,
we think that we shall have to tell him to look for other employment.
Married, no children.   Please turn to Page 189.

12   Patents

Original purpose

The value of a patent is that when properly registered it gives the patentee a monopoly of the process or product for a specific period. In English law the period was normally fourteen years until 1920 and sixteen thereafter.[1] This monopoly gives the patentee the opportunity of reaping a financial reward from his inventive efforts. To be sure of obtaining such a privilege, the patentee needs to submit the required documents to the Patent Office and pay the necessary fee.

The history of English patent law is tangled and combative. Early English monarchs used monopolies and patents as a method of raising revenue or rewarding loyal supporters. This brought patents into disrepute, aggravated by the practice of granting monopolies in the trade or production of basic necessities, rather than for a new idea or process. Resentment came to a head in the Civil War, when the king's use of such devices played a small but significant part in bringing about the break between him and Parliament. The basis of modern patent law was laid in the 1625 'Act concerning Monopolies and Dispensations with Penal Laws and Forfeiture thereof', more simply known as the Statute of Monopolies.[2] Although primarily intended to outlaw monopolies and privileges, section 6 of the Act specifically excluded from such a ban any 'true and first inventor within this realm'. This followed earlier speeches by Francis Bacon in 1601 and a court ruling in 1615 suggesting the only basis for a monopoly should be a new manufacture.[3]

The principle that an inventor should have exclusive use of his invention over a period of normally fourteen years was thus enshrined in an Act of Parliament. The process of registering a patent remained expensive, and the inventor was subject to a degree of hostility at least until the early nineteenth century because of the monopoly his patent gave. As it was normally granted with no specification other than the title, the defence of a patent before a jury could be expensive and time-consuming.

It was not until the 1852 Act[4] that the grant of a patent needed to be followed within six months by the filing of a specification, though the practice had become increasingly common. In so doing the inventor's defence of his patent and prosecution of any infringements was made easier. In 1883, legislation required a specification to be filed within nine months and checked by the Patent Office before the patent was granted as to 'whether the nature of the invention has been fairly described and the application, specification and drawings, if any, have been prepared in the prescribed manner'.[5] The 1902 Act, which applied from 1905, required the Patent Office to check that the patent had not 'been wholly or in part claimed or described in any specification published before' and although it gave the examiner power to insist on inserting references to any previous relevant patent, it did not allow refusal of a patent altogether.[6] This was rectified by the 1907 Act.[7] The 1949 Act merely brought together the outstanding pieces of legislation and codified them into one coherent Act.[8]

Thus the original purpose of a patent has remained the same since the seventeenth century, though the amount of information filed has varied depending on legislation and perceived self-interest. The cost of obtaining a patent has become less expensive in real terms over time; Charles Dickens, writing in the middle of the nineteenth century, suggested it could cost over £95 to register a patent for England, for the whole of the UK about £300.[9] The former represented well over two years' wages for a working man. After 1852 the cost came down to £175 for fees and stamp duty for the whole of the UK for fourteen years, was further reduced to £158 for the same protection in the 1883 Act, and fell to £95 under the 1892 Act.[10]

Sources

The best source of a patent is the Science Reference Library (SRL), see 'Useful addresses', which is a division of the British Library. The reading rooms currently contain printed copies of all patents since 1617 which are available with minimal delay, though the PRO holds the original drafts. The researcher needs only the number and the year of issue in order to locate the relevant patent. The National Library of Wales and a number of provincial libraries, such as Birmingham, Glasgow, Leeds, Liverpool, Manchester and Newcastle upon Tyne, receive full sets of printed patents, indexes and abridgements. Many other major libraries also used to receive these, but cost considerations mean they now only take the less bulky abridgements. However, many have retained their sets and have good historical collections. Although often in basements or stores, they should be available to historians without easy access to London. The researcher should not confuse the SRL and the Patent Office, the role of the latter being essentially to register, check and grant new patents of aspiring inventors.

The SRL contains a number of aids for finding patents. If the enquirer is ignorant of the patent number but knows the name of the patentee, there are annual indexes of patentees to consult. Some are now bound together and the years 1617 and 1852 are in one large volume. They are arranged alphabetically by the patentee's surname against which the patent number, a brief specification and the date lodged are given. If the researcher is interested in an industry or a particular type of machine, then the 'Abridgements' volumes can be used. These bring together all the patents for a particular industry or trade in chronological order. To discover in which 'abridgement class' a particular invention is likely to fall, it is necessary to consult the 'Abridgement Class and Index Key' held at the SRL. The Abridgement volumes list each relevant patent by year and number, giving patentee's name, a brief description of perhaps one paragraph, and a single drawing. They also contain both name and subject indexes. The Abridgement volumes from 1855 are on the open shelves at the SRL, earlier volumes can be obtained at 10–15 minutes' notice. Thus, providing the researcher is based in or near London, access to patents is not difficult.

Some patents survive in the papers of scientists and inventors who either filed them or consulted them with a view to carrying the work further. They are also often preserved in the archives of the individual business which worked the patent. Because of their legal significance and because they were perceived as an asset of the firm, they have frequently been kept for long periods, perhaps by the company secretary or in the legal department. However, there is no guarantee that such sources will contain all the relevant material; the great strength of the SRL is the comprehensiveness of its collection: all patents ever issued survive there.

The information they contain

All patents have to contain certain basic information such as the date filed, its number, the title of the patent, and the name, occupation and address of the patentee. Thereafter the amount of information depends upon the date patented and the preference of the patentee. Before the late eighteenth century the amount of detail given in patent applications was often very brief. In the late eighteenth century it became more common to give a detailed specification and after the 1852 Act it was an essential pre-requisite for full registration.

Where a specification is given, it has two main components: the technical description of the invention and an explanation of what is new about this process or product. The aim of the description was not to give such detail as to allow a user to build the machine or work the process, indeed this would have been counter-productive. Rather the intention was to record only sufficient detail to ensure protection from any piratical imitator or subsequent inventors working on the same lines, but not enough information to allow easy copying of the technology. The example reproduced, registered in 1898, is for a process to produce viscose fibres suitable for use in the textile industry. Its importance lies in it being one of the earliest patents relating to the development of artificial fibres such as rayon which became a major part of the textile industry in the twentieth century. Stearn's patent was not novel in the process for producing the basic cellulose solution, for he acknowledged the earlier patent 8700 of 1892 taken out by Charles Cross, Edward Bevan and Clayton Beadle. Rather it was the manufacture from cellulose of filaments of varying degress of fineness which were suitable for textile manufacture which was innovatory. To obtain proper protection, he needed to ensure certain key variables were mentioned in his patent: the nature of the precipitating solution, the use of an orifice or jet through which the filament is drawn, the variation in speed to obtain varying thickness, and the use of rollers to wind up the extruded filaments. In addition, because the patentee had encountered and overcome difficulties in the precise composition of the solution, he stressed the need for purity and endeavoured to obtain patent protection for these breakthroughs.

The second part of the specification stressed the uses to which he envisaged putting these filaments or threads, namely as a textile yarn capable of being woven into fabrics. Stearn's patent is unusual in having no drawings or plans attached to it. Most patent specifications had a series of plans to show either the machinery to be used or the product to be manufactured and the specifications referred to these plans.

Thus the patent is a technical document, outlining the process or product, indicating the uses to which it is to be put and stressing the unique aspects of the specification. It does not need to cover the economic or social implications of the invention as this is not required to obtain protection.

Uses

The early patent applications, that is before the middle of the nineteenth century, were couched in legal terms which can be off-putting. However, the researcher should not be deterred as often only the preamble is expressed in legal bombast, while the specification is written in everyday language. Patents are of great value to the historian of science and technology. They can indicate who was the first person to develop a particular product or process and shed light on the nature of scientific discovery itself. Questions could be tackled such as: how far one invention is firmly based on previous breakthroughs; the extent to which technical progress is an accretion of small steps each built on preceding discoveries; the degree of simultaneous discovery of similar answers to common problems by different inventors working independently. Patents can also show which areas were considered to be of especial concern at a particular period: the large number relating to velocipedes, tricycles and tyres in the 1880s demonstrates the concern to develop safe, reliable and comfortable bicycles. By aggregating the number of patents applied for in each year, some historians have purported to show the 'inventiveness' of a country over time and thus trace upturns in scientific enquiry or opportunities for economic development. A study of the patents of a particular inventor will show the range of his interests, whether he roamed over wide areas, as Bessemer did, or concentrated on one industry with patience and determination as in the case of James Watt. The technical drawings are of use both to the technological historian and the industrial archaeologist trying to restore arcane pieces of equipment from little more than a pile of rusty components apparently in random order.

Business history is also critically concerned with patents. Many business histories have stressed the importance of a patented invention in giving a firm a monopoly of a machine, process or product which enabled them to make supra-normal profits and dominate a particular market: the Bonsack cigarette-making machine for W. D. & H. O. Wills, the viscose process for Courtaulds, and the float glass process for Pilkington Brothers.[11] However, this is exactly where the patent reveals itself to be a poor source, for the application and specification did not need to state anything about the social, economic or business implications of the invention. This is quite understandable as it would have required the inventor to gaze into his crystal ball and predict likely outcomes, which is an unreasonable expectation. It is precisely these areas which are of most interest to the general historian. He is less concerned with the techniques of how something worked and more with its impact upon employment patterns, the organization of industry, the size, structure and profitability of firms, the pattern of overseas trade and so on. About these the patent reveals nothing.

Apart from the researcher interested in the development of science and technology for its own sake, patents are a narrow source which need to be supplemented by many other types of material. Even then, another drawback is that they contain no indication of the effectiveness of the process. Many relate to misconceived discoveries, the personal whims of eccentric inventors and there is no assurance either that the process actually worked, or that there was any real demand for the product. It may have been a technological or commercial blind alley. Thus many have little or no technological or economic significance. It has been estimated that only 5 per cent of patents in the late nineteenth century were thought worth renewing for the full fourteen-year life.[12]

It should not be supposed that all inventions were patented, and this is another problem with using patents as a source. Some famous inventions do not appear at all in the patent records because their inventors were either ignorant, too poor or too concerned of being copied to make their discovery public. Some other inventors were opposed to the principle of patents, perceiving them as barriers to progress and bastions of privilege. Josiah Wedgwood, for example, refused to patent any of his many improvements in pottery and opposed that taken out by William Cookworthy and Lord Camelford for the exclusive use of Cornish china clay and stone which the former had discovered in Boconnoc in 1774.[13]

A residual use of patents is when a firm and its archives have completely disappeared. Since all patents have survived, they can be relied upon to provide some very basic information about firms which registered them. They indicate the activities in which the firm was involved, its address, some of the entrepreneurs or personnel involved and the period in which it was most technologically active. Where all other sources have failed, because of their comprehensiveness the patents may provide some material.

Cross-references to other documents

Wherever a firm or individual has been granted a patent, there is always the possibility of a licence agreement (q.v.) resulting. If a licence agreement does exist it is an indication that the patent was perceived of commercial importance by more than just the inventor and therefore increases the likelihood that it was technically feasible and commercially worthwhile. The number and extent of licences granted may give an idea of the significance of the process patented and the method chosen to exploit it, such as the degree to which the inventor decided to work it personally and how far this responsibility was delegated to other firms. Thus if licences exist, they may answer some of the questions about the economic significance of the patent which the records themselves cannot address.

The balance sheet (q.v.) of a company may indicate the existence of patents owned by a particular firm, for they were considered among the assets of a business and placed on the credit side of the balance sheet until quite recently. In modern accounting it is considered unwise to assign a money value to intangible assets such as trademarks or patents and include them on the balance sheet because of the difficulty of arriving at an objectively determinable value. However, such inhibitions were not common before the Second World War and firms did include such intangibles among their assets, but the researcher would be most foolish to take any notice of any money value placed on such 'assets'. For a start, patents were often compounded with all the other intangibles and one value placed on the whole lot. Secondly, these often remained surprisingly static over several years. Thirdly, there was no way in which their value could be calculated and was an entirely subjective estimate: the figures inserted were chosen more for their ability to balance the account than their real value. So the best that a balance sheet can do is draw attention to the existence of patents which the researcher may follow up.

Prospectuses (q.v.) may be able to perform a similar function. Where a company was set up, going public or seeking additional capital in order to exploit a particular patent, it was likely to make this clear in its prospectus, for it might be an attractive hook on which to impale the investor. Thus some mention of the patent and its economic value was bound to appear. Again the researcher should beware of placing too much faith in the prospectus for it was likely to over-emphasize the value of the invention, but at the least it indicates that there is a source worth pursuing.

The chairman's speech (q.v.) or the printed version in the more recent annual report and accounts may refer to any discovery that has been patented which is likely to improve the company's profit prospects. It might be a quite invaluable adjunct to the patent specification as it may answer some of the questions the latter cannot, such as how long the research has been under way, the market niche at which the product is aimed, and the costs and anticipated returns on the process. Of course, since the report is in part a public relations exercise, the claims of the chairman need to be treated with some circumspection. A more objective source is likely to be the letter books (q.v.). These may contain letters between the firm and its solicitors or patent agents which might have information on the significance of the process, where other patents might impinge on it, if other firms or inviduals are working on similar lines, any problems encountered in working the process and perhaps the economic and social significance of the invention. Certainly if the letter books survive it will be worthwhile to examine the correspondence around about the time the patent is being sought and registered.

Finally, because patents were frequently contested and the patentee often perceived infringements, to follow up their later history the researcher needs to consult legal cases concerning patents. This could be done through the law report pages of a quality paper such as *The Times* or the law abstracts, but this would be a tedious and time-consuming process. There are a few guides to such cases, for example T. Webster, *Report and Notes of Cases on Letters Patents for Investors* published in 1844 and 1855, and T.M. Goodeve, *Abstract of Reported Cases related to Letters Patent for Invention* of 1876 and 1884. From 1884 there is an annual *Report of Patent, Design and Trade Mark Cases*. However, although these summarize the cases and list the people involved, they are not indexed either as to patent number or subject so it is still not easy to find if a particular patent is under attack. A degree of determination is required from the researcher. Another useful source is the *Patents Journal*, which appeared initially in 1854 as *The Commissioners of Patents' Journal* issued bi-weekly, with information on the stages which each application has reached, any alterations in specifications, and such matters. It is indexed by name annually. Its name changed in 1884 to the *Official Journal of the Patent Office* and it became weekly.

Works using this source

Until recently there was no comprehensive study of the patent system although a number of works used the number of patents registered to give 'a rough index' of inventive activity.[14] This gap has in part been filled by a recent work on the patent system in the period of British industrialization.[15] Dutton's work is definitive, wide-ranging and comprehensive and the reader is recommended to consult it. It does, however, still leave the last century and a quarter uncovered and this is a significant omission for any student of patent history.

A large number of business histories have drawn on patent records to tell at least a part of their tale. For many firms the registering of a patent was the foundation of their commercial success: for example, James Watt's patent on the separate condenser was crucial to the foundation of the Boulton and Watt steam engine manufacturing partnership.[16] Some firms considered their patents so important that they incorporated them into their names, such as the Patent Desiccating Co or the Patent Shaft and Axletree Co. In other cases the profitability and stature of a firm was transformed by its purchase of exclusive use in the UK of a patent developed by others. Wills' purchase of Bonsack's patent on a cigarette-making machine in 1873 and Courtaulds' purchase of the patents owned by the Kew-based Viscose Spinning Syndicate in 1904 are good examples of long-established businesses which were given a massive boost by their purchase of patent rights.[17] Industrial archaeologists have used registered patents to investigate the pre-history of successful inventions. Mounfield, interested in the development of shoe-making machinery, examined four prescient patents in the period 1790 to 1853 to show how successful equipment evolved from near misses.[18]

Patents seem to have played an important role in the development of the rubber industry. One historian considered patent rights to be 'one of the most important aspects in the development of this industry'.[19] He was concerned with the conflict between two patentees: one was taken out by Thomas Hancock of Manchester in 1843 and the other by Stephen Moulton of Bradford-on-Avon in 1847. The former hoped, by proving to the courts that his patent was a master, to put Moulton out of business and gain a virtual monopoly of the rubber industry. In fact Goodyear, Moulton's ally, outmanoeuvred him by establishing a factory in Glasgow where the English patent did not apply. From these and other patents, Woodruff shows that all the important breakthroughs in rubber manufacture were made in the first half of the nineteenth century: 'there are no major developments in the period 1850–1900 worth recording'.[20] Another historian, exploring the role of rubber in railway engineering, also devotes a whole chapter to patents in order to trace product innovation. Mainly interested in the inventions of George Spencer using rubber cones, blocks and cylinders for springing on railway rolling stock, Payne draws on patent specifications and drawings to describe the products and show their uses to the multitude of mid-nineteenth-century railway companies. Spencer was also astute in the commercial exploitation of his ideas and acted as a merchant for some of the rubber products manufactured by Moulton.[21] Thus in two works on the rubber industry, patent records were used to show what products looked like, explain how they evolved and were used, analyse how the raw material was processed into a usable form, and investigate the conflict over priority of invention and hence patent rights.

The example

As explained in the section on 'The information they contain', this example is among the earliest patents which led to the commercial production of artificial fibres. In the second third of the nineteenth century, chemists became aware of cellulose, the essential ingredient of all plant tissue. Work proceeded in a number of countries on parallel lines searching for uses for this product. One facet of this was the discovery of nitro-cellulose or guncotton which led to a whole range of new blasting agents for mining and propellants for military purposes. Another aspect of this research was to find a strong uniform fibre which could be used as the filament in the newly discovered electric lamp. Sir Joseph Swan was the first to produce a cellulose-based fibre for this purpose at Newcastle upon Tyne. In the next year, Hilaire Chardonnet, a pupil of Louis Pasteur in France, produced cellulose fibres using a spinneret, based on the spinning gland of the silkworm. However, this process used a highly inflammable chemical, nitro-cellulose, which made it a high-risk method. Chardonnet, unlike Swan, was searching for a fibre that could be used in the textile industry, preferably as a silk substitute, and thus could be seen as 'the technical father of the rayon industry'.[22] In 1890 an alternative process to make artificial fibres was developed in Germany and France using cuprammonium, in the former for electric lamp filaments and in the latter by Louis Despeissis for textiles. In 1892, Charles Cross, Edward Bevan and Clayton Beadle patented yet another method, known as the viscose method, using caustic soda and carbon bisulphide on cellulose:[23] it did not use inflammable ingredients but, rather, cheap raw materials. Later, Cross went into partnership with Charles Stearn to exploit this process. Stearn was interested in producing filaments for his electric lamp factory, Cross was involved in paper-making, another cellulose-based industry. They both also perceived the value of the process for the textile industry and set up the Viscose Spinning Syndicate at Kew on the outskirts of London in 1899. This firm was bought by Henry G. Tetley for Courtaulds, the long-established, Essex-based silk crepe firm, in 1904 for £25,000. This purchase marked a turning point in Courtauld's fortunes and location. Within a decade it had switched from relying on mourning crepe for its profits to the new artificial fibre. It gained a virtual monopoly of the product in the UK market and then proceeded to do the same for the US market, establishing its own wholly-owned subsidiary, the American Viscose Co. in Pennsylvania. The profits from the new Coventry factory and the American subsidiary poured in and Courtaulds became one of the largest and most successful textile groups in the UK.[24]

Notes

1. 9 & 10 Geo. V c. 80, clause 6.
2. 21 Jacobi I c. III.
3. P. Meinhardt, *Inventions, Patents and Trademarks* (Gower, 1971) p. 21.
4. 15 & 16 Vict. c. 83.
5. 46 & 47 Vict. c. 57, clause 6.
6. 2 Edw. VII c. 34.

7.   7 Edw. VII c. 29, clause 7.

8.   C. Lees, *Patent Protection* (Business Pubns, 1965) p. 16; 12 & 13 Geo. VI c. 62.

9.   Charles Dickens, 'A poor man's tale of a patent', *Reprinted Pieces* (Macmillan, 1925) pp. 64–70.

10. B.M.D. Smith, 'Patents for Invention: The National and Local Picture', *Business History*, Vol. 4, No. 2 (1962) pp. 111–12.

11. B.W.E. Alford, *W.D. & H.O. Wills and the development of the UK tobacco industry* (Methuen, 1973) chap. 7; D.C. Coleman, *Courtaulds: An Economic and Social History*, Vol. 2, Part 1 (Oxford UP, 1969); T.C. Barker, 'Business Implications of Technical Developments in the Glass Industry, 1945–65' in B.E. Supple (ed.), *Essays in British Business History* (Oxford UP, 1977) chap. 10.

12. I. Winship, 'Patents as a Historical Source', *Industrial Archaeology*, Vol. 16, No. 3 (1981).

13. J. Quick, 'Cornish China Clay', *Quarterly Journal of Science*, Vol. 14, article 4 (1877) p. 502.

14. T.S. Ashton, 'Same Statistics of the Industrial Revolution in Britain', *Manchester School*, Vol. XVI (1948); W. Bowden, *Industrial Society in England towards the End of the Eighteenth Century* (Macmilan, 1925); A.E. Musson (ed.), *Science, Technology and Economic Growth in the Eighteenth Century* (Methuen, 1972) pp. 49–56.

15. H.I. Dutton, *The Patent System and Inventive Activity during the Industrial Revolution, 1750–1852* (Manchester UP, 1984).

16. H.W. Dickinson, *James Watt, Craftsman and Engineer* (Augustus M. Kelley, 1967) p. 89.

17. As footnote 11 above.

18. P.R. Mounfield, 'Early Technical Innovation in the British Footwear Industry', *Industrial Archaeology Review*, Vol. 2, No. 2 (1978).

19. W. Woodruff, *The Rise of the British Rubber Industry during the Nineteenth Century* (Liverpool UP, 1958) p. 133.

20. Ibid., p. 144.

21. P.L. Payne, *Rubber and Railways in the Nineteenth Century* (Liverpool UP, 1961) chap. 2.

22. D.C. Coleman, 'Courtaulds and the Beginning of Rayon' in B.E. Supple, *Essays in British Business History* (Oxford UP, 1977) p. 89.

23. Patent No. 8700 of 1892.

24. This section draws heavily on D.C. Coleman, *Courtaulds: An Economic and Social History* (Oxford UP, 1969) Vol. II, part 1.

Nº 1020　　　A.D. 1898

Date of Application, 13th Jan., 1898

Complete Specification Left, 10th Oct., 1898—Accepted, 23rd Dec., 1898

PROVISIONAL SPECIFICATION.

Improvements in the Manufacture and Production of a Filamentary Material, and Fabrics therefrom.

I, CHARLES HENRY STEARN, of 47, Victoria Street, in the City of Westminster, Electrician, do hereby declare the nature of my invention to be as follows:—

The object of my invention is to manufacture a filamentary material and fabrics therefrom by the employment of a solution of cellulose made by treating
5　cellulose with strong alkali and then with carbon bi-sulphide and dissolving the product in water. A process for the production of such a preparation is described in the Specification of Letters Patent No. 8700 of 1892. I precipitate the cellulose in filamentary form by projecting the solution thereof into a precipitating solution such for instance as alcohol, brine, chloride or sulphate
10　of ammonium or other suitable precipitant and by providing means whereby the cellulose solution can be drawn rapidly through the precipitating solution the filaments formed can be obtained of a degree of fineness in accordance with the speed adopted. The filaments may be produced singly or in any required number simultaneously and can be wound on spools or bobbins and be woven
15　or otherwise combined to form the required fabrics.

The solution of cellulose should be as perfect as possible and any impurities or imperfectly dissolved cellulose be filtered out before use.

After precipitation the product can be purified by sulphites or sulphurous acid or other reagents and be bleached for instance with sodium hypochlorite.

20　Dated this 13th day of January 1898.

JOHNSONS & WILLCOX,
47, Lincoln's Inn Fields, London, W.C., Agents.

COMPLETE SPECIFICATION.

Improvements in the Manufacture and Production of a Filamentary
25　Material, and Fabrics therefrom.

I, CHARLES HENRY STEARN, of 47, Victoria Street, in the City of Westminster, Electrician, do hereby declare the nature of this invention and in what manner the same is to be performed, to be particularly described and ascertained in and by the following statement:—

30　The object of my invention is to manufacture a filamentary material, and fabrics therefrom, by the employment of a solution of cellulose made by treating

[Price 8d.]

---

12. Patent specification No. 1020 of 1898; Charles Stearn's patent for producing viscose yarn for fabrics.
Source: British Library. Science Reference Division.

cellulose with strong alkali and then with carbon bisulphide and dissolving
the product in water. A process for the production of such a preparation (which
is commonly known as viscose) is described in the Specification of British Letters
Patent No. 8700 of 1892. I precipitate the cellulose in filamentary form by projecting the solution thereof into a precipitating or setting solution, or liquid, 5
alcohol, brine and sulphate of ammonium solution, for example, are precipitating,
or setting liquids, or solutions, but I have found that a solution of chloride of
ammonium gives the best results, as, at the proper strength, it is of a specific
gravity which will allow the cellulose solution to pass downwards therein and
it has the effect of immediately setting the said cellulose solution. By providing 10
means whereby the cellulose solution can be drawn rapidly through the precipitating or setting solution the filaments formed can be obtained of a degree of
fineness in accordance with the speed adopted (the size of the orifice, or jet, and
the pressure on the vessel, being the same). A suitable strength of the chloride
of ammonium solution is one of a specific gravity of 1.050 to 1.060, but I do not 15
limit myself to this particular strength. The filaments may be produced singly,
or in any required number simultaneously, and can be wound on rollers, as a
preliminary to bringing the filaments into the form of hanks, in which form
they are more conveniently handled in the subsequent treatments for fixing,
purifying, bleaching and dyeing. 20
In the preparation of the viscose solution the greatest care must be taken
to render the solution perfectly homogeneous and free from all undissolved
particles of cellulose.
The ordinary viscose of commerce generally consists of a mixture of a true
solution of cellulose with a jelly-like substance, and contains many undissolved 25
fibres, or parts of fibres. This character remains in the viscose even after the
most careful filtering and if filaments be made of such a material the outlines,
when viewed under the microscope, will be seen to be more, or less, wavy, or
sinuous, presenting sections of unequal diameter, and of unequal strength, in
various parts of the filament. 30
The non-homogeneous nature of such a solution is clearly apparent by the
variations in colour displayed when viewed under the microscope in a thin film,
or layer, under polarised light.
A perfectly homogeneous solution can be obtained as follows:—
I first obtain the purest bleached cellulose and subject it to the action of alkali, 35
as in the well known process of mercerisation, continuing the process until the
solution of alkali has thoroughly penetrated through the mass. The cellulose
used should be as loose in structure as possible so as to admit readily of the
penetration of the alkali solution. When the mercerisation is thoroughly accom-
plished, the excess of alkali is squeezed out and the alkali-cellulose is treated 40
with carbon bisulphide. When the reaction is complete sufficient water is added
to make a solution containing say from 9½ to 10 *per cent.* of cellulose, and the
mixture is thoroughly stirred for a considerable time by means of a mixer
revolving at high speed, the vessel containing the viscose being kept cool during
stirring. 45
The mixture must then be filtered very thoroughly and freed from air by the
air pump.
The solution, if carefully prepared and treated as aforesaid, will be perfectly
clear and structureless, or homogeneous, and of high viscosity, and is fit for
precipitation, or setting, as aforesaid, and filamentary material of great tensile 50
strength, and of even section through its whole length, is obtained.
The cellulose solution can be squirted through the jet under any suitable
pressure (air, or hydraulic, or mechanical,) into the precipitating or setting solution, or liquid, the orifice in the jet being of the requisite diameter to give the
size of filamentary material required which can be allowed to coil upon itself, 55
or be drawn off by a revolving pulley as may be desired.
The filament should be placed, and remain from 6 to 12 hours, in fresh chloride

Manufacture and Production of a Filamentary Material, and Fabrics therefrom.

of ammonium solution, or other setting solution or liquid, so as to remove soluble
products as thoroughly as possible.

After digestion in the cold the filamentary material is then removed from the
liquid and introduced for a few minutes into a boiling solution of the same
5 liquid, to regenerate the cellulose, by completing the decomposition of the sulpho-
carbonate, after which it is washed in boiling water to remove all traces of the
chloride. The resulting cellulose may then be purified in any suitable way, the
following being suitable. The thread is immersed in a hot solution of sodium
carbonate, (washing soda), and is left for some time in the solution. From this
10 it is well washed and immersed in a solution of sodium hypochlorite, or other
bleaching agent, till colourless. It is then thoroughly washed and may then
be treated with dilute acids and washed. It is then dried in the air under tension, or passed under tension through a heated chamber.

By providing a number of jets, or orifices, more than one filament can be
15 made at the same time, and if desired these may be twisted together to make
a compound thread or yarn, preparatory to the subsequent treatments for purifi-
cation, bleaching and dyeing.

The filaments produced may be reduced, polished, or otherwise acted upon by
passing them between rollers.

20 Having now particularly described and ascertained the nature of this invention and in what manner the same is to be performed, I declare that what
I claim is:—

1. The manufacture, for textile purposes, of filamentary material by projecting the aforesaid solution of cellulose (viscose) through a small orifice into
25 a precipitating or setting solution or liquid.

2. The manufacture, for textile purposes, of filamentary material by projecting
the aforesaid solution of cellulose (viscose) through a small orifice into a solution
of chloride of ammonium.

3. The manufacture, for textile purposes, of filamentary material by projecting
30 the aforesaid solution of cellulose (viscose) through a small orifice into a precipitating or setting solution, or liquid, and drawing it therethrough.

4. The preparation of a filamentary material for textile purposes by first sub-
jecting the aforesaid solution of cellulose (viscose) to stirring and filtering, and
then projecting it from a small orifice, into a solution of chloride of ammonium
35 and drawing the same therethrough.

5. A filamentary material for textile purposes prepared from the aforesaid
solution of cellulose (viscose) substantially as hereinbefore set forth.

6. Fabrics made from filamentary material prepared from the aforesaid solution of cellulose (viscose) substantially as hereinbefore set forth.

40 Dated this 10th day of October 1898.

JOHNSONS & WILLCOX,
47, Lincoln's Inn Fields, London, W.C., Agents.

Redhill: Printed for Her Majesty's Stationery Office, by Malcomson & Co., Ltd.—1899.

12. Patent specification No. 1020 of 1898; Charles Stearn's patent for producing
viscose yarn for fabrics.
Source: British Library. Science Reference Division.

13 Licences

Original purpose

In general, a licence is merely a grant of permission to do something. So a TV licence allows the holder to use his TV set, a driving licence permits the licensee to drive a motor vehicle on the public roads. In the commercial world, a licence has the same general meaning: it is the granting of permission by one firm or individual to another to undertake a business activity. Nowadays it is prudent for a company to protect any product or process it develops by obtaining a patent; similarly, if the firm evolves a design or trademark or brand name, it is registered in order to ensure exclusive use. If the company then chooses to allow another firm to exploit this protected asset, the two businesses will normally draw up a licence which is the legal agreement between the two parties defining the extent of the permit and the method of compensation. The firm granting the licence will obviously wish to be paid for parting with this valuable right and it will define on what basis the payment is to be made, for example whether a lump sum or on a royalty basis or by a fixed annual payment.

The original purpose of a licence was to create a legal document, binding on both parties, which would stand up in a court of law in case of any dispute between the two firms. It is, therefore, written in legal English which often seems more intended to obfuscate rather than clarify. Until recently it was likely to carry stamp duty to demonstrate its nature as a legal record, and was completed by signatures and official company seals. Its most common use was when the holder of a patent chose to allow another firm to work that patent. This was particularly true when the patent holder lacked the capital fully to exploit the potential of its innovation, or where the patentee did not wish to work the patent itself in overseas countries but instead decided to make money from the invention indirectly by allowing a company based in the foreign country to work it 'under licence'. In some nations, such as France and Germany, a patent had to be worked in the country within a specified period of time or it became invalid. If a company lacked the resources or motivation to set up a factory locally, granting a licence to an indigenous firm was one method of maintaining patent protection. Similarly, if the authorities imposed terms for the construction and working of a wholly-owned subsidiary which did not suit the patent holder, it might choose to grant a licence to a native business in the belief that it would receive better treatment.

In the UK after 1883, licences began to feature in legislation. The Patents Act of that year gave the Board of Trade (BoT) power to order patentees to grant licences on terms of its own choosing if a patent holder refused 'to grant licences on reasonable terms' which led to the patent not being worked in the UK or 'the reasonable requirements of the public with respect to the invention' not being supplied. These became known as 'compulsory licences'.[1] These powers were enhanced in 1902 by the right to revoke a patent as an alternative to a compulsory licence in extreme cases and the conditions applied to all previous patents rather than merely those to come. However, the BoT lost its direct powers as cases were referred to a committee of the Privy Council which could issue an Order in Council requiring the patentee to grant a licence or, *in extremis*, revoke the patent. The grounds for such action by the Judicial Commitee of the Privy Council were the same as those in the 1883 Act, if spelt out in rather more detail.[2] This procedure was altered in 1907, when all cases of dispute were required to go before the courts instead of the Judicial Committee of the Privy Council, but the powers and grounds for action remained unaltered.[3]

The situation changed again in 1919 when the idea of 'licences of right' was introduced. A patentee could request the comptroller of patents to issue licences to any who applied, on terms determined by the comptroller. Such patents were endorsed 'licences of right'. The comptroller was required to balance on one hand the rights of the patentee to a fair return for his invention and on the other hand the need for the widest possible diffusion of the discovery in the UK. The advantage to the patentee was a halving of the renewal fees payable.[4] Additionally, if the comptroller was satisfied that the monopoly rights of a patent were being abused, he could unilaterally endorse a patent 'licences or right', or grant an exclusive licence, or revoke the patent.[5] Thus a patentee could find a licence had been granted to work his patent without his consent although he was given the opportunity to make representations against any such action. Both of these conditions were continued in the 1949 Act which laid down more clearly the grounds on which a case could be made out for a compulsory licence or even revocation of a patent entirely.[6]

So from 1883 a patent holder might be compelled to grant a licence on reasonable terms if he did not work the process assiduously himself or face the threat of having the patent revoked. This was another pressure to grant licences. In fact, not many applications were received either for licences of right or the grant of compulsory licences but this may have been because the Acts were effective in persuading patent holders to issue licences. There was an alternative stratagem to a licence agreement: a patent holder might choose to sell its patent rights to another firm or individual. An example of outright sale was when Courtaulds, the Essex silk manufacturer, bought out the Viscose Spinning Syndicate in 1904 for £25,000. Included in the price was the latter's 'set of patent rights covering the making of artificial silk'. This was of crucial importance to Courtaulds' future prosperity and in retrospect can be seen as a bargain.[7] A good example of a territorially limited agreement is the eponymous Bonsack cigarette-making machine. Developed by an American, he sold the exclusive rights in the UK to W.D. & H.O. Wills, the Bristol-based tobacco manufacturer, in 1883 for a mere £4000. Again this technical development was vital to the firm's future.[8] In both cases, rather than issuing a licence, the patent holder sold his rights direct to another company. The effects are similar to a licence, as was the legal document drawn up. Although this was an alternative, most of what is said about licences in this chapter also applies to such agreements.

Sources

There has never been any necessity under company law to lodge licensing agreements with any central authority. Although the Patent Office carefully preserves all patent applications, there is no concomitant requirement on it to lodge, or store, any licenses issued. Thus the preservation of licensing agreements depends entirely on the actions of individual firms. Fortunately, since they were legal documents, often relatively small in size and took up little room, and were current for long periods, they were likely to be kept carefully either by the company secretary or in the legal department of the firm. In some cases that is where both the older and more modern examples will still be found. Where a company has established its own archive, the more ancient examples whose term has long expired will probably have been transferred there. There is greater uncertainty of survival when a business has ceased to trade or been subject to a takeover. In some cases they may still survive with the absorbing firm, or the records of the firm taken over may have been lodged with a local record office and the licences can be found there. It may well be that a number of licences still exist with the firms of solicitors who acted for their corporate clients. Law partnerships are very reluctant to throw away any documents which may be of relevance at some remote future date but they are equally unwilling to reveal whether or not they have material appertaining to a particular firm or, if so, what sorts of documents are held. Without the written permission of the company involved, the researcher will certainly not gain any information. With that permission, his chances are still not good. After some time, lawyers tend to return old documentation to the company concerned so the older licenses may have been returned in this way.

The information they contain

Because of the *raison d'être* any licence must contain enough information to identify the parties fully. Thus the full legal name and registered address of each are spelt out. Additionally, the licence has to state if it supersedes any previous agreements and then list these in sufficient detail to make them easily identifiable. The main body of the document defines the precise terms of the licence. This includes the period for which it is to run; the geographical extent of the permission, for example when a foreign company is licensed to work a permit, whether it may establish factories outside its parent country; the precise process or product which is the subject of the agreement when any patents or registrations need to be delineated, often in an appendix or schedule; the method of payment for the licence indicating whether a one-off lump sum, or annual sum, or royalty payments are to be paid usually based on the output.

The example used contains much of this information. The period is defined as the current life of the patents. The geographical extent of the permit is given: the Austrian company may manufacture in Austria but may not set up a plant in the UK or its dependencies (to prevent competition with the UK-based Daimler company) but it is allowed to import and sell its Austrian-made chassis in the UK. The precise patents involved are listed in a schedule with their year, number and title, allowing easy identification. Payment for the privilege is by means of a royalty payment per unit depending on engine size subject to the patent holder receiving a minimum payment of £100 per annum.

The agreement also normally states whether there are any particular conditions on the working of the process. For instance, if it is a manufacturing licence the licenser may insist that the licensee works the process within a certain period — normally a year or two — and that a minimum level of output must be reached within a given time span. This is to protect the licenser from failing to gain any income from the licence. If the licensee has not achieved the stipulated conditions by the pre-determined times, the licenser is free to cancel the licence and seek a more successful partner. Another frequent and important clause is an undertaking to provide the licence holder with technical support for the product or process. If the licensee encounters problems in setting up plant or obtaining the right quality or quantity of output, he may be able to call on the greater expertise of the original producer to solve the difficulties. In similar vein some licences also entitle the holder to share in any future improvements in technique or technology which the licenser may make which relate to the particular process or product. In the Mercedes Daimler example shown, the licensee may use not merely the patents already in force but also any 'to be granted and any extension or promulgation thereof which can or may be obtained'. So the Austrian company is guaranteed use of any future technical breakthroughs made by either the German or UK company. This type of clause comes very close to a form of cartelization, but was not uncommon in some licence agreements, for example that in which Continental Can of the USA empowered Metal Box of the UK to make and use their automatic can-making, filling and sealing equipment in the 1930s.[9]

In addition to the precise terms of the agreement, there are often also details on what procedure is to be adopted if there are any disagreements between the two parties on the interpretation of the document. In some cases specified independent arbitrators may be called in, while in others internal committees may be created to adjudge the issue. In the example, conditions laid down include that the Austrian company may not pass on to any other firm the advantages of the licence nor may it sell chassis for use as buses or coaches in the London area. In case of disagreement, the parties bind themselves to go to arbitration under the 1889 Arbitration Act.[10] There is usually also a clause specifying how the agreement may be amicably terminated: whether there is to be a period of notice or any compensatory payment for the rupture by either party. Clause 11 of the Mercedes Daimler agreement stipulates a minimum period of one year, after which either party may give six month's notice of intention to terminate and then a new basis of payment comes into force.

Uses

As with other documents examined in this volume, a license is of greatest interest to researchers interested in discovering the commercial history of a specific business. A licence agreement will indicate whether the firm was a true innovator in the sense that it pioneered new techniques or products and then allowed others to buy the technology or whether it was a technology-imitator, buying in new processes from other, more inventive companies. In the nineteenth century we might expect British companies to have pioneered and sold their ideas to foreign firms, while in the twentieth century a reverse flow might be anticipated. An investigation of licensing agreements would shed significant light on this.

A study of a range of licence agreements might contribute to the debate on the process of invention and innovation. In the Industrial Revolution the UK led in both invention and innovation based on individualistic experimenters and small-scale businessmen. By the later nineteenth century, foreign competitors had begun to formalize research and development in company laboratories based on widespread scientific education. UK firms were slow to adopt this structure, with one or two worthy exceptions, compared to, say, German or American companies and research in the UK continued to be based on the lone experimenter. If this hypothesis is correct, the number of licences which were taken up by UK firms should increase in the late nineteenth century as they bought in their technical developments either from abroad or the experimenting individual or syndicate. Similarly, the number of licences granted by UK firms should decline if they were failing to invent.

Because they are predominantly about technical breakthroughs, licences are invaluable to research into the history of science and technology. They show how ideas were diffused from one company, or one country, to others. They show the type of firm that was granting licences and the types of organization that took up these new opportunities. They also show which countries were technology creditors and which were technology debtors and how this balance changed over time. Licences could also give a crude measure of the significance of a particular technology for, if a large number were granted, it may have been that many firms perceived the process or product as potentially profitable and so hurried to utilize the discovery. If, however, very few licences were granted, one reasonable deduction might be that the process was of limited utility. Of course, this depends on the nature of the licensing agreement. It may have been the policy of the licenser to licence only one company in each country, or even contintent, but the agreement should make this clear in its clauses defining the geographical extent of the accord. The licence can also be of importance to the economist studying the economic development process. As well as showing how the transfer of technology took place, an examination of the financial clauses may allow some evaluation of the cost of that technology transfer to the recipient country and therefore the degree of profitability or, alternatively, the element of exploitation by the more developed country of the less developed.

Where no other documentation survives for a firm, licensing agreements provide some idea of the level and type of technology employed, give an indication of the range of markets in which the firm operated and the sort of marketing policies pursued, that is whether it was a direct exporter, or set up foreign subsidiaries to manufacture locally or, as in the case of a firm granting licences, chose to leave local exploitation to quite independent firms, becoming itself almost a professional innovator on the lines of the Edison laboratory in the US. The main drawback of licence agreements is that they do not say why they were granted, whether the licenser lacked capital to exploit the idea fully or chose to accept a tempting offer for an unproved process that still needed much development and refinement, or whether political conditions were more conducive to local manufacture and control. It is just this sort of explanation which is most fascinating to the historian, but licensing agreements *per se* are unlikely to elucidate this and other documents will have to be sought to throw light on causality.

Thus the licence agreement is of most use in any discussion of the process of technological change, whether within the firm or in a more general context. However, because of the partial survival rate of licensing agreements and because they are not all available at any one location but rather are scattered in numerous repositories, it is much simpler to use the patent records, as explained in Chapter 12. Whereas a researcher can find easily all the patents for an industry, the same is not true for licences. The best method of approach is to use the patents to discover which firms had licenceable inventions and then see if they did in fact licence them. This will not work as well for registered designs or brand names, but a similar technique can be pursued.

Cross-references to other documents

Given what has already been said, the source which should be used in conjunction with licensing agreements is patents (q.v.). Since most licences arose from patented inventions, the best way to access licences is through an examination of the patent records. To understand what was being licensed it is necessary to consult the patents, for most licences only listed the patents which were involved and did not give details. Thus the researcher needs to track down the original patents to discover precisely what technology was being bought or sold and thus what is indicated about the level of technical development of the two firms. Prospectuses (q.v.) of companies set up especially to operate a licence may give an indication of the existence and broad content of a licence agreement. Similarly, if the firm had made a technical breakthrough which was likely to bring in additional income through licensing agreements, it would stress this in a prospectus. As this breakthrough might have already entailed the firm in considerable outlay which should result in future inflows of cash, that was a good time to go public and capitalize some of the anticipated future earnings.

Two sources which should give some useful background to the decision to issue licences or to take out a licence are the board minute books (q.v.) and the chairman's statement (q.v.). Although the latter will give a rather bland account as it is for public consumption, it may indicate why the decision was made. The board minute books, as they were not intended to be generally available, are likely to be more detailed and may, therefore, go into greater depth for the reasons behind the decision. They may indicate which director(s) was most in favour and why. They may give the minutiae of the negotiations and some indication of how long they took to come to fruition. Letter books (q.v.) are another source which may help throw light on licences if there was correspondence between the firms on the subject. In some cases the discussions were considered so delicate or the desire for secrecy was so great that nothing was committed to paper until the deal had been finalized; in others there is ample evidence to flesh out the bones of the licence.

Finally, once a licence agreement has been entered into there may be some sign of it in the company's financial records. A separate entry may be opened in the ledger (q.v.) to account for payments from a licensee or to a licenser. In the more recent past, the profit and loss account (q.v.) may have a heading for income earned through licence fees. This is less likely the further back in time the account originated because nineteenth and early twentieth centuries profit and loss accounts are often miracles of compression, lumping all income under a couple of headings and doing the same for expenditure. A careful search of the firm's financial records should show up some traces of licensing activity.

Works using this source

Licensing agreements are most commonly used as a means of allowing firms to work patents which are not owned by them. They rarely allow a broad vision of the companies involved but they are crucial to an understanding of their technical development. They have not usually been the central source for a technical history, for this will be the patents. But they are crucial to show how a firm exploited any patents it registered or adopted a technical breakthrough which it had not developed. A good example of the former from recent history is that of Pilkington Brothers, a UK-based flat glass manufacturing company, which developed a new process for making plate glass in the 1950s, later called the float glass method. Patent protection was obtained in 1954 for a large number of countries. Once the plant was fully operational and the rate of spoilt glass had reached acceptably low proportions, rather than work the process abroad themselves, Pilkington chose to licence foreign firms. The first was to the Pittsburgh Plate Glass Co of the USA in 1962. By 1976, over twenty liences had been granted to foreign firms.[11]

An example of a UK firm buying in technology via a licensing agreement is to be seen in the 1930s when, as mentioned above, Metal Box paid £50,000 to Continental Can of the USA for 'exclusive rights in Great Britain for fifteen years . . . to service and technical information, as well as patent licences'.[12] In this case the technological lead had passed to the US and the British company was buying in know-how. In some cases a firm which commenced life as a technology borrower via a licensing agreement went on to become a major generator of patents itself and hence granted licenses to others. The giant British chemical firm, ICI, can be counted among this number. One of the four firms which amalgamated in 1926 to form ICI was Brunner Mond & Co. It had started in 1873 manufacturing soda using a process invented and patented by the Solvay Brothers, who were Belgian. In 1872 the Solvays had granted Ludwig Mond a licence under their English patents to all their technical information. The conditions imposed were that he had to build a factory within one year and be producing good soda within two. He paid for this privilege by giving the Solvays a royalty payment of 8/- (40p) per ton of soda produced.[13] Nobels, another major component of ICI, started in a similar manner. It was founded in 1871 in Scotland as the British Dynamite Co Ltd to work Alfred Nobel's patents under licence. Nobel received payment for the licence partly in fully paid-up shares in the company issued to him free of charge, partly by a profit-sharing agreement which came into operation once a minimum level of return had been achieved. In 1877 the concern was reorganized as Nobel's Explosives Co Ltd and in 1926 went into ICI.[14] ICI of course had its own research laboratories and went on to become a licence issuer on a large scale.

The history of many companies contain a crucial technical breakthrough made sometimes by the company, sometimes bought in. Most of these innovations were protected by patents, and where there is one, there is a chance of a licence or some sort of agreement between two or more companies to trade the right to work the patent. Although not given as much prominence as the patent itself, licences were a crucial form of technological transfer for many firms.

The example

The licensing agreement featured is drawn from the archives of the Daimler Benz Motor Co in Unter Turkheim, near Stuttgart, West Germany. This company is a combination of two of the world pioneers of motor vehicles, Gottlieb Daimler and Carl Benz, who established separate firms to produce self-propelled vehicles in the 1880s. The two companies merged in 1925 but before then the model name Daimler had virtually disappeared in Germany and been superseded by Mercedes. The romantic story of how a special racing Daimler became known as a Mercedes need not detain us here,[15] and it is sufficient to say that the cars produced after the merger were the legendary Mercedes-Benz.

The licence is being granted jointly by the Mercedes Daimler Motor Co of Great Britain, which was the holder of the rights to the UK patents of Daimler and thus Mercedes, and the parent German Daimler Company to the Austrian Daimler Company. The Austrian company is permitted to use these UK patents to construct motor chassis which embodied these inventions and then to export them for sale in the UK, subject to certain restrictions. The idea of the licence plate in clause 5 is an ingenious way of checking on the number of chassis produced to ensure the licensors are not being cheated. Otherwise it is a fairly typical example of a licence agreement of this period.

Notes

1. 46 & 47 Vict. c. 57, clause 22.
2. 2 Edw. VII c. 34, clause 3.
3. 7 Edw. VII c. 29, clause 16.
4. 9 & 10 Geo. V c. 80, clause 2.
5. Ibid., clause 1.
6. 12 & 13 Geo. VI c. 62, clauses 13, 14 & 16.
7. D.C. Coleman, 'Courtaulds and the Beginning of Rayon' in B.E. Supple (ed.), *Essays in British Business History* (Clarendon, 1977).
8. B.W.E. Alford, *W.D. & H.O. Wills and the development of the UK Tobacco Industry 1786–1963* (Methuen, 1973).
9. W.J. Reader, *Metal Box: A History* (Heinemann, 1976) p. 54.
10. 52 & 53 Vict. c. 49.
11. Based on T.C. Barker, *The Glassmakers: Pilkington 1826–1976* (Weidenfeld & Nicolson, 1977) pp. 416–20.
12. W.J. Reader, op. cit.
13. W.J. Reader, *Imperial Chemical Industries: A History. Vol. 1: The Forerunners 1870–1926* (Oxford UP, 1970) pp. 46–7.
14. Ibid., pp. 11 & 24–31.
15. See A. Room, *Dictionary of Trade Name Origins* (RKP, 1982) p. 120.

This Indenture

made the *tenth*

day of *February* One thousand nine hundred and *thirteen* BETWEEN
THE MERCEDES DAIMLER MOTOR COMPANY LIMITED whose registered
Office is at 70a Basinghall Street in the City of London (hereinafter
called "the Licensors") of the first part THE DAIMLER-MOTOREN-
GESELLSCHAFT of Unterturkheim in the Empire of Germany (hereinafter
called "the German Company") of the second part and the OESTERREICHISCHE
DAIMLER MOTOREN ACTIEN GESELLSCHAFT of Wiener-Neustadt in the
Austrian Empire (hereinafter called "the Licensees") of the third part
W H E R E A S the Licensors and the German Company are the registered
owners of Letters Patent of the United Kingdom of Great Britain and
Ireland short particulars whereof are set forth in the Schedule hereto
AND WHEREAS the Licensors have agreed to grant and the Licensees
have agreed to accept a license under the Letters Patent set forth
in the said Schedule and under all Letters Patent of the United Kingdom
and of its Colonies and Dependencies (except Canada) relating to motor
cars or to parts thereof or to accessories to motor cars which the
Licensors may during the continuance of this license require (all of
which Letters Patent as well as those now owned as those which may
hereafter be acquired by the Licensors are hereinafter referred to as
"The said Letters Patent") upon the terms and subject to the conditions
hereinafter contained NOW THIS INDENTURE WITNESSETH that in
pursuance of the said agreement and in consideration of the royalties
hereinafter reserved and of the covenants on the part of the Licensees
hereinafter contained the Licensors with the consent of the German
Company hereby testified DO HEREBY GRANT unto the Licensees (but
subject to the restrictions and conditions hereinafter contained)
license and authority to import into and sell in the United Kingdom
of Great Britain and Ireland and the Isle of Man and the Colonies
(except Canada) and Dependencies of the United Kingdom (the whole of
which territory is hereinafter referred to as "the said territory")
chassis made as to any part thereof in accordance with any of the
inventions the subjects of the said Letters Patent TO HOLD the said
License and Authority unto the Licensees during all the residue now to

13. Licence agreement between Mercedes Daimler Motor Co Ltd, Daimler
Motorengesellschaft, and Oesterreichische Daimler Motoren Actien Gesellschaft,
10 February 1913.
Source: Daimler Benz Archives, Unter Turkheim, Stuttgart, West Germany.

come and unexpired of the terms of Fourteen years in and by the
said Letters Patent respectively granted or to be granted and any
extension or prolongation thereof which can or may be obtained but
subject to the restrictions and conditions hereinafter contained
AND it is hereby mutually covenanted and agreed by and between
the parties hereto each party covenanting and agreeing in respect
of their own acts only as follows that is to say :-

1.   THE Licensees shall during the terms of the said Letters
Patent granted or to be granted and any extensions or prolongatio
thereof pay to the Licensors as and by way of royalty upon all
chassis made as to any part thereof in accordance with any of the
inventions the subjects of the said Letters Patent and imported
directly or indirectly into or sold in the said territory under
the license the sums following that is to say :-

   (a)   The sum of Two pounds ten shillings for and in respect
         of each chassis of not exceeding sixteen horse power
         according to the formula of rating for the time being
         adopted by the Royal Automobile Club of the United
         Kingdom, and

   (b)   The sum of Five pounds for and in respect of each cha
         of more than sixteen horse power according to the sam
         formula of rating.

2.   THE Licensees shall keep or cause to be kept full and pro
books wherein shall be entered particulars of all chassis made a
to any part thereof as aforesaid and imported or sold as aforesa
under this license and will at all times produce all such books
to the Licensors or their authorised agent or agents and will
allow him or them to take copies thereof or extracts therefrom
and will at all times furnish to the Licensors free of charge
all information as to any item or items contained in the said
books or which ought to be contained therein.

3.   THE Licensees shall upon the usual quarter days in each y
or within twenty one days thereafter deliver to the Licensors
a statement in writing verified by the Certificate of the Licens
Manager containing particulars (including the horse power calcula
as aforesaid and the serial number) of all chassis imported into

or sold by them in the said territory during the preceding quarter
under this license and of the royalties payable in respect thereof
and shall at the same time pay to the Licensors the royalties so shewn
to be due The first of such statements shall be delivered to the
Licensors on the *25th* day of *March* One thousand nine hundred
and *thirteen* and shall include all such chassis so imported or sold
since the *25th* day of *December* One thousand nine hundred
and *twelve*.

IN the event of the royalties payable hereunder in respect of
any year ending the twenty fifth day of December not amounting to the
sum of One hundred pounds or to a proportionate part of such sum
in the event of there being a fraction of a year at the expiration
or earlier termination of this license the licensees shall within
twenty one days after the expiration of such year or upon the
expiration or earlier termination of this license pay to the Licensors
the amount of such deficiency so as to make up the minimum royalty
payable hereunder in each year during the terms of the said Letters
Patent as aforesaid to the sum of One hundred pounds and so in proportion for any period less than a year.

THE Licensees shall procure from the Licensors License plates
which shall be supplied free of charge by the Licensors and the
Licensees shall affix the said plates in a prominent position one of
such plates to each chassis imported or sold as aforesaid under this
License and if any chassis made as to any part thereof in accordance
with any of the inventions the subjects of the said Letters Patent
shall be imported into or sold in the said territory without having
a license plate affixed thereto in the manner aforesaid such chassis
shall be deemed to be infringing chassis and not protected by the
License hereby granted provided that no chassis shall be deemed to be
an infringing chassis by reason of the absence of a license plate if
the number of such chassis shall have been notified to the Licensors
in the proper quarterly statement as the number of a chassis imported
into or sold in the said territory and proper royalty shall have
been paid to the Licensors in respect thereof.

THE Licensees shall not without the previous consent in writing

13. Licence agreement between Mercedes Daimler Motor Co Ltd, Daimler
Motorengesellschaft, and Oesterreichische Daimler Motoren Actien Gesellschaft,
10 February 1913.
Source: Daimler Benz Archives, Unter Turkheim, Stuttgart, West Germany.

of the Licensors assign or mortgage or attempt to assign or mortgage this license or grant or attempt to grant any sublicense hereunder.

7.   THE Licensees shall not during the continuance of this license dispute or question the validity of the said Letters Patent or of any of them.

8.   THE Licensees shall not use any chassis imported or sold hereunder or allow or permit the same to be used upon or in connection with omnibuses chars-a-banc or other vehicles to be used as public service vehicles working for hire under the Metropolitan Stage Carriage license within a radius of twenty miles of the General Post Office in the City of London (such omnibuses chars-a-banc or other vehicles to fall within the definition of "stage carriage" contained in section 4 of the Metropolitan Public Carriage Act 1869 and not to include Hackney Carriages or Cabs) and the Licensees shall take all such steps as may be necessary to prevent the use of any such chassis so made and imported or sold as aforesaid for any of the purposes aforesaid and if the same are so used they shall be deemed to be infringements not protected by the license hereby granted.

9.   THE Licensors shall from time to time during the continuance of this license keep the Licensees informed of all Letters Patent of the United Kingdom or of its Colonies or Dependencies which may hereafter be granted to or acquired by the Licensors and shall also from time to time during the continuance of this License inform the Licensees of all or any of the said Letters Patent which may expire or be otherwise terminated.

10.   THE Licensors and the German Company shall be at liberty from time to time to apply at the Patent Office of the United Kingdom or elsewhere for leave to amend the Specifications of the said Letters Patent or any of them including the drawings forming part thereof by way of disclaimer correction or addition.

11.   EITHER party hereto may at the end of the year terminating on the twenty fifth day of December One thousand nine hundred and thirteen or on the same date in any subsequent year terminate clauses 1 and 4 of this License by giving to the other party six months previous notice in writing thereof and immediately after

14   Premises records

Original purpose

The heading 'premises records' covers a wide spectrum of individual documents ranging from deeds, leases or conveyances, as in our example, through maps, plans and photographs to tenders for building work, schedules of interior decoration, inventories of furniture and fittings and fire insurance policies. This range makes the present chapter different from most of the others in this book as it is not dealing with one specific document which has a standard, easily recognizable layout, but rather it examines a general category of records the format, contents and shape of which vary markedly. In some ways it is similar to the entry on staff records (q.v.) which also covers a number of different types of document.

   Although the shape and layout of the documents vary, the original reason for their creation evinces some unity of purpose. Essentially the most important function of these documents was to establish title to a piece of land or building. Deeds or conveyances certainly fit into this category. A deed was, and is, a legal document which indicated ownership of landed property. It is a type of contract and, to be binding, the agreement between the two parties must be put in the form of a deed. This meant that the agreement had to be signed by both parties, witnessed and preferably sealed. Conveyances were also legal documents showing the transfer of land or property from one owner to another and were a combination of invoice, receipt and delivery note rolled into one involving the payment of stamp duty to the authorities. A prospective purchaser asked to inspect the conveyance of the vendor from the previous owner of the land. If this was in order, the current owner was deemed to hold legal title and be entitled to sell it. Leases had a similar purpose in that they were again legally binding documents, in which the owner of freehold property gave another person possession of that property for a specified period for a regular remuneration — the rent — possibly with certain conditions or obligations imposed as covenants. The lease proved the freeholder owned the property but also demonstrated that the leaseholder had use of it for a time; the leaseholder could normally also sub-let this property. Thus the original purpose of these documents was to prove ownership of land or property for at least a period if not in perpetuity. As well as establishing legal right, a subsidiary purpose of some of these documents was to specify constraints on land or building use. If, for example, there were restrictive convenants on the property, these were recorded and made available to a potential purchaser prior to completion of the deal as they might influence the decision to buy. It was also important that the purchaser not merely knew of these covenants but was known to know them, so there was no excuse later for non-compliance on grounds of ignorance.

Deeds, conveyances and leases are frequently accompanied by plans and maps showing the exact location and extent of the land and buildings involved. Their original purpose was to clarify the verbal description given in the written document and they were often included as part of that agreement and had force of law, as with the plan in the example used here. This plan indicates another function of this class of record: not merely to establish title but also to describe and define the property in case of dispute with neighbouring land or property owners. Sometimes such maps or plans may have been drawn to show the position of land or buildings to the partners or board of directors of a firm which was contemplating a purchase or lease. Then these diagrams had no legal standing but were for clarification only. In some cases they may have been a subtle piece of marketing on the part of the vendor to try and make the land or building as attractive as possible and therefore encourage a sale; in these instances the plan may need to be treated with caution as a certain bias might have crept in. A more mundane purpose of some maps and plans was to indicate and record rights of way or ancient lights or, indeed, to show the layout and structure of a property to which state it had to be returned once the lease ran out.

Another common form of record about premises is the tender. This was a document prepared by the owner of land or property specifying the quantity and quality of work to be done on it. The potential contractor used this document to estimate the cost of the work and submitted his bid to the property owner. If the submission was accepted, the tender then became the contract between the two parties. The tenderer was required to adhere to the specifications laid down in the document and the customer retained a copy to show what was originally stipulated. Any agreed subsequent departures from this specification were likely to mean an extra payment to the contractor. Similarly, any omission by the contractor from the detailed provisions was likely to justify the client withholding part of the previously agreed payment. This type of document might have been drawn up not just for building works, but also for interior decorations and fittings. The original purpose was the same in both instances: to provide an agreed written basis on which the work was to be carried out. In any dispute, the two parties would refer back to this document and, if still in conflict, refer the matter to an independent arbitrator who would mediate using the original tender as prime evidence.

Another sort of record which often survives about industrial buildings is the architect's drawing and occasionally the scale model. These were created for a number of reasons. In some cases they were an attempt to obtain a contract to do a particular piece of work. The architect submitted outline drawings which were put before the board in competition with the schemes of other architects and designers in the hope of winning the order to carry out the design of the building. Thus their original purpose was to sell an idea, design or image to a particular company and so drum up work for the architects. A secondary purpose, if the scheme was successful, was to act as the overall plan from which many detailed drawings would be drafted which, in turn, would lead to a tender document via quantity surveyors. Such plans could equally well be drawn up for the conversion or renovation of an existing building, or the redecoration and remodelling of an interior, as for the construction of a whole new building on a green-field site. Another original reason for such plans may have been to guide millwrights, engineers or machine installers as to the positioning, spacing and orientation of the equipment needed in a factory. Edgar Jones has drawn on a number of such documents for cotton and woollen mills where the size and shape of the mill was dictated by the dimensions of the machinery to be used.[1]

Insurance firms were also interested in the layout of buildings and, before agreeing to take the risk on any particular premise, often insisted on the submission of plans and statements as to the whereabouts of fire hazards such as boilers, open fires, candle, oil or gas lights, and any inflammable material such as raw wool or cotton, pitch or turpentine. They certainly wanted details of any explosives, volatile substances or other high-risk articles. They were also concerned to know the method of construction of the building and the degree to which fire-proof materials had been used and this information was indicated on the surveyor's plan. The firm often kept a copy of any such document sent to the prospective insurer. The original purpose of these documents was to allow the insurance company to evaluate the degree of risk and either set an appropriate premium or refuse the business as too chancey. There was an obvious conflict of interest between the potential insurer and insured. The latter wished to convince the former to take on the business and was likely to be inclined to play down the risks involved whereas the latter wanted as full an exposition as possible of all hazards and sources of fire and flood. For this reason, many insurance companies insisted on sending their own surveyor to assess the risk and make a report, often accompanied by a plan. If agreement was reached between the two parties, a fire insurance policy was issued which was the legal contract between the insurer and insured.

Finally, some of the documents about premises served no other purpose than to record internal arrangements. Plans or drawings showing the position of various services — gas, water or sewerage pipes, electric or telephone cable runs — might be important in any future reconstruction of the building or in case of a breakdown. A reminder of when and how a room was decorated and fitted out was important in determining the time and type of redecoration. Photographs were taken or, earlier, drawings made of buildings, rooms, shop layouts or factory interiors, sometimes for publicity purposes to impress customers with the modernity, cleanliness or prestige of the firm; sometimes, especially just before a radical transformation was about to ensue, to record what had been before it was swept away. Interior designers often kept photographs of their work for use as advertising for future business.

Thus the original purposes for drawing up premises records are as various as the types of material involved. In some cases they were legal documents to provide a basis for work undertaken and to act as the 'bible' in any dispute. Sometimes they were more like marketing documents convincing a board of directors of the beauty or efficacy of a design; in others they were meant to be objective records of design, layout or fittings for the company's own purposes of maintenance, repair or refurbishment, or for external parties such as insurers or contractors. Some of these purposes are liable to lead to bias and the researcher needs to be aware of these.

Sources

Unfortunately the central government never required the submission of any returns relating to premises other than the address of the registered office of a company. Thus there is no single source easily available and maintained over a long period. For a particular company, as we have suggested for many other documents, the best source is that company itself: it may have an in-house archive or it may know where its records have been deposited. If that leads to nothing, it might be worth trying the solicitors who acted for the firm at the time for it may be that they hold deeds, leases and conveyances in a basement strong box. As we have also noted before, because of the value lawyers place on confidentiality they are usually very reluctant to allow any access to their holdings. At the minimum it will require written permission from the business specifying which documents may be examined; at the worst, access may be refused entirely or the presence of any document denied.

A useful source in terms of plans and drawings of buildings is the British Architectural Library at the Royal Institute of British Architects (RIBA). As well as holding printed books on all aspects of architecture, they also collect the papers of the more famous architects and have over 400,000 drawings.[2] If a particular architect was known to have been commissioned to do a design for a specific company there might be a plan, drawing, specification or some other reference in his papers which may be at the RIBA. Even where the RIBA does not hold the papers of a particular architect, it may know their location or if indeed they survive. Another source for similar information is the NRA at the HMC. As well as having catalogues arranged by name of the individual, they also have them arranged by trade or profession. The annual journal of the BAC, *Business Archives*, for the last decade or so has carried annual lists of records deposited with various archives extracted from the HMC publication, *Accessions to Repositories and Reports added to the National Register of Archives*, and classified by type of industry or service. One of the classifications is 'architects'. If it is known that a particular architect was involved there is, therefore, no real excuse for not discovering whether his papers or drawings still exist and are open to study. They may shed some light on the company which commissioned him and his relation with it. Similar lines of enquiry could be pursued when a civil engineer was involved in the construction of a factory, mill or railway. The Institute of Civil Engineers is the obvious first stop to try and locate relevant papers. The Science Museum in London also collects the papers of eminent engineers and, though most of these are mechanical, electrical or hydraulic rather than civil, it does hold the papers of some civil engineers who might be of interest if investigating a railway, shipping or dock business.

The insurance companies in the last decade or so have begun to make their records available to the researcher and they contain a wealth of information on building construction, plans, maps, drawings, specifications, letters, policies and reports on the state of the buildings. Unless it is known from some other source that a particular firm was insured with a specific insurance company, these records can be difficult to use for there is no overall index of the firms for whom insurance was undertaken. To ascertain if any records relevant to a particular company survived, the researcher will have a tedious search through each insurance company's catalogues or card indexes. A very useful guide has been published to the records of insurance companies and the reader is recommended to consult it before embarking on any such search.[3] There is no doubt that the records of the insurance companies do contain much material of relevance to anyone interested in premises records, although tracking down an individual company or building is a daunting task. As Cockerell and Green say, 'insurance records can yield more "physical" information about defunct businesses and factories than any other single source'.[4]

For more recent history, another source of material about premises is the records of local government. Since the introduction of planning permission and building regulations, any firm intending to build from scratch or alter an existing building has had to provide documentation to the authority including maps and plans to show the work to be done and that it complies with regulations. To obtain access to these records will mean ascertaining the relevant local authority and whether the records are open. They are usually deposited in the local county or city record office.

The information they contain

Because of the wide range of documents being discussed under this heading, the information that they can contain is equally broad. Conveyances include a definition of the property, often both in words and on a map or plan. They state the names and addresses of the parties involved in the transaction, the consideration, or sum of money being paid, information about neighbouring property or its owners which will help locate the particular piece, the precise property, that is whether land alone or whether there are also buildings on the site and what sort, an estimate of the total size in acres or square yards, the date, signature and seal, if any, plus a witness and his or her name and address. They are written in obtuse legal language and contain many phrases of importance in law about idemnities, enjoying the use of the land and so on which lengthen the document but, because they appear regularly in any such item, add little information. Title deeds contain very similar material, again stating names, addresses, details of the property involved, any restrictive covenants or rights of way, usually accompanied by a map or plan, again witnessed and wrapped up in verbose phraseology. Leases bear a passing similarity to both these documents in that they share the same legal language, are signed, stamped and witnessed and contain very similar details with the addition of the length of the lease, the precise conditions of each party in terms of repair, maintenance and decoration, whether the rent is fixed or subject to regular reviews, whether it can be terminated by either side on giving a period of notice, what state the property must be in at the end of the period of lease and whether the lessee is liable for dilapidations and returning the property to its original state. Any restrictions, for instance on sub-leasing or type of use, are also stated.

Plans, architect's drawings and models, as well as being useful illustrative material, often also contain details of the materials used in construction, the uses of various rooms, the location of key features in a factory such as the engine house, boiler room and chimney, the offices and counting house. When such plans were drawn up for insurance purposes they were particularly careful to note fire-proof materials such as brick, iron or steel joists and to pinpoint fire hazards such as the boilers, stores of 'oily waste' and bales of wool or cotton. 'The fire offices appointed surveyors to assess properties which contained major fire hazards or exceeded a stated value. The surveyors inspected building materials, production methods, raw materials for manufacture, and located sources of power, heat, and light. A number of surveyors' plans of workshops and factories have survived.'[5] If factories were built on 'fire-proof' principles, the owners enjoyed lower insurance premiums. Some plans also noted the nearest source of water — a river, spring or pool which could be used by a fire appliance attending a conflagration. These plans, especially in the more modern period, also contain details of services installed, such as gas pipes, electrical cables and phone wires. Many plans included a description of the methods of construction: the thicknesses and dimensions of various materials, whether stone or brick is to be, or has been, used.

This is particularly true of architect's drawings, where the architect was concerned to demonstrate solidity of design and longevity, and insurance proposals, where the firm wished to minimize premium payments by emphasizing fire resistance. Tenders give precise details of the method of construction and the quantity and quality of materials to be used. Where they survive, they contain a wealth of evidence on the nitty-gritty of building methods down to mortar mixes, types of wooden joint and types of plaster.

Some inventories are of great value in listing interior fixtures and fittings, the number and position of oil lights, gas mantles or candle holders, the layout of machinery, the distances between machines, and the positioning of various departments of a factory relative to each other. A number also contain details of the interior decoration of the building. Not all Victorian industrial buildings were plain and functional; many were built with an eye to enhancing the prestige of the firm or its owners and money was spent on appearance as well as function, with cupolas, finials and quoins. This largesse occasionally extended to the interior, and pumping stations or engine houses in particular were decorated tastefully to match the engines themselves, which were usually polished, painted and kept gleaming, with stained glass, fancy window shapes and colour-washed walls.

Where a firm owned property abroad, the surveyor or property manager of the firm, when visits or revaluations were being made, often took it upon himself to comment not merely on the state of the land and buildings but also upon local economic and political conditions which might affect the value of the company's property. The market value of land or property pre-supposes there to be an active market in that commodity; if the political situation is so unstable that no one wishes to invest in the country, the book value of the property may be quite unrealistic and thus figures recorded in the published accounts (q.v.) may be suspect. Similarly, if there are local labour problems or a lack of adequate transport to the area, its economic value might have been significantly diminished. The more astute and aware surveyor took these wider considerations into account and in so doing provided the latter-day researcher with an unexpected bonus.

Uses

Property records are of obvious value to the student of architectural history. If interested in the work of particular famous architects, it is possible to trace individual buildings and begin to understand how the designer's style evolved and developed, to show the range of buildings an individual designed and whether he specialized, for instance, in banks or cotton mills or showed eclectic tastes. A good example is Edwin Lutyens who designed a number of buildings now occupied by the Midland Bank Group.[6] It may be possible to trace 'schools' of architecture, or at least the adoption of common styles by virtue of a common function, locality or building material. One or two recent historians have argued that the design of industrial architecture should be seen as deriving at least in part from fashions and styles in other sectors such as churches, country houses and commercial buildings[7] and use of property records might demonstrate common styles or designs and indicate any explicit carry-over from other buildings.

Similar considerations apply to any study of the history of design. Although industrial architecture is not likely to be a very rich source, commercial buildings such as banks, insurance companies and offices may provide insights into the layout of interiors, the type of furniture used, its design and materials, the shape, size and type of light fittings, the use of ornaments such as vases, clocks or mirrors, the colour schemes used on interiors and whether walls were papered, painted or distempered, whether decorative friezes, dado lines or ceiling roses were used. From such details the student of design history can build up a general picture of how styles and fashions evolved, spread and disappeared; the degree to which materials or function dictated design and how far there was commonality between industrial, domestic and commercial design.

The industrial archaeologist is particularly indebted to premises records as his main areas of interest are the buildings and the machinery that they housed. If wishing to discover the precise functions which occurred in each room, the superstructure which was originally erected on what is now only a ground plan, how the use and layout of a building changed over time, the relationship between various buildings in a complex such as a group of forges and furnaces, then the obvious place to seek elucidation is among the premises records of the original firm and any which took over the site or building. Premises records are a great help to industrial archaeologists when they consider restoration of a particular historic building or group of structures. In order to encourage study of industrial history and celebrate the design of the buildings, many have been restored as living museums to educate, inform and amuse visitors. Prime sites are those in which it is possible to recreate the activities which originally took place there. Thus many beam engines are apparently back in service pumping water or raising loads, although the power is now often provided by an electric motor. Some still use coal or coke, boilers and steam power, but minimize the effort required by reducing the work the pump has to do. Some buildings in the City of London such as Whitbread's brewery have been lovingly restored; engine houses, from fenland pumps to keep the low-lying levels drained to Cornish beam engines once used to raise men and ores from the mines, have been refurbished to act as tourist attractions; some sites have been restored to demonstrate living and working habits of a century or more ago, such as the award-winning Ironbridge Gorge Museum or the forge, water wheel and hammers in Sticklepath, Devon, or the complex of workshops, cottages and sheds showing how hand tools were crafted just outside Sheffield. The accurate restoration of any of these would have been very much more difficult without use of the relevant premises records. Groups such as the Historic Buildings Division of the GLC, and its successor, and the similar departments in other local authorities find this class of records of especial value when restoring or maintaining specimen buildings.

Those scholars interested in construction history can draw much material from premises records. The Construction History Group, as well as the history of individual building firms, is interested in innovations in the use of materials, where and when a particular material such as steel or concrete or type of construction was first used; how rapidly the technique spread or whether it was abandoned as impractical; the height and size of buildings, whether factories dominated the surrounding houses or merged in; the extent to which builders concentrated on residential or industrial construction or worked equally happily in either; these sorts of questions can be in part answered from premises records. Similar usage can be made by the industrial historian of this type of document. He may wish to discover the way in which a factory was laid out, whether there was logic in the way the various departments were positioned in order to ensure a steady flow of part-completed work around the factory, or whether it was thrown together higgledy-piddledy with no attempt to minimize movement of materials or semi-finished components. These documents may show if the process was batch production, as most were in the early nineteenth century, and when a change was made to continuous production requiring assembly lines, flows of work through the factory and perhaps a total reorganization. Some firms such as Boulton and Watt were innovative in arranging a logical layout of their factory to ensure the work progressed in such a way as to minimize distance travelled. Others, such as Kenricks, seem to have had little idea of these principles even in the 1920s or 1930s.[8] Another area of prime importance is the source of power used by firms to drive their machinery; this can be investigated from premises records. The timing and speed of transition from one power source to another is crucial. Some firms such as Courtaulds shifted from horse to water power and then to steam power in a very short period, even if the initial use of the steam engine was to pump the water back when it had worked the water wheel to drive it again.[9] In the late nineteenth century the adoption of gas engines and electric power can be traced and explained with plans of factory layouts. Similar investigations could be made of the types of machinery used in particular industries, the dating of the introduction of ring spinning, its speed and methods of transfer, or the adoption of open-hearth furnaces for steel production. A whole range of important areas on the border of industrial and technological history could be investigated in part using premises records. Sometimes photographs can be used to show machine layout and type with the name of the maker obligingly displayed. Premises records may also be able to contribute to the debate about capital formation in the process of industrialization. Questions have been raised as to the relative importance of fixed versus circulating capital, whether the British experience was much different from continental imitators, which industries were capital-intensive, the complementarity and timing of investment inputs.[10] Where values can be ascertained from surviving records about premises, it may be possible to contribute to this discussion at least at the level of individual sites or firms.

A number of other specialist areas of historical research can benefit from using primary sources such as premises records. The historian of insurance will find details of construction and layout relevant to assessing fire risk, as already mentioned.[11] There may also be references to actual fires to give an indication of the frequency and seriousness of such forces. There may be mention of premiums paid and the insurance companies used, discussion of how to guard against fire and whether the firm had their own fire-fighting appliances, as many did. For the urban historian, there may be maps showing how an area developed, indicating whether there were specifically industrial areas or residential and industrial were intermixed, whether there was any formal or more likely informal planning by the local authority. It was claimed that the Borough of Ealing in west London excluded any manufacturing industry from its boundaries in the early twentieth century in order to preserve a genteel, residential ethos unpolluted by factory smoke or sound. Many towns have produced detailed development plans at some time, and these usually indicate the attitude of the planners to industrial and commercial development.[12] The early development of a species of town planning can be traced through the premises records of industrial concerns as the earliest examples were tried by entrepreneurs such as Sir Titus Salt, the Cadbury Brothers, William Lever and the Rowntrees.[13] Their sites in Saltaire, Bournville and Port Sunlight were essays in providing reasonable residential dwellings for their workers alongside light, airy, clean and safe factories, and also a set of amenities such as a library, swimming pool, sports grounds and parks. Thus the prime sources for studying early urban planning are to be found in company archives. This area is also of concern to those studying labour conditions in industry because the activities of paternalists like Cadbury or Lever indicate not merely their concern with the material welfare of their employees but also an attitude of mind which was likely to be reflected throughout their firms, perhaps in worker consultation, reasonable wages and high-quality working conditions. Although they may not be typical of late nineteenth-century employers, they throw doubt on the hypothesis of the emisseration of the workers and in part offset the appalling conditions inflicted by some inhumane employers. Some idea of working conditions can also be gleaned from 'action' photographs of the works. It has to be remembered, however, that these were not spontaneous but very much posed pictures and the area displayed was often packed with more staff than would normally have been there, and they were well turned out knowing they were on camera.

Finally, these records can be of value to a more glamorous group of researchers: those who are designing a stage, film or TV set may locate some of their action in an industrial or commercial setting. In order to check what is appropriate to a period and locality, they are well advised to consult the archives of a relevant firm, especially where there is a photograph or drawing collection. These will ensure the right period feel and historical accuracy which is increasingly considered of importance to a good presentation.

Because of the great range of documents, plans, maps and photographs covered in this chapter, their uses are manifold. We have not been able to cover all of them here but merely pick out the more interesting or those where most material is likely to be found. They are a very rich and varied source for historians of many persuasions and interests.

Cross-references to other documents

The land, buildings and leases owned by a firm represent long-term fixed assets and as such should appear on their annual balance sheet (q.v.). They needed to be assigned a value to so appear and for many companies until very recent times the normal practice was to allocate historic cost, that is the cost of the initial purchase or construction, less some element of depreciation. It was very rare for firms to revalue their real estate to ascertain current market rates or engage outside surveyors to do this. Therefore the values placed on this form of asset can be quite inaccurate and represent 'book' figures only and have no relation to market values. Another problem in using property values in balance sheets is that they were not always separated out from a hodge-podge of other assets. It was not unusual to lump together goodwill, trademarks, patent rights, freehold and leasehold property and then assign one value for the whole lot. Furthermore, not infrequently this value remained substantially unaltered over long time periods, such as decades. Until the 1928 Companies Act this was quite legal and it was only after that legislation that companies were required to show goodwill, patents and trademarks in one separate heading, assets in subsidiaries in another, and real estate was left as another separate heading. Even after this date it was not unusual to put all such property under one heading so it is very difficult to arrive at a market valuation of any particular factory or mill.

More detail can sometimes be found when a firm depends on its land more wholeheartedly than the average manufacturing firm. If the main activity of a business is a plantation, mine or timbered forest, it is likely to place greater emphasis on land values. Some such companies append maps or plans to their reports and accounts to show the extent, position and degree of exploitation of such a natural resource. The Assam Company, whose main business was tea growing, did this on a number of occasions. Thus it may be of value to consult reports and accounts to throw light on premises and land values.

Most of the other documents dealt with in this book may shed some light on land and premises. The board minute books (q.v.), for instance, may contain discussions about whether to open new branches or factories; the need to close a building and rebuild because of obsolesent design or falling demand; which design to adopt for a mill and which architect or builder seems the best. There may be high-level decisions on whether to sink new shafts to an existing mine, buy more land on which to grow additional tea or rubber, and when an existing premise needs a complete renovation and redecoration. Generally this source is likely to be concerned with strategic decisions and those involving considerable expenditure, but some boards descended to surprisingly low-level minutiae on some occasions. Similarly, letter books (q.v.) often contain correspondence relating to premises, letters to and from architects and builders, insurance firms, decorators and local authorities, or the impact of war and natural disasters on company property; there are a host of possibilities too numerous to mention here.

A whole class of specialized business records which are invaluable to any study of premises, to which numerous references have already been made, is that of the various insurance companies. The policy registers of these companies are 'the most important source . . . of descriptions and valuations of insured property . . . These records were the head office compilations of orders for insurance from all branches and agencies. They summarised relevant information about the building or contents underwritten . . . including details of ownership, construction and value . . . most entries . . . describe building materials, neighbouring properties, and occupational hazards associated with each insurance.'[14] As such they are invaluable to any researcher interested in buildings or their contents, but the problem of locating an individual firm or factory has to be emphasized, since most registers are not indexed or classified.

Finally, a useful adjunct to any study of premises or sites is a large-scale ordnance survey map of the area involved. The 6 inches to the mile gives a very large scale which will make it possible to locate individual factories if they are of a reasonable size. These maps go back some time and by using the appropriate edition it is possible to obtain a pretty good idea of what an area looked like at a particular period, how the area developed and how industry fitted into the locality.

Works using this source

Stanley Chapman pioneered the use of the insurance companies' records to attempt to determine the amount and nature of fixed capital used in the process of industrialization. He used the Sun Fire Office valuations of the Peel family's manufacturing interests at the end of the eighteenth century for this purpose. The Sun insured many of the Peel properties and details of these policies have survived, as have the detailed inventories on which the Sun insisted.[15] A more comprehensive survey of the value and limitations of fire insurance records for calculating the types and values of fixed capital was written by Dr Chapman a few years later.[16] Resulting from this, others have used these records to ascertain the types of power source used in factory industry. Dr Jenkins used the country registers of the Sun Fire Office for the West Riding of Yorkshire to see how scribbling machinery was powered, and to trace the shift from hand power to more inanimate forms.[17] He found that many types of power source were used — hand, horse, water and steam — but that the most common was water power. In the same volume, Chapman pushed his own work using insurance records further.[18] He used 'the first hundred volumes of the Sun Fire Office series [of insurance policy registers which] cover the period 1710–50, each volume containing hundreds of policies, many of them for the textile industries . . . [after 1728 they] also give an outline inventory of his property and its contents, with a separate valuation of each item. Policies readily divulge the insured person's interest in various branches of industry . . . and his investment in property.'[19] From this mammoth study he concluded it was an 'easy matter to transfer capital from one industry to another within the region . . . because entrepreneurs maintained a high proportion of their assets in liquid form and their fixed capital investment avoided heavy commitment to any one industry'.[20] There is a growing literature drawing on the vast and largely untapped records of insurance and insurance companies.

Historians dealing with many manufacturing and processing concerns have used this type of document, especially where complex machinery required particular conditions, or the shape, size and extent of the premise dictated output levels and productivity. Barker in his study of Pilkingtons uses, among many other documents, leases to show how the glassworks began in a disused iron foundry near the Sankey Canal[21] and an abstract of title to indicate that the St Helens Building Society lent the six initial partners in the venture £400 each to help them construct their glassworks;[22] when two of the founders, J.W. and Thomas Bell, sold their shares in the business to finance their defence in a case brought against them by the Excise for defrauding the public purse, these shares were bought by the remaining four partners.[23]

Premises records relating to docks, shipyards and slipways have been used by maritime historians to show the amount of capital equipment required, the degree to which inanimate power was supplanting manual labour, and the changes which were brought about by the switch from wooden hulls and sail to iron and steam.[24] There are also many works on industrial archaeology which drew on premises records to supplement and explain the remaining physical evidence which can be examined on field trips and explored in excavations.[25] Although the use of premises records is not always emphasized, because of their legal status they have tended to survive to a greater extent than some other classes and so give clues as to the location, buildings, value and partners of early firms when other sources are not available. Because of this they are always consulted when writing the history of a particular business.

The example

The example illustrated here is of a conveyance drawn up in 1847. In it Timothy Thorney sold a timber yard and bonding wharf to the Hull Dock Company for £10,898 10/-. The Company obtained a private Act of Parliament to allow it limited liability and to compel property owners to sell the land which it required to construct the new docks and quays. It contained a rough sketch plan as well as a verbal description of the land, buildings, boundary markers and adjoining property. The vendor attested that he was entitled to sell and indemnified the purchaser against any claims arising in the event of his not being the rightful owner.

This property was ultimately acquired by Joseph Rank, the flour miller, possibly in 1890 when he first built a mill direct on the quayside to ease access to imported grain. This followed Rank's entry to milling in 1875 and his use, first of steam power in 1880 and then roller milling in 1885. Ranks took corporate form in 1899 and became a public company in 1933. In 1962 it acquired Hovis McDougall to become Ranks Hovis McDougall Ltd and thus the conveyance passed into this corporate archive.[26]

Notes

1. Edgar Jones, *Industrial Architecture* (Batsford, 1985) pp. 144, 166 & 167.
2. An immensely valuable guide to the contents of the RIBA has just been published: A. Mace, *The Royal Institute of British Architects: A Guide to its Archive and History* (Mansell, 1986).
3. H.A.L. Cockerell & E. Green, *The British Insurance Business 1547–1970* (Heinemann, 1976).
4. Ibid., p. 18.
5. Ibid., p. 20.
6. Edwin Green, 'Bank Archives for Historians', *Business Archives*, No. 49 (1983) p. 3.
7. Jones, op. cit.
8. E. Roll, *An Early Experiment in Industrial Organisation* (Cass, 1968) pp. 186–8; R.A. Church, *Kenricks in Hardware* (David & Charles, 1969) pp. 205–6.
9. D.C. Coleman, *Courtaulds: An Economic and Social History Vol. I* (Oxford UP, 1969) chap. V.
10. There is a huge literature on this topic. A good idea of the debate and a useful bibliography is to be found in F. Crouzet (ed.), *Capital Formation in the Industrial Revolution* (Methuen, 1972).
11. See also L.M. Wulcko, 'Fire Insurance Policies as a Source of Legal History', *Local Historian*, Vol. IX, No. 1 (1970).
12. For example, see C.H. James & S.R. Pierce, *Royal Leamington Spa: a plan for development* (priv. pub., 1947) which is typical of many such works on towns which were redeveloped in the 1940s and 1950s.
13. J. Reynolds, *The Great Paternalist: Titus Salt and the Growth of Nineteenth Century Bradford* (Maurice Temple Smith, 1983); I.A. Williams, *The Firm of Cadbury* (Constable, 1931) chaps. 3 & 4; C. Wilson, *The History of Unilever. Vol I* (Cassell, 1954) chap. 10.
14. Cockerell & Green, op. cit., pp. 26–7.
15. S.D. Chapman, 'The Peels in the Early English Cotton Industry', *Business History*, Vol. 11, No. 1 (1969).
16. S.D. Chapman, 'Fixed Capital Formation in the British Cotton Manufacturing Industry' in J.P.P. Higgins & S. Pollard (eds), *Aspect of Capital Investment in Great Britain 1750–1850* (Methuen, 1971) pp. 57–119.
17. D.T. Jenkins, 'Early Factory Development in the West Riding of Yorkshire 1770–1880' in N.B. Harte & K.G. Ponting (eds), *Textile History and Economic History: Essays in Honour of Miss Julia de Lacy Mann* (Manchester UP, 1973) chap. 10.
18. S.D. Chapman, 'Industrial Capital before the Industrial Revolution: an analysis of the assets of a thousand textile entrepreneurs c. 1730–50' in Harte & Ponting, op. cit.
19. Ibid., p. 155.
20. Ibid., p. 136.
21. T.C. Barker, *The Glassmakers, Pilkington: the rise of an international company 1826–1976* (Weidenfeld & Nicolson, 1977) p. 25.
22. Ibid., p. 33.
23. Ibid., pp. 34–5.
24. R. Craig, 'William Gray & Company: a West Hartlepool shipbuilding enterprise, 1864–1913' in P.L. Cottrell & D.H. Aldcroft (eds), *Shipping, Trade and Commerce: Essays in memory of Ralph Davis* (Leicester UP, 1981) pp. 165–91.

25. The David & Charles series *The Industrial Archaeology of the British Isles*, in several volumes, is a good starting place to this subject.

26. D.J. Jeremy (ed.), *Dictionary of Business Biography, Vol. 4* (Butterworths, 1985) pp. 828–36; R.G. Burnett, *Through the Mill: the Life of Joseph Rank* (Epworth, 1945); *The Master Millers. The Story of the House of Rank* (Harley, 1956) a commemorative volume issued on the company's eightieth anniversary.

D A T E D   6th August

23.

No. 101.   Vol. 44.

Mr. TIMOTHY THORNEY

to

THE DOCK COMPANY
at Kingston upon Hull.

C O N V E Y A N C E.

of a Timber or Bonding Yard Wharf
or Quay Clough and Hereditaments
situate on the East side of the
River Hull.

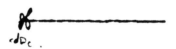

14. Pages from a conveyance of a timber wharf by Timothy Thorney to
The Dock Co at Kingston upon Hull, 6 August 1847.
Source: Ranks Hovis McDougall Records Centre, Windsor.
(The RHM Records Office is *not* normally open to members of the public
for research purposes)

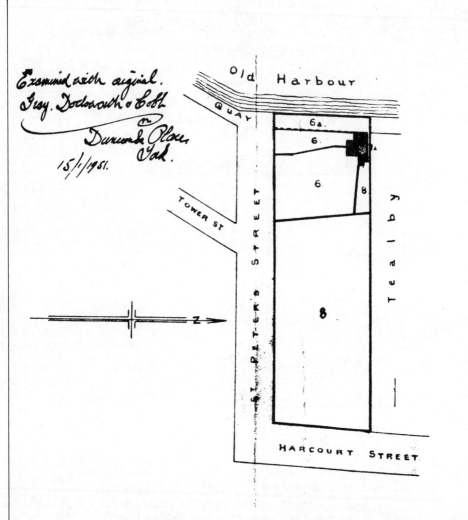

COPY OF PLAN ON CONVEYANCE FROM Mᴿ TIMOTHY THORNEY
TO THE DOCK COMPANY AT KINGSTON UPON HULL OF A
TIMBER OR BONDING YARD WHARF ON QUAY CLOUGH AND
HEREDITAMENTS SITUATE ON THE SIDE OF THE RIVER HULL.
DATED 6ᵀᴴ AUGUST, 1847.
Nᵒ 101 VOL.44.

14. Pages from a conveyance of a timber wharf by Timothy Thorney to
The Dock Co at Kingston upon Hull, 6 August 1847.
Source: Ranks Hovis McDougall Records Centre, Windsor.
(The RHM Records Office is *not* normally open to members of the public
for research purposes)

I TIMOTHY THORNEY OF THE Borough of Kingston upon Hull Timber
Merchant in consideration of the sum of TEN THOUSAND EIGHT
HUNDRED AND NINETY EIGHT POUNDS AND TEN SHILLINGS paid to me
pursuant to an Act passed in the eighth year of the Reign of Her
Majesty Queen Victoria intituled " An Act for making New Docks
and other works connected therewith in addition to the present Docks
at Kingston upon Hull and for amending the Acts relating to such last
mentioned Docks" by the Dock Company at Kingston upon Hull (which
said sum of Ten thousand eight hundred and ninety eight pounds
and ten shillings is the full value or purchase money of or for the
Hereditaments and premises hereby conveyed DO hereby convey to the
said Dock Company their successors and Assigns ALL those pieces or
parcels of Land Timber or Bonding Yard Wharf or Quay Timber Pond
Clough Entrance and passage to the Timber Pond Hereditaments and
premises situate and being on the Garris-on side in the Borough of
Kingston upon Hull and bounded as to the said Timber or Bonding
Yard on the West by the Quay or Wharf hereinbefore mentioned on
the south by a certain Street called Saint Peters Street on the
East by the Timber pond hereinafter mentioned and on the North by
land or premises now or lately belonging to or occupied by Mrs.
Elizabeth Tealby and Mr. Robert Chapman Tealby or one of them
and by the passage to the said Timber Pond hereinafter mentioned
and bounded as to the said Wharf or Quay on the West by the River
Hull or Old Harbour on the North by part of the Harbour Quay on
the East by the said Timber or Bonding Yard hereinbefore described
and on the South by other part of the said Harbour Quay and Saint
Peters Street and bounded as to the said Timber Pond on the West
by the Timber or Bonding Yard hereinbefore described on the South
by Saint Peters Street aforesaid on the East by a certain other
Street called Harcourt Street and on the North by a certain
Timber Pond and premises now or lately belonging to or in the
occupation of the said Elizabeth Tealby and Robert Chapman
Tealby or one of them ALL of which said pieces or parcels of
Timber or Bonding Yard Wharf or Quay Timber Pond Clough Entra
and Passage Hereditaments and premises are more particularly
delineated and described on or in the Map or Plan and Boo

(— 4 —

Reference thereto relating deposited by the said Company in the Office
of the Clerk of the Peace of the said Borough of Kingston upon Hull
and Also in the Plan drawn in the Margin of these presents and
Numbered in such Maps or Plans and Book of Reference 6. 6a 7a and
8 and in such last mentioned Plan coloured Pink TOGETHER with
all Houses Outhouses Counting houses Lath shops Workshops Sheds
Offices Buildings or Erections Clough Entrances Passages Sluices
paths Ways Fences Hedges Ditches Rights members easements and
appurtenances to the said pieces or parcels of Land Timber or Bond
Yard Wharf or Quay Timber Pond Clough Entrance or Passage and eve:
of them in upon or belonging or held used and occupied or enjoyed
therewith respectively and which said pieces or parcels of Land
Timber or Bonding Yard with the Counting House Lath shop and
erections thereon and the said Wharf or Quay and the said Timber
Pond Clough and Entrance severally distinguished on the said plans
and Book of Reference by the Numbers 6.6a. 7a and 8 contain
together by estimation Three thousand four hundred and forty six
square Yards and four feet or thereabouts be the same more or less
AND of and in all ways rights and appurtenances to the said
Hereditaments and premises hereinbefore described or any of them
belonging and all such estate right title and Interest in and to the
said several Hereditaments and Premises hereinbefore particularly
described and each and every of them and every part and parcel
 thereof respectively as I am or shall become seized or possessed
or am by the said Act empowered to convey TO HOLD the said pieces
or parcels of Land Timber or Bonding Yard Wharf or Quay Timber Por
Clough Entrance and Passage to Timber Pond and Hereditaments and
all and singular other the premises hereby conveyed unto the said
Company their Successors and Assigns for ever according to the
true intent and meaning of the said Act and of the several Acts
therein recited relating to the Docks at Kingston upon Hull
aforesaid AND I the said Timothy Thorney for myself my heirs
executors and Administrators Covenant and agree with the said
Company their Successors and Assigns by these presents in manner
following (that is to say) That for and notwithstanding any Ac

-?-

14. Pages from a conveyance of a timber wharf by Timothy Thorney to
The Dock Co at Kingston upon Hull, 6 August 1847.
Source: Ranks Hovis McDougall Records Centre, Windsor.
(The RHM Records Office is *not* normally open to members of the public
for research purposes)

deed Matter or thing whatsoever by me or by any of my Ancestors
made done omitted committed or willingly suffered to the Contrary
I the said Timothy Thorney now have in myself good right and
absolute authority to convey the said pieces or parcels of Land
Timber or Bonding Yard Wharf or Quay Timber Pond Clough Entrance
and passage to Timber Pond Hereditaments and Premises hereby
conveyed or intended so to be with their Appurtenances unto the
said Company their Successors and Assigns for ever in manner
aforesaid according to the true intent and meaning of these presents
AND that it shall be lawful for the said Company their successors
and assigns from time to time and at all times hereafter peaceably
and quietly to have hold possess and enjoy the said pieces or parcels
of Land Timber or Bonding Yard Wharf or Quay Timber Pond Clough Entrance and passage to Timber Pond Hereditaments and Premises hereby
conveyed or intended so to be with their Appurtenances and to have
received and take the rents issues and profits thereof and of
every part thereof for their own use and benefit without any lawful
let eviction interruption claim or demand whatsoever of or by me or
my Heirs or of or by any other persons or person lawfully or
equitably claiming or to claim by from under or in trust for me or
any of my Ancestors and that free and absolutely acquitted and
discharged or otherwise by me my Heirs executors or administrators
well and sufficiently saved kept harmless and indemnified from and
against all and all manner of former and other estates Titles Debts
troubles charges and Incumbrances whatsoever either already or to
be hereafter made occasioned or suffered by me or my Heirs or any of
my Ancestors or by any other person or persons lawfully or equitably
claiming or to claim by from or under or in trust for me or them
or any of them AND FURTHER that I the said Timothy Thorney and my
Heirs and all other persons claiming or to claim any estate right
title or Interest claim or demand at Law or in Equity in to or out
of the said pieces or parcels of Land Timber or Bonding Yard Wharf
or Quay Timber Pond Clough Entrance and Passage to Timber Pond s
Hereditaments and Premises hereby conveyed or intended so to be or
any part thereof by from under or in trust for me or any of my
Ancestors will from time to time and at all times hereafter upon

-3-

every reasonable request to be made for that purpose by and at the
Costs of the said Company their Successors or Assigns make do or
execute or cause to be made done and executed all such further
lawful and reasonable Acts deed things Conveyances and Assurances
for the further and more absolute conveying and assuring the
said pieces or parcels of Lands Timber or Bonding Yard Wharf
or Quay Timber Pond Clough Entrance or passage to Timber Pond
Hereditaments and Premises hereby conveyed or intended so to be
and every part and parts thereof with their and every of their
Appurtenances unto the said Company their Successors and Assigns
in manner as aforesaid and according to the true intent and
meaning of these presents as by the said Company their Successors
or Assigns or their Counsel in the Law shall be reasonably devised
advised and required so that no such further assurance contain or
imply any further or other covenant or Warranty than against the
person or persons who shall be required to make or execute the same
 and his her or their heirs executors or Administrators acts and
Deeds only so that the party or parties who shall be required to
make or execute such further or other assurance or assurances
be not compelled or compellable for the making or doing thereof to
go or travel from his her or their usual place or places of abode
IN WITNESS whereof I have hereunto set my hand and Seal the sixth
day of August in the Year of our Lord one thousand eight hundred
and forty seven

Signed sealed and delivered   )
(being first duly stamped) by the)
within named Timothy Thorney in the)   Timothy Thorney
presence of :-   )

        Jno Thorney
          Tho. Hindes (Sworn)
             Clerk to Charles Frost
             Solicitor, Hull.

A Memorial of the within written Deed was   )
Registered at Beverley the fourteenth day of August)
Eighteen hundred and forty seven at two in the   )
Afternoon in Book G.H. Page, 349 and number, 368.)

             Maister.
               Registrar.

                 -:-

14. Pages from a conveyance of a timber wharf by Timothy Thorney to
The Dock Co at Kingston upon Hull, 6 August 1847.
Source: Ranks Hovis McDougall Records Centre, Windsor.
(The RHM Records Office is *not* normally open to members of the public
for research purposes)

```
Received on the day and year within written      )
of and from the within named Dock Company        )
the sum of Ten thousand eight hundred and ninety  )   £      s   d
eight pounds and ten shillings being the consideration) 10.898.  10.  C
money within mentioned to be paid by them to me.  )


Witness                         Timothy Thorney.

      Jno Thorney,

          Tho. Hindes
```

15 Dealers and agency agreements

Original purpose

The main reason for the creation of dealerships or agencies was to allow one firm to delegate part of its business operations to another. This allowed greater specialization and permitted separate organizations to concentrate on a limited range of business activities, such as one company manufacturing a product and another undertaking the selling and marketing of it, as in the example. In other cases it might be because of geographical separation of the two spheres of activity, for instance a London-based company running ships to the Far East might appoint agents who were on the spot and had a sound knowledge of local laws, markets and economic conditions to act for them. Another reason for using dealerships or agencies was to minimize the amount of capital needed in a business. The principal firm avoided the cost of setting up retail outlets or starting its own branches abroad if it delegated these functions to a separate firm. This might be especially important in the early stages of a business when it required much capital to establish itself before significant profits begin to flow in. The agency system is still in use today, especially in difficult or peculiar markets such as the People's Republic of China or parts of Malaysia.

In a sense this relationship was a form of sub-contracting in which the main firm appointed another to act on its behalf and the specific agreement was a legal document which defined the extent of the delegation and the fees to be paid for the services performed. Agents usually had wide powers to act on behalf of the principal firm, whereas dealerships were usually restricted to marketing and selling a product or range of products made by the principal firm. It was unusual for a firm to appoint an agent at home but quite normal for it to use agents in foreign markets; it was more normal for dealerships to operate in the home market. While dealers usually only acted as merchants or retailers for a manufacturer, an agent had a much fuller role, providing market intelligence and research, arranging the advertising of the principal's product, and making deals with other companies on behalf of the principal firm on a full range of business activities. Since the agreement was intended to be binding on both parties, it was drawn up in legal language with great care taken to cover all aspects of the arrangement in terms which would stand up in a court of law should there be any dispute. The advantage to the agent or dealer of such undertakings was that he was given exclusive rights to perform the service for the principal company in a given geographical area. Therefore if the dealer was selling a range of products, he knew he would encounter no competition from other retailers selling the same branded product in his region. This did not eliminate competition because, of course, there might well be other brands or makes of the same product, but if the dealer perceived his brand to have unique advantages he could reap the benefit of all sales in that area.

Thus dealership and agency agreements were formal documents drawn up to define the services to be performed, the geographical area to be covered, the basis of remuneration and any other aspects of the relationship between the two firms.

Sources

Since these documents were perceived as binding agreements on both parties, they were likely to be carefully preserved by each side during the currency of the compact. Normally the company secretary would keep them in his strong box or safe. In some cases copies might also be lodged with the solicitors of the two parties for safekeeping. Thus the first place to look for any dealership or agency agreement would be the principal company or agency where they survive, or the firm which has absorbed the original business if it has been subject to takeover or amalgamation. If this fails, it might be worth approaching the partnership of solicitors who acted for either party at the date of the agreement, though it has to be said that solicitors are understandably wary of allowing access to any of their records or, indeed, even admitting that specific documents still exist.

Firms may preserve agreements which are no longer current, but this is less likely as they become more remote from the present. If the company is still in existence, it is worth starting the search there; however, it may be that the documents have been destroyed by one of the many baleful influences affecting record survival — war, flooding, salvage drives and lack of interest. A few have found their way into public repositories such as city or county record offices or even museums when the specimens are particularly interesting. To locate these the researcher should try each such institution near to the location of the firm involved or, if there is one, an archive specializing in the particular industry or trade. It is also worthwhile using the BAC and NRA to try to locate any surviving collections or relevant business records. The finding aids which they maintain may well indicate if there are any agency or dealership agreements among the collection.

Unfortunately, since this form of covenant never came under the scrutiny of company law, there was never any requirement to lodge copies or abstracts with the Registrar of Companies and thus it is not possible to access a large number of such documents in one readily available archive. However, there is one source which may be worth trying: the manuscripts department of the Guildhall Library where the London Stock Exchange has deposited the bulk of its historical records. These include the papers lodged with the Stock Exchange by companies seeking a listing for their securities on the official market. One of the Stock Exchange requirements was that all agreements which might have a bearing on the value of the business were declared at the time the company sought a listing or quotation. This included any agency agreements or dealerships. These records will be found in Ms 18000 'Applications for Listing' and there is a card index of the companies covered in alphabetical order at Ms 18001. Obviously this source will only contain public companies whose paper was traded on the London market, and in some cases the actual agreements may not survive, but only an abstract of them or their import.

Sometimes these agreements may be found bound inside other volumes of records, for instance within letter books or files of correspondence relating to the dealer or agent. Where this occurs, the researcher has a bonus in that there may well be additional information about why the agreement was made, how the relationship worked out, and why or how it was terminated. As these documents were often substantial and kept in strong linen-backed envelopes, they may stand out from the mass of flimsies and so make such a search less daunting than it at first sounds.

The information they contain

Because they were binding legal agreements, these documents tried to be as comprehensive as possible in laying down all the rights and obligations of the contract, the penalties for non-compliance and the circumstances under which they might be terminated. Among the information any such compact normally contains are the full names and addresses of both parties; the goods to be sold or the service to be performed, in the example 'Austin cars or chassis'; a definition of the territory for which the agent or dealer was responsible; clauses on the degree of exclusivity of the deal, in this case the dealer may not take on the agency for any other make of car and Austin agree to pay a commission to the dealer for all cars sold in his territory irrespective of whether he sells them direct so he is effectively exclusive Austin dealer in that specified region; financial arrangements such as the method of payment by the principal to the agent for providing the service, in this instance since the dealer is selling cars and spares he receives them at a discount on list price and then must retail them at that set price; details of the records to be kept by the dealer or agent about his activities which are to be open to the inspection of the principal company; and the conditions under which the agreement may be ended by either side, in the particular example if the dealer breaks a number of the clauses termination may ensue, death and bankruptcy are also sufficient causes, and in any eventuality it is only valid for nine months when it runs out anyway.

In addition to these general points, each agreement is likely to contain a number of sections particular to the specific trade or business. Financial minutiae may loom large since this was the core of the deal. The period within which payment had to be made may be specified, whether deposits or sureties are required (dealers in the motor industry are handling goods with a high unit value and thus deposits and sureties are a prominent feature), whether there were any performance-related bonuses — in the example the quarterly rebate can be seen as this, though it should be noted that no such bonus comes into effect until well over 160 cars per annum have been sold. If there were different rates of commission for different types of good or service this was made explicit, as was any obligation on the part of the dealer to provide particular back-up services to the main activity, in the example the dealer is required to spend 1 per cent of his sales revenue on advertising the product and must provide suitable premises not merely as a showroom but also for service and repairs to the vehicles. The question of damages for any breach of the agreement may be stated, as may the amount of time the agent is expected to spend on the principal's business and whether he may employ other staff to aid him or sub-contract any of the work to sub-agents.

Uses

The main value of these documents is the light they shed on the marketing functions of the companies involved, since all dealerships were agreements between a manufacturer and a firm which was to sell its products, and agencies had a major role in marketing goods and services for their principals. Therefore, to a researcher interested in the development of sales and marketing, these records are particularly useful. They are equally of importance to the historian who is researching a specific company for the detail they contain on that particular company's marketing methods.

Agency and dealership agreements can give an idea of the geographical extent of a product's distribution, whether it was sold throughout the UK or limited to certain areas; whether it was sold abroad and, if so, the type of foreign markets in which it was acceptable. This in turn demonstrates how far a commodity had ceased to be solely regional or national and had created an international market and was moving towards being a universal brand. These papers also give an intimation of the variety of articles made by the manufacturing company and the range of goods or services handled by the agent. They can also show whether this range expanded or contracted over time, indicating whether the firm was diversifying into a wider spread of goods or concentraing on a few main items. Similarly, the number of agency agreements made or dealers appointed can be important, for it is another indicator of the popularity of the product or service and also hints at the policy of the manufacturer or principal on agencies. Some firms, such as Ford UK, believed in appointing large numbers of small to medium dealers and limiting the number of Ford outlets held by one organization so ensuring that the balance of economic power was tilted in their favour. British Leyland, on the other hand, or at least those predecessor firms which later amalgamated to make up BL, was willing to appoint a few large chains of dealers who took a high proportion of the manufacturer's output. This placed them in a better position to deal with the manufacturer on more equal terms and to strike more equitable bargains.

These records can also be used to assess how far this balance of power changed over time: whether the tail (the agent or dealer) began to exercise greater influence or power over the dog (the manufacturer). This type of shift can be seen in the relationship between the Blue Funnel Line, which ran steamships to the Far East, and their agents in Shanghai and Hong Kong, Butterfield and Swire, later John Swire and Son. Initially the Holt brothers who founded and managed Blue Funnel were innovative and entrepreneurial and Swire was their agent in the Orient following their instructions and lead. However, after a decade or so of operations it was the agents, especially John Samuel Swire himself, who were urging on the Holts the need for faster, larger ships built in steel rather than iron if they were to compete effectively with the opposition.[1] Use of agency agreement or dealerships may also provide an insight into the growing strength of a manufacturer in marketing terms, or vice versa. If a company chose to take away all of its dealerships or agencies in order to market the product or service itself, it could be an indication that it had come of age in sales terms and felt sufficiently competent and moneyed to undertake this aspect direct. A recent example of this in the UK is BMW. Initially, BMW sold its cars and motorbikes through local agents. Once the market had been established and the number of units sold justified it, the German company bought out the main dealers and took over the marketing operations itself. The reverse trend may also be detected. If a manufacturer did not maintain product quality, failed to deliver on time or made increasingly obsolete goods, the number of dealers or agents in that product may have declined so showing general disillusion with the firm and that it was on a downward slope to economic perdition.

Dealer and agency agreements may be of importance in gauging the efficiency of the British economy as a whole. One aspect of the debate which has raged for several decades over the performance of the late-Victorian economy is the degree to which British entrepreneurs adopted their selling methods when they exported. One view is that, compared to their German or American competitors,

British businessmen relied too much on agents and failed to take a firm and positive lead in selling, advertising and distributing their products abroad. This contention has, inevitably, been hotly disputed.[2] An examination of some of the documents under discussion should indicate the precise terms between principal and agent and whether in fact the British agency agreement differed greatly from the examples of other countries, or if the conditions imposed on agents were very lax or failed to specify important details which would have ensured greater sales.

Finally, agency agreements and dealership contracts are of value to the historian interested in the development of law or, indeed, the lawyer interested in the history of his profession. They were intended as a legal document and the clauses they contain and how these vary over time indicate how solicitors adopted such agreements to take account of changes in statute law or, more importantly since they came under the law of contract, the precedents handed down by the courts. An examination of these records would show the speed of adoption to such cases, the looseness of wording which might give rise to disputes, and evolution of tighter drafting to cover problems which arose previously. Although agency and dealer agreements are mainly of use to study the marketing aspects of business, this should not be seen as minimizing their value. This side of operations is crucial to the success of a firm and has been relatively little studied in the aggregate, although many case studies exist of individual firms, entrepreneurs or products.

Cross-references to other documents

Background information about the origins of an agreement may be discovered in correspondence in the archives of both companies, for example in letter books (q.v.) or letter files or, in the event of especially valuable and important contracts, these may be announced to shareholders at AGMs and feature in the published reports and accounts (q.v.) or be the subject of press releases. These sources may indicate how and why a particular agent was appointed or why a specific territory was chosen. Advertisements of products by the agents on behalf of the manufacturer may be found in the trade press or, in the case of fast-moving consumer items, in the daily papers.[3] Records of individual travelling salesmen, if available, may add to our knowledge of the problems encountered by the agents in trying to sell particular goods.

The holding of an extremely valuable agency by a company counts as one of its assets and may be one of the reasons why it is attractive to other companies making take-over bids. So, letters to shareholders advising them why a company should sell out or, conversely, purchase another company may mention certain agencies. The researcher could then seek out the particular agreement for more information. Board minute books (q.v.) may also help flesh out the bare agreements in that they may have recorded discussions about the policy to be adopted in marketing a product. Why the agency route was chosen rather than selling direct, why the particular agents were chosen for that specific territory, why certain clauses were inserted in the document, are the sort of questions that may be answered. The minute books may also show how the agreements worked out in practice, whether both parties were pleased with the outcome or one side was constantly trying to alter the basis of the accord because it felt hard done by, and what were the problems of keeping to the terms.

Finally, although not strictly business documents, some public records may be a valuable adjunct, especially those among the Foreign Office papers dealing with consular reports about local market conditions, or correspondence from ambassadors or other diplomats commenting on British business methods and businessmen. These may mention individuals, partnerships or companies acting as agents and pass judgements on their efficiency and success. Consular reports were until very recently an almost unused source and this led the International Historical Congress at Edinburgh in 1978 to devote a whole session to them. The reader is recommended to the report of this session which looks not merely at UK consular reports but also those of many other developed countries.[4]

Works using this source

The current debate on Britain's economic performance in the late-Victorian and Edwardian periods had drawn attention to agency agreements. One component of the debate revolves around Britain's falling share of world exports in manufactured goods. This has been seen as evidence of British entrepreneurial failure, and the British businessman has been castigated on his choice of methods for selling overseas. Quite frequently this involved some variant of the agency system. Munting has shown that the agents employed by the agricultural engineering firm, Ransomes of Ipswich, were of a high standard, able to speak the language and often exclusive to Ransomes.[5] In a later article, Munting paints a similar picture but with a broader brush showing that British agricultural engineering firms in general picked their agents carefully and gave comparable credit terms, discounts, commissions and back-up as their rival German or American firms. Munting draws on a number of agency agreements *inter alia* for this study.[6] At an even more macro-level, Nicholas rejects the view that Britain employed the wrong institutional arrangements for selling goods in the international market and, drawing on agency agreements among other sources, supports Munting's conclusions for a wide range of markets, types of industry and firm sizes.[7]

Reference has already been made to the role of agents in shipping firms like Blue Funnel.[8] Any UK-based shipowner sailing to distant parts needed a good agency system if it was to be successful in finding return cargoes, ensuring sale of the outward freight, supervise repairs, fuelling and stores and numerous other tasks which were facilitated by knowledge of local customs and conditions. This is shown in business histories of merchant shipping partnerships and companies such as Harrisons[9] and also from the viewpoint of the numerous small agency partnerships such as Rathbones of Liverpool,[10] some of which were later to become major trading concerns such as the Inchcape Group and Jardine

Matheson.[11] Although the various agency agreements were only one of the sources that were used in these books, they were a vital starting point.

All agencies were not, however, acting as merchants for firms reluctant to sell direct in foreign markets. The agency system could be and was used in the UK. One example of this is the firm of George Spencer. Spencer invented, patented and sold rubber-based products for the suspension of railway carriages and wagons.[12] He chose to use agents to sell these products in the domestic market for three main main reasons: to motivate them, for their 'remuneration depended solely upon their commission'; to minimize the costs of selling at a time when the firm was new and relatively weakly financed; and to take advantage of agents who already had connections with railways and engineering companies.[13] Payne paints a fascinating picture of the way this agency system worked, the use of railway officials working for Spencer on the side — the 'confidential agents'; the expenditure on little presents such as pipes, tobacco, cigars, pocket books and liquor 'to make things pleasant' when calling on officials and managers, the regular use of entertainment such as dinners and lunches as a more suitable place to discuss business; and the eventual decline of this form of marketing in the 1870s when the firm's finances were stronger, the products well established and the business felt able to take over marketing direct.[14] This account of one domestic agency system draws on agency agreements often included in correspondence or amplified by it.

The example

The dealers' agreement shown here is between the Austin Motor Co Ltd of Birmingham and the Wimbledon Motor Works, in respect of the sale of 20, 12 and 7 horsepower cars, and is dated 1922–3.[15] Austin were aware that they would need to make many such agreements and were keen to cover themselves completely — this agreement leaves little to chance.

Wimbledon Motor Works was founded by William Oats at the turn of the twentieth century and operated from premises in High Street, Wimbledon, including one of the earliest roadside petrol pumps in south London. The business thrived under Oats' direction, who died as late as 1953, and in the early 1960s the firm was bought up by Mann Egerton Co Ltd, large British Leyland dealers based in Norwich since 1900.[16]

Two general points come out from the example quoted. First, the manufacturer seems to be in the dominant position in that there are many clauses specifying penalties incurrable by the dealer for breaching the agreement but none for the manufacturer; also, whereas the dealer's role is very fully specified, the manufacturer is free to deliver or not as he chooses, raise prices, and is left untrammelled. This reflects the relative economic strength of the two parties. Motor cars were new products with a huge potential market in the 1920s; Austin could pick and choose his agents who were keen to acquire such a dealership. Secondly, clause 23 states quite explicitly that the dealer is not an agent so we know what we are dealing with. The reason for this clause was that agents had legal powers to act on behalf of another party and bind that second party to agreements as if the principal had entered into the contract personally. Obviously Austin did not want its dealers to have any such powers and inserted this clause as a disclaimer. It brings out the difference between an agent who had a much wider brief to act on behalf of his principal than a dealer who merely acted as a retailer or merchant for another firm or individual.

Notes

1. F.E. Hyde, *Blue Funnel* (Liverpool UP, 1956) and S. Marriner and F.E. Hyde, *The Senior, John Samuel Swire 1825–98* (Liverpool UP, 1967).
2. S.J. Nicholas, 'The Overseas Marketing Performance of British Industry, 1870–1914', *Economic History Review*, 2nd ser. Vol. 37, No. 4 (1984).
3. Advertisements have been used most effectively by historians, for example see E. Williams, *The Story of Sunlight: Centenary of a Famous Soap 1884–1984* (London, 1984) or P. Hadley, *The History of Bovril Advertising* (Bovril, 1972).
4. Much of *Business History*, Vol. 23, No. 3 (1981) is given over to reporting the papers on consular reports given at the Edinburgh Congress.
5. R. Munting, 'Ransomes in Russia: An English Agricultural Engineering Company's Trade with Russia to 1917', *Economic History Review*, 2nd ser. Vol. 31, No. 2 (1978) pp. 260–3.
6. R. Munting, 'Agricultural Engineering and European Exports before 1914', *Business History*, Vol. 27, No. 2 (1985) pp. 127–31.
7. Nicholas, op. cit.
8. Hyde, op. cit.
9. F.E. Hyde, *Shipping Enterprise and Management, 1830–1939: Harrisons of Liverpool* (Liverpool UP, 1967),
10. S. Marriner, *Rathbones of Liverpool 1845–73* (Liverpool UP, 1961).
11. S.K. Jones, *Two Centuries of Overseas Trading: The Origins and Growth of the Inchcape Group* (Macmillan, 1986); M. Keswick, *The Thistle and the Jade* (Octopus, 1983).
12. P.L. Payne, *Rubber and Railways in the Nineteenth Century* (Liverpool UP, 1961).
13. Ibid., p. 72.
14. Ibid., chap. 5.
15. The history of this firm is briefly referred to in Jones, op. cit; further information is in the Mann Egerton archives, 5 Prince of Wales Road, Norwich.
16. K. Richardson, *The British Motor Industry 1839–1939: A Social and Economic History* (Macmillan, 1977) pp. 217–18.

The

MOTOR
COMPANY
LIMITED

DEALERS

AGREEMENT

1922-23

20 H.P.   12 H.P.   7 H.P.

15. Pages from a dealers' agreement between the Austin Motor Co Ltd
and the Wimbledon Motor Works, 1 February 1923.
Source: Mann Egerton archives, Norwich.

Memorandum of Agreement made

this *1st* day of *February* 1923, BETWEEN

THE AUSTIN MOTOR COMPANY LIMITED OF LONGBRIDGE WORKS, NORTHFIELD, IN THE CITY OF BIRMINGHAM (hereinafter called the " Company ") of the one part and

> Messrs. Wimbledon Motor Works,
> 29, High Street,
> Wimbledon

—(hereinafter called the " Dealer ") of the other part.

Whereas this Agreement is one of a large number of similar Agreements entered or to be entered into by the Company, and strict observance of the same by the Dealer is essential to the success of the Company's undertaking, and, consequently, any breach by the Dealer of any of the provisions herein contained will necessarily inflict serious damage on the Company, the extent whereof will be difficult of ascertainment, and, accordingly, the parties have agreed upon the various sums hereinafter expressed to be payable as liquidated damages as being fair and reasonable amounts for the damage which will accrue from the breach of the respective provisions hereinafter contained.

Now this Agreement Witnesseth :—

CONTRACT.

1.—(a) The Dealer will purchase from the Company and *Fifteen* Austin Cars or Chassis when required of not less than ....20-h.p. ....12-h.p. ....7-h.p. Austin Cars or Chassis, and pay in cash on delivery of the same, and also of the parts named in Clause 6 hereof, during the period commencing at this date and ending October 31st, 1923. In the event of the Dealer not accepting and paying for the Cars and Chassis and parts in cash on delivery, the Company shall have the power by notice in writing to be given to the Dealer within 7 days from the due date to determine this Agreement at the expiration of 28 days from the due date, but such notice shall have no effect if the Dealer accepts and pays for the Cars within such 28 days. And in the event of such determination the deposit on all Cars and Chassis contracted for and not accepted and paid for up to the date of cancellation shall be forfeited to the Company.

(b) The Company will use their best endeavours to deliver the said Cars or Chassis unless prevented by strikes, war, or other causes out of their control, but delay in delivery from any cause beyond such date shall not give the Dealer any right to damages. If, however, such delay exceed one calendar month the Dealer may cancel the orders thus affected on giving notice in writing to the Company, in which case the deposits shall be returned less any deductions which the Company are authorised to make under this Agreement.

DEPOSIT.

(c) The Dealer will pay to the Company upon the execution hereof a deposit of £5 per unit as a guarantee of the full and faithful performance by the Dealer of all the terms and conditions of this Agreement. The Company may retain and apply the whole of this sum or any part thereof towards the liquidation of any due accounts or other legitimate claims arising by reason of the Dealer failing to perform all or any of the obligations of this Agreement ; the balance (if any) of the said deposit shall be returned to the Dealer at the termination of this Agreement. If the Dealer shall commit any breach of this Agreement the said deposit shall be unconditionally forfeited to the Company.

15. Pages from a dealers' agreement between the Austin Motor Co Ltd and the Wimbledon Motor Works, 1 February 1923.
Source: Mann Egerton archives, Norwich.

2.—(a) The Cars and Chassis to be delivered under clause 1 (a), and hereinafter sometimes called the product, are sold to the Dealer for retail re-sale to and use by residents in the United Kingdom only and/or its Cars and Chassis so detailed as aforesaid for sale to *bona-fide* Motor Traders in accordance with the provisions of Clause 10 hereof in the following territory only :—

TERRITORY FOR TRADE SALE.

That portion of the County of Surrey enclosed in a line drawn from the London County Border at Beverley Brook to Lower London, thence east to Mitcham Station, thence to Norbury Park and along the county border to Beverley Brook.

(b) During the continuance of this Agreement the Dealer undertakes not to contract for directly or indirectly for the sale of Motor Cars or Chassis made or dealt in by any other Motor Manufacturer or Dealer without the consent in writing of the Company first obtained, but this Clause shall not apply to any Agencies which the Dealer may have at the time of this Agreement.

EXPORT PROHIBITED.

(c) In the event of the Dealer re-selling the Company's product for export or to any person in the United Kingdom who either transports or disposes of such product so that it is delivered beyond the United Kingdom within three calendar months from the date of such re-sale the Dealer will repay to the Company all discounts and rebates allowed or paid by the Company in connection therewith.

PREMISES.

3.—(a) The Dealer will maintain on his own account and at his own expense a place of business efficiently staffed in *Dunton* for the purpose of conducting the re-sale of the Company's product and rendering efficient service in connection therewith. Such place of business will include Garage, Showroom, and a properly-equipped Territorial Service Station and Repair Shop stocked with an adequate supply of renewal parts in accordance with the provisions of Clause 6. The Dealer will affix a notice to his premises in a conspicuous position stating that he is a Dealer in the Company's product.

DELIVERY CHARGES.

(b) The Dealer will maintain and pay the fixed charges for transportation of Austin Cars or Chassis from the Company's factory where delivery is complete, to the place of destination, as the Company shall from time to time establish and communicate to the Dealer. From the time when the Cars or Chassis leave the Company's Works the Company shall not be responsible for any damage which may happen thereto.

ADVERTISING.

(c) The Dealer will advertise the Company's product effectively in such manner as the Company shall from time to time communicate to the Dealer, and the Dealer will expend on such advertising a sum not less than one per cent. of the retail list price of each Car or Chassis agreed to be purchased hereunder always excepting the Cars or Chassis sub-contracted for by *bona-fide* traders as provided in Clause 10. He will give his immediate and careful attention to all enquiries and will not advertise or trade in the Company's product in such a way as to be an annoyance or injurious to the product and organisation of the Company or to any of its duly appointed Dealers and will instantly withdraw any advertisement on being notified by the Company that objection is taken to same and will not repeat any such advertisement or publish any form of advertisement containing matter to which the Company has objected. When the expenditure under this clause has to be incurred by advertisements in the public press or any approved periodical then only specialised advertisements dealing solely with Austin products will be deemed to be in relief of this obligation. The Dealer will if requested produce printers' proofs of the advertisements and details of the expenses.

DEMONSTRATION CAR.

(d) The Dealer will during the currency of this Agreement retain in stock in proper running condition not less than one Austin Motor Car or Chassis unused for exhibition purposes, and, in addition, in proper running condition and in good clean order and repair, not less than one Austin Motor Car for the sole purpose of demonstration and exhibition to intending purchasers.

ALTERATION TO DESIGN AND REPAIRS.

(e) The Dealer will not alter or interfere with or add to the design or working of any Austin Car or Chassis and will execute any repairs required to any Austin Car or Chassis within such time limitation and at such charges as shall be scheduled by the Company and communicated to the Dealer from time to time.

DISCOUNT

4.—The Company will allow the Dealer the following discounts from the Current British Catalogue Prices of the Cars or Chassis, that is to say :—A discount of $12\frac{1}{2}$% on each of the first Two Motor Cars or Chassis, and 15% on every additional Car or Chassis taken by him under this Agreement. Delivery of all Cars or Chassis to be taken at the Company's Works, or, if at the request of the Dealer, delivery is made otherwise, then all expenses and freight charges to be paid and borne by the Dealer which expenses shall, in accordance with the provisions of Clause 7 hereof, be charged by the Dealer to the purchasers from him of the Cars or Chassis.

REBATES.

5.—At the expiration of each quarter of a year (except as herein provided) of the Agreement and subject to the full and faithful observance and performance by the Dealer of all the provisions hereof, the Company will pay or allow the Dealer the following rebate on the net price of Cars and Chassis purchased, of which delivery has been taken by the Dealer hereunder during such quarter of a year —

If the net turnover during such quarter is £10,500			..	..	..	A rebate of	1%.
Ditto	ditto	£21,000	..	..	..	,,	$1\frac{1}{2}\%$.
Ditto	ditto	£33,000	..	..	..	,,	2%.
Ditto	ditto	£45,500	..	..	..	,,	$2\frac{1}{2}\%$.
Ditto	ditto	£57,000	..	..	..	,,	3%.
Ditto	ditto	£69,000	..	..	..	,,	$3\frac{1}{2}\%$.
Ditto	ditto	£81,000	..	..	..	,,	4%.
Ditto	ditto	£105,000	..	..	..	,,	$4\frac{1}{2}\%$.
Ditto	ditto	£140,000	..	..	..	,,	5%.
Ditto	ditto	£175,000	..	..	..	,,	$5\frac{1}{4}\%$.
Ditto	ditto	£210,000	..	..	..	,,	$5\frac{1}{2}\%$.

At the end of the last quarter of a year of this Agreement, if the Dealer has taken delivery of and paid for the aggregate number of Cars and Chassis agreed to be purchased by him during the year, the total net turnover shall be ascertained and an additional rebate allowed to him of the difference between the quarterly rebate previously allowed according to the above Scale and the higher rebate mentioned in the same Scale as if the whole of such Cars and Chassis had been taken in the last quarter.

The Company shall (and is hereby authorised by the Dealer so to do) deduct from the said rebates any sums due to the Company by the Dealer and any and all rebates, discounts, or allowances due and payable to Retail Dealers appointed under the provisions of Clause 10 hereof.

DISCOUNT AND
DISTRIBUTION
OF PARTS.

6.—The Company will allow to the Dealer a discount of 20% from the list price of all parts of Cars or Chassis manufactured by the Company and a discount of 15% on factored goods and accessories, but where a Distributing Service Depot is established by the Dealer then on condition of his maintaining a stock of spare parts of a minimum value consistent with the number of Cars delivered within the territorial area, and in quantities to be decided by the Company, the rate of discount shall be 25% from the list price of all parts manufactured by the Company and 15% from the list price of all factored goods and accessories.

In the event of the expiration of the contractual relationship of the Dealer and the Company all spare parts that are returned within 28 days in a new and saleable condition will be purchased or allowed for by the Company at the trade price to the Dealer ruling at such time.

RETAIL PRICE
MAINTENANCE.

7.—Excepting in accordance with the provisions of Clause 10 hereof the Dealer will not offer for sale or sell or supply any Austin Car or Chassis at a price other than that ruling at the time of delivery and published on the M.T.A. protected price list, plus freight charges and delivery expenses from the Company's works or warehouses at Northfield or elsewhere to place of destination nor by paying commission to any person or rendering any service or supplying any goods either gratis or at reduced prices or doing or permitting any other act soever directly or indirectly reduce the said retail prices.

In the event of breach of this clause the Company shall have the right immediately to terminate this Agreement and the Dealer shall pay to the Company the sum of £100 (one hundred pounds) as liquidated damages for every such breach, such sum being the agreed damages which the Company will sustain.

RETAIL PRICE
MAINTENANCE.

8.—Excepting in accordance with the provisions of Clauses 6 and 10 hereof the Dealer will not offer for sale or sell or supply any Austin parts at prices below the advertised retail list prices thereof current at the date of delivery, plus freight charges and delivery expenses, if any, from the Company's works or warehouses at Northfield or elsewhere to place of delivery nor by paying commission to any person or rendering service or supplying any goods either gratis or at reduced prices or doing or permitting any other act soever directly or indirectly reduce the said retail list prices. In the event of breach of this clause the Company shall have the right to immediately terminate this Agreement and the Dealer shall pay to the Company in respect of each part sold a sum equal to three times the retail list price thereof as liquidated damages, such sum being the agreed damages that the Company will sustain.

EMPLOYEE
DEFINED.

9.—The Dealer will not pay any commission in respect of the sale of an Austin Car or any Austin part except to persons whose whole time is bona-fide devoted to the service of the Dealer. In the event of breach of this clause the Company shall have the right immediately to terminate this Agreement and the Dealer shall pay to the Company in respect of each breach the same damages that would be payable under Clauses 7 and 8 respectively, if the said sale had been also a breach thereof.

DEALERS.

10.—The Dealer undertakes to negotiate the appointment of Retail Dealers acceptable to the Company in all localities throughout the territory assigned to the Dealer under this Agreement and prior to the sale or delivery of any of the Company's product to such parties will require such parties to execute an Agreement in a form to be furnished by the Company and will only allow and pay to such parties the discounts and rebates set out in the form of Agreement aforesaid. The Dealer will immediately upon the execution by the Retail Dealer of the Agreement aforesaid transmit such Agreement to the Company for approval and upon being approved by the Company one copy shall be retained by the Company and one by the Retail Dealer. The Dealer will not make any Agreement affecting the Company or the supply of the Company's product nor sell or supply or cause to be sold or supplied to any person or persons unless at the Company's full retail list prices the Cars or Chassis of the Company excepting in accordance with the provisions of this clause. Notwithstanding anything herein contained the Company has the right to appoint dealers and allot territory to such Dealers within the territory above mentioned provided that such Dealers enter into an Agreement with the Company as herein provided and in consideration thereof the Company will pay to the Dealer a sum equal to the difference between the discount and rebate allowed to the Dealer as above defined and the amount of discount and rebate payable to the Dealer hereunder. All Cars and Chassis so sold shall be credited to the Dealer for the purpose of calculating the scale of rebate to be paid or allowed to the Dealer under Clause 5 hereof in respect of the Cars or Chassis actually purchased by the Dealer and in relief of the obligations of this contract.

15. Pages from a dealers' agreement between the Austin Motor Co Ltd and the Wimbledon Motor Works, 1 February 1923.
Source: Mann Egerton archives, Norwich.

Bibliography

Primary sources

Acts of Parliament affecting the creation of documents and their deposit with the Companies Registrar as discussed in the text. Their 'short titles' have been used.

Companies acts

7 & 8 Vict. c. 110	An Act for the Registration, Incorporation and Regulation of Joint Stock Companies, 1844.
19 & 20 Vict. c. 47	The Joint Stock Companies Act, 1856.
20 & 21 Vict. c. 14	The Joint Stock Companies Act, 1857.
25 & 26 Vict. c. 89	The Companies Act, 1862.
30 & 31 Vict. c. 131	The Companies Act, 1867.
63 & 64 Vict. c. 48	The Companies Act, 1900.
7 Edw. VII c. 50	The Companies Act, 1907.
8 Edw. VII c. 69	The Companies (Consolidation) Act, 1908.
7 & 8 Geo. V c. 28	The Companies (Particulars as to Directors) Act, 1917.
18 & 19 Geo. V c. 45	The Companies Act, 1928.
19 & 20 Geo. V c. 23	The Companies Act, 1929.
11 & 12 Geo. VI c. 38	The Companies Act, 1948.
16 Eliz. II c. 81	The Companies Act, 1967.

Acts of Parliament relating to patents and licences using their short titles:

15 & 16 Vict. c. 83	The Patent Law Amendment Act, 1852.
46 & 47 Vict. c. 57	Patents, Designs and Trade Marks Act, 1883.
2 Edw. VII c. 34	Patents Act, 1902.
7 Edw. VII c. 29	Patents and Designs Act, 1907.
9 & 10 Geo. V c. 80	Patents and Designs Act, 1919.
12 & 13 Geo. VI c. 62	Patents and Designs Act, 1949.

Secondary sources

Works on the creation and uses of business documents:

T.S. Ashton, W.T. Baker *et al.*, 'The Publication of Business Records', *Archives*, Vol. 1, No. 6 (1951).

T. Barker, 'Consular Reports: A Rich but Neglected Source', *Business History*, Vol. 23, No. 3 (1981).

T.C. Barker, R.H. Campbell, P. Mathias & B.S. Yamey, *Business History* (Historical Association, 1971).

T. Cole, *The Nature of Business Records*, Record Aids, No. 4 (Business Archives Council, 1985).

M. Collins, 'The Business of Banking: English Bank Balance Sheets, 1840–80', *Business History*, Vol. 26, No. 1 (1984).

P.L. Cottrell, *Industrial Finance 1830–1914* (Methuen, 1979).

T. Daff, 'Patents as History', *Local Historian*, Vol. 9, No. 6 (1971).

H.I. Dutton, *The Patent System and Inventive Activity during the Industrial Revolution, 1750–1852* (Manchester UP, 1984).

H.C. Edey & P. Panitpakdi, 'British Company Accounting and the Law 1844–1900' in A.C. Littleton & B.S. Yamey (eds), *Studies in the History of Accounting* (Sweet & Maxwell, 1956).

J.R. Edwards, 'The Accounting Profession and Disclosure in Published Reports, 1925–1935', *Accounting and Business Research*, No. 24 (1976).

J.R. Edwards & K.M. Webb, 'The Influence of Company Law on Corporate Reporting Procedures, 1865–1929: An Exemplification', *Business History*, Vol. 24, No. 3 (1982).

J.R. Etor, 'Some Problems in Accounting History, 1830–1900', *Business Archives*, No. 38 (1973).

J.H. Harvey, 'Architectural Archives, *Archives*, Vol. 2, No. 11 (1954).

J. Imrie, 'National Archive Sources for Business History' in P.L. Payne (ed.), *Studies in Scottish Business History* (Cass, 1967) pp. 3–29.

J. Kitchen, 'The Accounts of British Holding Company Groups: Some thoughts on development in the early years', *Accounting and Business Research*, No. 6 (1972).

G.A. Lee, 'Historical Business Accounting Records', *Business Archives*, No. 46 (1980).

T.A. Lee, 'Company Financial Statements: An Essay in Business History, 1830–1950' in S. Marriner (ed.), *Business & Businessmen: Studies in Business, Economics, and Accounting History* (Liverpool UP, 1978) pp. 235–62.

L. McDonald, 'Appraisal Criteria: Application to Business Records', *Records Management*, No. 11 (1985).

S. Marriner, 'Company Financial Statements as Source Material for Business Historians', *Business History*, Vol. 22, No. 2 (1980).

J. Mason, 'Accounting Records and Business History', *Business History*, Vol. 24, No. 3 (1982).

P. Mathias, 'Historial Records of the Brewing Industry', *Archives*, Vol. 7, No. 33 (1965).

E.V. Morgan & W.A. Thomas, *The Stock Exchange: Its History and Functions* (Elek, 1962).

K. Newman, 'Financial Advertising Past and Present', *Three Banks Review*, No. 140 (1983).

P.L. Payne, 'Business Archives and Economic History: the Case for Regional Studies', *Archives*, Vol. 6, No. 29 (1963).

H. Pollins, 'Aspects of Railway Accounting before 1868' in A.C. Littleton and B.S. Yamey (eds), *Studies in the History of Accounting* (Sweet & Maxwell, 1956); reprinted in M.C. Reed (ed.), *Railways in the Victorian Economy* (David & Charles, 1969).

C. Prestige, 'Historical Records in Solicitor's Offices', *Archives*, Vol. 14, No. 64 (1980).

T. Rath, 'Business Records in the PRO in the Age of the Industrial Revolution', *Business History*, Vol. 17, No. 2 (1975).

A. Room, *Dictionary of Trade Name Origins* (RKP, 1982).

H.A. Shannon, 'The First Five Thousand Limited Companies and their Duration', *Economic History*, Vol. 2 (1931).

B.D.M. Smith, 'Patents for Invention: The National and Local Picture', *Business History*, Vol. 4, No. 2 (1962).

G. Stanley, 'Registration of Companies and Businesses' (unpub. PRO typescript, 1985).

W.A. Thomas, *The Provincial Stock Exchanges* (Frank Cass, 1973).

I. Winship, 'Patents as a Historical Source', *Industrial Archaeology*, Vol. 16, No. 3 (1981).

Business histories

We have not attempted to compile a comprehensive list of published books or articles on business history but rather have referred to the most appropriate in each section. Good bibliographies, at their date of publication, are contained in the Historical Association's booklet by T.C. Barker, R.H. Campbell & P. Mathias on *Business History*, last revised in 1971 and issued in an updated form in 1984 by Debrett's Business History Research Ltd; P.L. Payne's *British*

Entrepreneurship in the Nineteenth Century (Macmillan, 1974); and K.A.
Tucker's *Business History: Selected Readings* (Cass, 1977) appendix three,
which is less parochial than the previous two works and includes works from
American and antipodean scholars as well as British.

A bibliography of books published in the broad area of business history appears
annually in *Business Archives*, the journal of the Business Archives Council. The
Economic History Review in its November issue contains a list of both books and
articles on British economic history and section 3 of this classified bibliography on
'Industry and Internal Trade' contains many works relevant to business history.
Currently Francis Goodall at the Business History Unit of the London School of
Economics is compiling a comprehensive bibliography of all books, articles, and
booklets published in a wide definition of business history, including privately
published company histories. Once this work is completed it will be a very
valuable adjunct to currently available lists and should supersede them.

Guides to collections of business records

J. Armstrong (comp.), *Directory of Corporate Archives* (Business Archives
Council, 1985).
H.A.L. Cockerell & E. Green, *The British Insurance Business, 1547–1970*
(Heinemann, 1976).
Janet Foster & Julia Sheppard, *British Archives: A Guide to Archive Resources
in the United Kingdom* (Macmillan, 1982).
P. Hudson (ed.), *The West Riding Wool Textile Industry: A Catalogue of
Business Records from the Sixteenth to the Twentieth Centuries* (Pasold
Research Fund, 1975).
C.A. Jones, *Britain and the Dominions: a guide to business and related records in
the UK concerning Australia, Canada, New Zealand and South Africa* (G.K.
Hall, 1978).
A. Mace, *The Royal Institute of British Architects: A Guide to its Archives and
History* (Mansell, 1986).
P. Mathias & A.W. Pearsall (eds), *Shipping: A Survey of Historical Records*
(David & Charles, 1971).
L.S. Pressnell & John Orbell, *A Guide to the Historical Records of British
Banking* (Gower, 1985).
L. Richmond & B. Stockford, *Company Archives: The Survey of the Records of
1000 of the First Registered Companies* (Gower, 1985).
L.A. Ritchie, *Modern British Shipbuilding: A Guide to Historical Records*
(National Maritime Museum, 1980).

In addition, *Business Archives* contains an annual list of business records deposited
in the preceding year with public repositories which is drawn from the Stationery
Office publication *Accession to Repositories and Reports Added to the National
Register of Archives* by kind permission of the Historical Manuscript Commission.

Archives, the journal of the British Records Association, also contains articles on specific sets or types of records and occasionally these collections are of relevance to the business historian. For example:

R. Craig, 'Shipping records of the Nineteenth and Twentieth Centuries', Vol. 7, No. 36 (1966).

A.E.J. Hollaender, 'A London Merchant's Letter Book 1698–1704', Vol. 3, No. 17 (1957).

P. Mathias, 'Historical Records of the Brewing Industry', Vol. 7, No. 33 (1965).

Useful addresses

Britain

British Library, Reference Division, Newspaper Library, Colindale Avenue, London NW9 5HE. *Telephone*: 01–200 5515

Business Archives Council, 185 Tower Bridge Road, London SE1 2UF. *Telephone*: 01–407 6110

City Business Library, 55 Basinghall Street, London EC2V 5BX. *Telephone*: 01–638 8215

Companies House, 55–61 City Road, London EC1Y 1BB. *Telephone*: 01–253 9393

Guildhall Library, Aldermanbury, London EC2P 2EJ. *Telephone*: 01–606 3030

National Register of Archives, Royal Commission on Historical Manuscripts, Quality House, Quality Court, Chancery Lane, London WC2A 1HP. *Telephone*: 01–242 1198

Public Record Office, Ruskin Avenue, Kew, Richmond, Surrey TW9 4DU. *Telephone*: 01–876 3444

Science Reference Library, 25 Southampton Buildings, Chancery Lane, London WC2A 1AW. *Telephone*: 01–405 8721

International

Baker Library, Harvard Business School, Soldiers Field, Boston, Massachusetts, USA 02163.

Business Archives Affinity Group, Society of American Archivists, 330 S. Wells Street, Suite 810, Chicago, Illinois, USA 60606.

Eleutherian Mills Historical Library, Greenville, Wilmington, Delaware, USA 19807.

Hudson's Bay Company Archives, Provincial Archives of Manitoba, 200 Vaughan Street, Winnipeg, Manitoba, Canada R3C OV8.

Archives of Business and Labour, Australian National University, PO Box 4, Canberra 2600, Australia.

Business Archives Coordinator, Manuscript Division, Public Archives of Canada, 395 Wellington Street, Ottawa, Canada K1A ON3.

Central Institute for Business Archives, Mikkeli, Finland.

Gesellschaft fur Unternehmensgeschicte e.v. Geschaftsfuhrung, Schonhauser Strasse 62, 5000 Koln 51, West Germany.

Nederlands Economisch Historisch Archief, Herengracht 218–220, Amsterdam, Netherlands.

Statens erhvervshistoriske Arkiv, Vester Alle 12, DK 8000 Arhus C, Denmark.

Westfalisches Wirtschaftsarchiv, Markische Strasse 120, Postfach 871, D–46000 Dortmund, West Germany.

Index